CHOOSIN   OR?

Choosing to Labour?

School-Work Transitions and Social Class

WOLFGANG LEHMANN

McGill-Queen's University Press

Montreal & Kingston • London • Ithaca

© McGill-Queen's University Press 2007

ISBN 978-0-7735-3280-9 (cloth)
ISBN 978-0-7735-3306-6 (paper)

Legal deposit third quarter 2007
Bibliothèque nationale du Québec

Printed in Canada on acid-free paper that is 100% ancient forest
free (100% post-consumer recycled), processed chlorine free

This book has been published with the help of a grant from the
Canadian Federation for the Humanities and Social Sciences,
through the Aid to Scholarly Publications Programme, using funds
provided by the Social Sciences and Humanities Research Council
of Canada. Funding has also been provided by the J.B. Smallman
Publication Fund and the Faculty of Social Science, The University
of Western Ontario.

McGill-Queen's University Press acknowledges the support of the
Canada Council for the Arts for our publishing program. We also
acknowledge the financial support of the Government of Canada
through the Book Publishing Industry Development Program
(BPIDP) for our publishing activities.

Library and Archives Canada Cataloguing in Publication

Lehmann, Wolfgang, 1965-
    Choosing to labour?: school-work transitions and social
class / Wolfgang Lehmann.

Includes bibliographical references and index.
ISBN 978-0-7735-3280-9 (bnd)
ISBN 978-0-7735-3306-6 (pbk)

1. School-to-work transition – Canada. 2. School-to-work transition –
Germany. 3. Vocational guidance – Canada. 4. Vocational guidance
– Germany. 5. High school students – Canada – Economic
conditions. 6. High school students – Germany – Economic
conditions. I. Title.

LC1037.L43 2007   331.702'330971   C2007-901883-1

Typeset by Jay Tee Graphics Ltd. in 10.5/13 New Baskerville

Contents

Figures and Tables

Acknowledgments

Financial support for this research was provided through a doctoral fellowship by the Social Sciences and Humanities Research Council of Canada (SSHRC) and a doctoral research grant by the Department of Sociology at the University of Alberta. I also acknowledge the assistance of the J.B. Smallman Publication Fund and the Faculty of Social Science at The University of Western Ontario.

Select findings from this research have been published in different formats elsewhere: an article on the policy implications of youth apprenticeships appeared in *Work, Employment and Society*; the *Journal of Youth Studies* published an article on risk and uncertainty in school-work transitions; and an article on young people's rationalization strategies in the transition from high school can be found in the *Canadian Journal of Sociology*.

The research on which this book is based would not have been possible had it not been for the support, cooperation, advice, and guidance of a great number of people. Foremost, I want to thank the 105 young men and women in Edmonton and Bremen who agreed to participate in the interviews and focus groups on which this book is based. Thanks also go to the school principals, counsellors, and teachers who invited me to their schools and gave me permission to speak to their students. I am particularly grateful for the support I received from Walter Heinz, Helga Krüger, Andreas Witzel, and Werner Dressel at the Universität Bremen. Walter Heinz and Helga Krüger, in particular, not only established important research contacts in Bremen but also opened their doors during the weeks I spent in Germany collecting data. I am also greatly indebted to Eva Quante-Braun, Elisabeth Mahlberg-Wilson, Anne

Grothrian, and Manfred Breden from the "Bleib Dran" team at the Akademie für Arbeit und Politik at the Universität Bremen for taking me into vocational schools and introducing me to principals and teachers.

Thanks also go to Scott Davies, Gerald Taylor, Alison Taylor, Ray Morrow, Graham Lowe, and Harvey Krahn, who provided comments on and insights into the manuscript at various stages, from when it took shape as a dissertation until its publication. I especially thank Alison Taylor for the opportunity to work, present, and publish together at a crucial point in my academic career. But most of all, my heartfelt thanks go to Harvey Krahn, who has been a generous and inspiring supervisor, mentor, colleague, and friend.

At McGill-Queen's University Press, I wish to thank Philip Cercone, Brenda Prince, Anushka Jonian, and Joan McGilvray. In particular, I benefited from the thoughtful editing of Lesley Andrassy.

And finally I thank Audrey, who is the greatest friend and companion anybody could ask for. Your insightful comments and edits on various drafts of the manuscript were invaluable, but your patience, sense of humour, and love made it possible. And, of course, a special thank you to Rudy.

CHOOSING TO LABOUR?

Introduction

I've always enjoyed working in a trade. It's just what my family does.

Tim, Edmonton youth apprentice

[M]y dad would come home from [construction] work and I'd see what he looks like ... You know, my whole life he's told me not to get into this.

Trent, Edmonton academic-track high-school student

[M]y mom and dad both teach ... And my mom ... by the time she retires, I'll be pretty much into that field. I'd love to take over her class, maybe team-teach with her for a couple of years ... We were talking about that, my mom and I, and we thought that would be so neat.

Lisa, Edmonton academic-track high-school student

Let us begin by looking at three high-school students in Edmonton. Tim has just completed his first year of a high-school-based youth apprenticeship and is excited about continuing a family tradition of employment in the trades. Trent has decided to attend university, partly in reaction against his father's experiences of hard physical labour on construction sites. Lisa, too, is planning to attend university to become a teacher like her mother, whom she greatly admires. Some key questions regarding the relationship between social-structural determinants and active choice in school-work transitions emerge from these three cases. How did the career plans of Tim, Trent, and Lisa develop? What shapes their dispositions during school-work transitions? Are these dispositions the result of their active and reflexive engagement with their social and institutional environment, or the result of social class, economic conditions, and educational streaming processes over which they have little control?

The last year of high school is an important period in school-work transitions as students begin to seriously consider life after school, narrow their educational and vocational options, and reinforce dispositions toward specific career destinations. All this takes place against the backdrop of economic and labour market change, which has had, in countries like Canada, particularly drastic effects on the employment prospects of young people. Youth unemployment in Canada has been a persistent labour market problem throughout most of the past two decades. Youth unemployment rates, even in times of economic recovery, have been approximately double that of adults. Being young alone, however, does not completely explain these high levels of unemployment of Canada's population below the age of twenty-five. Educational attainment is recognized as one of the most important contributors to labour market outcomes. High levels of educational attainment are increasingly associated with career success, good incomes, and employment security. Low levels of education are seen as a sure-fire way into the vicious spiral of unstable, contingent employment with low salaries and little chance of advancement. Not surprisingly, educational policy-makers have been particularly concerned with those who have been labelled the middle majority (Benson 1997; Grubb 1996) or the forgotten half (Rosenbaum 2001): those students destined neither for university nor for unskilled employment. This concern has been intensified by the shortages of skilled workers in the trades and other technical occupations experienced in boom provinces like Alberta. Riding out a very favourable oil market, employers in Alberta are facing the dual challenge of an aging workforce and a lack of young people to fill jobs in the oil and construction industries.

A skilled workforce is considered a necessary cornerstone for a province or country to successfully compete in a technologically advanced, global marketplace. Alberta's youth apprenticeship program (Registered Apprenticeship Program, or RAP) – introduced in the early 1990s – is designed to address both issues: it offers high-school students an alternative to traditional post-secondary education or immediate workforce entry, while also attempting to create interest in the trades as a career option. RAP allows high-school students to begin an apprenticeship with an employer as early as Grade 11 (when the student is fifteen or sixteen years old), fulfilling requirements for high-school graduation and a journeyperson certification at the same time. Depending on workplace demands, RAP apprentices may work and go to school during the same term. Alternatively, they may spend one term exclusively at school, taking all their required courses, and the following term exclusively at work. Upon high-school graduation, RAP students have the option of continuing their apprenticeship training. Generally, they will have completed the equivalent of a first-year apprentice's work hours and will receive advanced standing once they take up their apprenticeship training full-time. However, if a RAP student drops out of high school or fails to graduate, the Alberta Apprenticeship and Industry Training Board voids his or her accumulated work hours. This policy is considered an essential element of RAP's stay-at-school purpose, at once attracting non-academic students to a more experiential alternative to completing high school and providing an incentive for sticking with the program.

Proponents of initiatives such as RAP argue that they make school experience more meaningful and offer a way out of the downward spiral of low levels of schooling and labour market failure (e.g., Alberta Apprenticeship and Industry Training Board 1996; Buechtemann, Schupp, and Soloff 1994; Economic Council of Canada 1992; Evans, Taylor, and Heinz 1993; Hamilton 1990). Critics charge such programs with reinforcing existing social inequalities by streaming lower-class children into marginalized career options (Kantor 1994). However, the lack of empirical data on youth apprentices and their motivations for entering these programs makes it virtually impossible to draw any conclusion regarding the pro- or anti-apprenticeship arguments. Furthermore, both proponents and critics of youth apprenticeships have used the German *dual system* of vocational education in support of their arguments, all too often without a proper understanding of its historical, cultural, economic, and political foundations and functions (Lehmann 2000). This book addresses both of these concerns.

From an educational policy perspective, we need a better understanding of why students participate (or not) in programs such as RAP, how parents and peers may influence this decision, and what external social factors play important roles. Such an understanding may help policy-makers and school staff to provide a more effective mix of school-work transition programs, as well as better counselling and advice to individual students. Furthermore, an important goal of these programs is to make school experiences more rele-

vant to less academically inclined students, thereby reducing the
incidence of program attrition and improving those students'
future position in the labour market. Therefore, policy-makers,
administrators, teachers, and parents should be interested in learning whether such programs effectively reach their target groups
and whether participation in them does have the potential to contribute to students' educational attainment, rather than diverting
them from the mainstream.

Although policy debates scarcely scratch the surface of the theoretical problems that underlie them, this book hopes to provide just
such knowledge. The theoretical literature on school-work transitions tends to follow two general streams: a human capital or rational
choice approach, both of which assume a relationship between education, cost-benefit calculations, and labour market outcomes; or a
social-structural approach, which often over-emphasizes the capacity
of social and institutional structures to reinforce inequality.

Within the rational choice tradition, inequality is explained as
the result of individuals' informed choice. For instance, participation
in youth apprenticeship programs or enrolment at university are
seen to be based on careful cost-benefit calculation, in which family
income, social expectations, and labour-market opportunity structures, including credential requirements, are weighed against the
cost and likelihood of success of participating in a specific program
(Boudon 1974; Goldthorpe 1996). The sociological school-work
transitions literature has been characterized by a more structural
approach that investigates relationships between variables such as
socio-economic background, gender, and ethnicity and school-
work transition outcomes. Most prominent in this tradition are
social stratification and status attainment theories. For instance,
recent stratification research has found that the influence of class-
based structural variables has persisted over time (Andres et al.
1999; Friebel et al. 2000) and that socio-economic status (SES) is
still the strongest determinant of educational attainment (Davies
2004).[1] Moreover, gender and race have been found to circum-
scribe both educational and occupational aspirations and attainment (Alba et al. 1994; Geller 1996). Somewhat similarly, status
attainment models (Blau and Duncan 1967; Duncan and Hodge
1963; Jencks, Crouse, and Mueser 1983; Looker and Pineo 1983)
have found evidence that parents' (usually fathers') educational
and occupational attainment have a significant influence on the

educational attainment, first job, and further occupational life course of their children.

These structural approaches have been criticized for overemphasizing the capacity of institutional structures to reinforce social inequality. Critics have argued that structural explanations lack insight into the actual decision making of individuals and disregard difficult-to-measure variables, such as specific institutional structures (in both education and the labour market) or high-school curriculum. In response, researchers have begun to explore the intricate interrelationships between individual choice, or agency, and social context, or structure. They have tried to explain either how individuals themselves are actively implicated in the reproduction of inequality or why at least some young people manage to escape the shackles of social origin. Willis's influential study *Learning to Labour* (1977) is the most famous explanation of individuals' own part in reproducing their social status. As the basis for resistance theory, Willis's work has inspired similar research in many countries, including Canada (Davies 1995; Tanner 1990). Although little evidence was found to support Willis's claims that the social order is reproduced through working-class youths' active resistance to the middle class culture of educational and social mobility (see Davies 1994, 1995), these studies highlighted the need to expand the analysis of social reproduction beyond exclusive consideration of either structure or agency. Working within the more recent theoretical notions of *risk society* (Beck 1992) and *late modernity* (Giddens 1990), researchers have developed concepts of agency and *individualization* that assume a continued influence of structural factors such as class, gender, and race, although at a much less deterministic level than in much of the social stratification and status attainment literature (Evans 2002; Roberts, Clark, and Wallace 1994; Rudd and Evans 1998).

Following these approaches, the starting point for the research discussed in this book was the assumption that a young person's socio-economic background, conceptualized as parents' educational and occupational attainment, family income, and various measures of cultural capital, has a very strong, early influence on school placement. Breaking through more structuralist notions that see life-course chances determined by an individual's socio-economic background and other institutional and structural factors, I propose a more nuanced approach that investigates the influence of an individual's social environment (e.g., parents, peers, teachers, and other potential role models) and institutional environment (e.g., education system, labour market structures, economic situation), as well as young people's own perception and understanding of these contexts, on the active formation of their dispositions toward certain transition paths.

More specifically, my analysis offers answers about what high-school students consider to be important influences during their transition processes and whether participation in a youth apprenticeship is the result of a young person's active and reflexive negotiation with his or her environment. Are young people actively entering youth apprenticeships because they see in them an alternative to post-secondary education or unskilled labour? Are the same young people aware of the debates surrounding the shortages in skilled trades and similar occupations? Or do young people participate, as the opponents of youth apprenticeships argue, because they were already streamed into vocational high-school programs or because their socio-economic background effectively precludes them from entering university or community college? In addition to these core questions about structure and agency, and social reproduction of inequality, this study also investigated how youth apprentices' early integration into adult roles affects their lifestyles, attitudes, and future career plans. Finally, it considered how these empirical findings can help us to develop better educational policy.

The comparison with Germany should prove particularly useful for policy-makers, as Germany's dual system of vocational education is often discussed as a successful model, because of Germany's low rates of youth unemployment and its highly skilled workforce. The policy and implementation process of RAP was certainly informed by the German dual system. The education system and labour market in each country, however, are very different and a proper understanding of these differences is generally missing. Germany's dual system is framed by a highly streamed secondary-school system and a credential-driven, occupationally stratified labour market: the school system feeds students into apprenticeship training from one end, and the labour market creates incentives for apprenticeship credentials at the other end. A comparison of Canadian and German youth apprentices provides a rare critical look at how these differences affect individual experiences in education and the labour market. Furthermore, critics of youth apprenticeships have also used the German dual system in support of their arguments, highlighting the socially reproductive outcomes of the country's heavily streamed education system. All too often, however, the dual system is discussed without a proper understanding of its historical, cultural, economic, and political foundations and functions.

THE STUDY

The answers to these questions come from a mixed-method, comparative study of 105 young people in Edmonton (Alberta, Canada) and Bremen (Germany). Between November 2001 and October 2002, 65 apprentices and 40 academic-track students were interviewed, using either one-on-one semi-structured interviews or focus groups. All interviews and focus groups were held at the participants' schools, usually in a conference room or available classroom. At the end of the interviews or focus groups, all participants completed a questionnaire, which included items regarding parents' educational and occupational attainment, participants' own educational achievements, and other background data. The following paragraphs offer a brief overview of the sampling and data-collection procedures. More detail is provided in Appendices A and B.

RAP apprentices were the "base" group against which all comparisons were made. Hence, the sampling procedure was driven by gaining access to students enrolled in the program. Despite increasing enrolment in RAP, the program still attracts less than one per cent of the total high-school student population in Alberta (Alberta Apprenticeship and Industry Training Board 2002). The Edmonton sample was drawn from four different schools, chosen because of their above-average enrolment in RAP. This group included first and second year youth apprentices (Grades 11 and 12) who had started their apprenticeship program in high school through RAP. Interviews and focus groups were arranged through the four schools' RAP co-ordinators. The students' work status at the time of interview determined whether they could be included in the study or not. While some RAP students work and attend school at the same time, others work for one semester and attend school the next semester. All participants were drawn from among part-time students or from those who were currently in their school semester. Given these restrictions (i.e., relatively low levels of enrolment and school-workplace scheduling), student availability eventually determined which trades and occupations were covered in the study. However, the range of occupations that resulted from this sampling process and the fact that the distribution of occupations reflects that of adult apprentices in Alberta leave me confident that the study participants are reasonably representative of the larger population of RAP students. Twenty-nine Edmonton youth apprentices participated in the study; only six were women, all of whom apprenticed as hairdressers. The twenty-three men apprenticed as automotive technicians, heavy equipment technicians, carpenters, welders, electricians, and chefs.

Twenty-three academic-track students – also in Grades 11 or 12 – were interviewed at the same four schools. Although the teachers and principals insisted on taking an active role in selecting students for these focus groups – largely in an effort to minimize interruptions to students' learning – the academic-track sample came to include a mix of female and male students from varied socio-economic and ethnic backgrounds, with various higher-level post-secondary goals.

The German comparison groups were found in Bremen, a city in northern Germany that is similar in size to Edmonton and is, like Edmonton, a provincial (*Land*) capital. While Edmonton's industrial base is in the oil and gas industry, Bremen is located just downstream of the North Sea coast and has an important (albeit somewhat declining) seaport and shipbuilding industry. Although recently Bremen, like the rest of Germany, has had higher levels of unemployment than Alberta, the city does have an industrial base that provides apprenticeship-training possibilities in similar or identical trades to those studied in Edmonton.

The Bremen sample of apprentices was selected to include apprentices in occupations identical or similar to those in Edmonton. This group included thirty-six first, second, and third year apprentices (aged sixteen to twenty) within Germany's dual system. As all apprentices in a specific occupational cluster attend the same vocational school for their technical training, data collection was arranged through these schools. In addition, seventeen academic-track students were interviewed in Bremen. This group included Grades 11 and 12 *Gymnasium* (grammar school) students. As I will discuss shortly, Germany has no comprehensive schools and youth apprentices have already left the secondary-school system by the time they start their apprenticeship. This makes comparison a little more difficult, as I was unable to draw the academic-track sample from the same schools as the apprentices. However, schools and students were selected to approximate the types of schools included in Edmonton and to ensure that participants came from a cross-section of socio-economic backgrounds.

The analysis presented in this book is largely focused on the qualitative data gathered through interviews and focus groups, but is supplemented by background survey data as necessary.

STRUCTURE OF THE BOOK

Chapter 1 serves as an entry point into the key issues discussed in this book, as it presents findings from both the survey and the individual and focus group interviews. The presentation of data in this chapter remains strictly descriptive and focuses on one key contradiction: quantitative data offers convincing evidence that participation in either youth apprenticeships or academic streams is related to social status, yet individuals' narratives are infused with notions of choice, independent decision making, and agency. These are hardly new or surprising findings. However, they are important as the foundation on which the later interpretive analysis rests.

Chapter 2 adds an additional element to the descriptive presentation of findings in the previous chapter by providing an in-depth analysis of how school-work transitions are affected by specific institutional arrangements. It includes brief descriptions of Alberta's Registered Apprenticeship Program (RAP) and the German dual system and explains how both programs are integrated into the school system and the labour market. Of central importance are the concepts of *transparency* and *flexibility*, since they form the basis for understanding the institutional differences that frame school-work transitions in Canada and Germany. Germany's highly streamed and socially reproductive yet very transparent secondary-education system is shown as both enabling and constraining. This understanding becomes important when analysing the influence of institutional structures on agency. These findings are extended in chapter 3, as I highlight how gendered expectations affect educational dispositions and choices, and how different welfare-state arrangements in Canada and Germany contribute to gendered school-work transition processes.

The findings in chapter 4 suggest that participants' initial insistence on the independent, purely interest-based formation of dispositions toward post-high-school plans is open to question if one probes a little deeper into these relationships. Bourdieu's notions of *habitus* and *cultural capital* assume central importance in the analysis of both reproductive processes and individual strategies (Bourdieu 1977; Bourdieu 1990; Bourdieu and Wacquant 1992). The interpretive analysis in this chapter shows that young people's career plans were overwhelmingly characterized by culturally reproductive processes. My interpretation of their stories reveals how cultural capital and habitus were formed, reinforced, and altered in the home, within their peer groups, in schools (in relation to teachers and curriculum), and in other institutional arrangements.

Chapters 5 and 6 offer more integrated views of the findings in terms of their implications for policy and theory. In chapter 5, I discuss the policy implications of this study and offer a number of suggestions for improving practices in youth apprenticeships. These policy suggestions address the potential for apprenticeship training to go beyond mere preparation for the workplace to envision a much broader form of vocational education that encompasses the potential for academic, critical, social, and emancipatory learning. This policy discussion is contextualized through recent critiques of the German dual system. Ironically, as youth apprenticeship programs modelled to various degrees after the Germany system have become increasingly popular in North America, apprenticeship training in Germany has been under siege for some time. Germany's dual system has been described as outdated and archaic, narrowly skill-based, and more concerned with antiquated virtues of discipline, punctuality, and cleanliness than with the more broadly defined demands of new, post-industrial workplaces.

Chapter 6 provides insights into the complex inter-relationship between individual choice and active decision making in the transition from high school to employment or further education. Throughout the previous chapters, I demonstrate that agency is always situated in a framework of institutions, objective structures, cultural practices, and ideologies. Furthermore, agency is circumscribed not only by the social reality in which individuals live but also by the way in which they construct and interpret this reality. Obviously aware of a pervasive public discourse that equates life-course success with increasingly high levels of formal education, most youth apprentices in both Canada and Germany felt it necessary to justify their choice to enter the trades as one that is actually advantageous. Youth apprentices talk about the financial advantages of earning money rather than spending money for their education. They talk about their preferences for manual work and the joy they experience at work. They also talk about how being at work makes them more responsible and better equipped to deal with the demands of adult life. In most cases, these forms of rationalization by youth apprentices reflected a stronger sense of agency than did the educational and career dispositions of their academic-track peers. I therefore propose in this final chapter that individuals engage with their structural, institutional, and cultural environment and history to form dispositions that reflect their understanding of their position in this social structure. Such a conceptualization of agency helps explain how reproductive outcomes can still be infused with individual agency, just as agency is always informed by the agent's social background (or habitus).

In his introduction to *Learning to Labour*, Willis (1977: 1) writes that "the difficult thing to explain about how middle class kids get middle class jobs is why others let them. The difficult thing to explain about how working-class kids get working-class jobs is why they let themselves." He concludes that his "lads" are actively involved in reproducing their own social disadvantage by embracing working-class identities and resisting the dominant middle-class school culture. In contrast to this pessimistic notion of *Learning to Labour*, I more optimistically propose that most youth apprentices in my study, in both countries, were indeed *Choosing to Labour.*

1

When Structure Met Agency

Despite the massive expansion of the Canadian post-secondary education system in the past four decades, and a resulting wider range of educational outcomes within each socio-economic category, aggregate Canadian data show that SES is still the strongest determinant of educational attainment. Whether measured by high-school dropout rates, achievement on standardized tests, or university attendance, working-class youth do not fare as well as do youth from middle- and upper-class backgrounds (Davies 2004: 139). Recent stratification research in Canada has found that the influence of class-based structural variables on educational attainment has persisted over time (Andres et al. 1999). Compared to young people from families in which neither parent had been to university, those with university-educated parents are still more likely to participate in academic-track programs in high school, and to attend and complete university (Andres and Krahn 1999). These disadvantages in the transition from high school to further education or employment tend to be perpetuated well into individuals' life courses, as recent longitudinal Canadian research has shown (Anisef et al. 2000; Krahn 2004). For instance, the national survey of 1995 graduates carried out by Statistics Canada and Human Resources Development Canada (HRDC) clearly shows a relationship between social origin (father's education) and educational attainment (Taillon and Paju 1999). Thirty-one per cent of university graduates in 1995 had a father with a university degree, compared with only 8 per cent of graduates from a trade/vocational program (Taillon and Paju 1999: 16). Similarly, German data show that, of all first-year university students in 2002, only 17 per cent came from a family in which fathers fell into the occupational category of "worker" (performing blue collar, manual labour), even though manual workers represent 34 per cent of the labour force (Bundesministerium für Bildung and Forschung 2005: 180).

These findings raise a number of serious questions regarding the different functions of youth apprenticeships. From a strictly economic perspective, policy-makers should only be concerned with the need to supply the labour market with much-needed young, qualified, skilled workers. But for school-work transitions, youth apprenticeships issues become a lot murkier. Are we seeing in youth apprenticeships a sinister streaming process that formalizes a social class-reproductive process by removing lower-achieving, working-class high-school students from the academic mainstream and thrusting them prematurely into the workplace? Or do youth apprenticeships offer a non-academic alternative to more practically oriented students that allows them to get a head start on gaining a positive vocational identity, without closing the door to higher education? And where do young people see themselves fitting in these largely institutional scenarios? Are they being streamed into apprenticeships by "the system," without their full knowledge of what is happening to them? Or are they actively engaged in decisions that reflect their own preferences and dispositions toward their careers and life courses?

One first step to answering these questions is to look at who participates in apprenticeship and academic-track programs and the terms in which young people discuss their educational dispositions.

AGENCY AND DISPOSITIONS IN THEIR OWN WORDS: "MY PAYCHEQUE IS MORE THAN YOUR MOM'S"

Brochures to promote RAP distributed in high schools across Alberta highlight money, work experience, and high-school credits as the key advantages of participation. The brochure's cover reads "Earn while you learn." RAP is promoted as a way to: "become an apprentice and gain credits toward both an apprenticeship program and a high-school diploma at the same time. It's like having it all! ... Paid career training before you leave school."

These promises are not lost on those young people who have decided to enter the program. Nathan, who apprentices as an electrician in Edmonton, sums up all the key incentives when he explains what he liked about RAP and what motivated him to enter the program:

NATHAN: There's a lot [I like about] the RAP program. I mean, you get a [credit for a] course out of it if you complete all your hours. You do get credits out of it ... as well as getting paid. And on top of that ... you finish all your hours and you have your first year [of apprenticeship training] completed. You get out of school and you're a year ahead of all your other classmates. You're out there; you're making [money] ... you have a job already. You don't have to go out and decide what you want to do. You already have your mind made up. You're out there; you're working towards what you want to be doing for the rest of your life ... I took a look at that and decided that by doing this, I would be ahead of most other people before I even got out of high school.

For some high-school students, receiving credits for working becomes a lifeline. Curtis apprentices as an automotive mechanic and has severe problems with some of his high-school courses. To him, participating in RAP does indeed increase the potential of successful graduation:

WL: And what did you like about [going into RAP as an automotive apprentice]? What sounded interesting to you?
CURTIS: Oh, for one thing, I get credits for it. And I need all the credits I can get.

While credits do play an important role in RAP students' decision to apprentice, their importance is quickly overshadowed by the reward of receiving a steady paycheque. Money becomes important in two ways: earning money to afford certain lifestyles and to buy consumer goods; and earning money while getting an education, rather than actually spending money to get an education. Nathan and Riley, two RAP students who had apprenticed as electrician and millwright respectively for some months by the time I spoke to them, comment on both reasons:

WL: What were some of the things you liked most about RAP, what sold you on going into RAP?
RILEY: Paycheque at the end of the week.

NATHAN: Coming to school, you get your marks. But really, to me, the marks were just numbers on a piece of paper. I can write numbers on a piece of paper, too. Whereas I was going to work and after my first paycheque, it was just like "wow, hey," these are numbers, but these numbers can get me something. And they can get me something right now. And that's what really … that really hit home … I get up in the morning now, and it's like "oh, I got to go to school today." Whereas it was getting up in the morning, "yes, I can go to work today, and get some more money so that next paycheque I can go out and get this, or get that." You're seeing something for what you're doing, and that's really what made the difference. I really liked working compared to school …

RILEY: But if you think about it, when you go to university, ok, university costs way more than [technical school, for apprenticeship training], right? OK, now you got all the student loans. See with us, we go, we start work, right. Maybe it takes you four years to complete your university course, then you have to look for a job. After our four years, we're already up at twenty-five bucks an hour, if not thirty. You're [university graduates] starting off at the bottom after your four years of trying to go up there. We, after our four years, can take another ticket and then we're up at like forty dollars an hour.

NATHAN: That's kind of how I looked at it, too. I mean, university … you go every year and you pay 5,000 to 10,000 dollars. Whereas, you go and take a [trades] ticket, and in your first year … I can easily make 5,000, 6,000, 7,000 dollars. Whereas that exact same money is what you will be paying to go to university. And after the first year, you go into your second year, you can easily make, you know, 8,000, 9,000, 10,000 dollars [with emphasis]. And I figured out by the time you're done university and by the time you've done your trade, university will have cost you somewhere around 20,000, 25,000 dollars, whereas in the trades, you could have made 30,000, 35,000, 40,000 dollars by that time. I mean, you're 80,000 dollars ahead of the other person.

Making an income not only becomes an important marker of maturity, but also of possible superiority over other high-school students who decide to go on to college or university. Riley, the mill-wright apprentice, puts it rather succinctly when he comments on people who may question his choice to enter the trades:

RILEY: I laugh at people [who study]. It's like, yeah, you work …

NATHAN: yeah, you think you're so smart ...
RILEY: you work in a clothing store and you think you make lots of money. It's like, my paycheque is more than your mom's, don't talk to me.

Thus, earning a regular income is seen as asserting your status as a mature individual, able to chart a more discerning path on your life course, understanding your potential and what you are worth, but also increasingly defining who you are:

TED: Exactly, that's your money, you know. That's what I am. You know, you worked; you made that money, so you worked for what you have.

Despite the differences between Canada's training program and Germany's dual system, the youth apprentices in Bremen gave remarkably similar reasons for having chosen a career in the trades, as this excerpt from a focus group of electricians attests:

WL: Did any of you think about continuing at school?
SEBASTIAN: That wasn't an issue for me.
WL: Why not?
SEBASTIAN: Don't know.
MARKUS: Because I wasn't good enough at school ...
TORSTEN: And you want to get your hands on money as soon as possible ...
SEBASTIAN: As a student at grammar school [*Gymnasium*], you have no money. You might get a bit of an allowance from your folks, maybe a small job on the side or so. You might get 200 Euro ... no, that's already too much ... maybe 100 Euro in a month or so. And we definitely get a bit more than that.
KARL: And we also learn to really work. Not like them, packaging vegetables or whatever it is they do [laughs].

Youth apprentices' comments about getting paid for education (rather than having to pay for it), getting a head start in a career, and still receiving high-school credits bring to mind notions of rational choice such as those theorized by Goldthorpe (1996) or Boudon (1974). According to Boudon (1974) people attempt to maximize the utility of their educational decisions based on costs, expected benefits, and the probability of success of various alternatives. As success is defined in terms of subsequent return on the initial investment in education, and as this definition depends on one's income and SES, individuals from different class locations arrive at different conclusions: "As a result of economic inequality in society, different social locations give rise to different costs, benefits and probabilities of success. It is the rational evaluation of these, rather than class cultural factors, which generate class differences in transition propensities" (Hatcher 1998: 10).

A number of rational considerations operate at this level. First, and most obviously, working-class families' participation in education comes at a higher relative cost, given their economic disadvantages compared to middle- or upper-class families. Therefore, leaving school earlier or not participating in higher post-secondary education may be a rational decision. Second, the more affluent middle classes not only have better means to finance further education but also have more to lose by not going on to higher education. Not taking advantage of higher-education options may lead to social demotion for middle-class kids, whereas working-class youth can maintain their class position even without great investment in education (ibid.: 10). What these rational decisions lead to, of course, is an effective reproduction of class location.

Goldthorpe (1996) has built on Boudon's notion of rational choice by explaining why, despite the massive expansion of educational opportunities in most industrialized countries, class differences in participation have remained essentially the same. Goldthorpe argues that these inequalities have hardly changed because the cost-benefit balances for members of different classes have hardly changed. For members of the working class, unsuccessful participation in higher education would be far more costly than for members of a family with a higher SES. Vocational programs or courses, from a cost-benefit perspective, provide a much safer protection against unemployment or unstable, unskilled labour. Goldthorpe concludes by proposing a weak version of rational choice theory, in which individuals choose courses of action based on some assessment of probable costs and benefits rather than "unthinkingly following social norms or giving unreflecting expression to cultural values" (ibid.: 485).

In a large quantitative study of Italian youth and their educational choices, entitled *Were They Pushed or Did They Jump*, Gambetta (1987) asked whether educational decisions are the result of a "push from behind" (i.e., structural determinants) or a "pull from the front" (decisions as a result of intentional, rational behaviour).

Leaning heavily on various notions of rational choice, he found
that subjects applied various forms of rationality to evaluate educational choices, but that these evaluations were also "distorted" by
specific class biases. Answering his initial question about whether
the young people he studied were pushed or whether they jumped,
Gambetta (1987: 187) concludes that: "They jumped as much as
they could and as much as they perceived it was worth jumping.
The trouble, though, is that not all children can jump to the same
extent and the number of pushes they receive in several directions,
shaping their opportunities as well as preferences, varies tremen-
dously in society."

The insistence of rational choice theorists on rational decisions
exclusively based on cost-benefit calculations finds little resonance
with most people's everyday experiences. For instance, Brown's
(1987) study of working-class secondary students' aspirations shows
how non-monetary rewards, such as interesting work, good work-
mates, and good working conditions, are more important to decision making than an understanding of the cost-benefit relation of
possible alternatives. And the perceptions of these rewards are
strongly influenced by the social and cultural conditions in an individual's life. The data in the present study confirm this view. Youth
apprentices and academic-track students considered both intrinsic
and extrinsic factors when choosing their careers (or when considering the careers they hoped to choose), suggesting that rational
choice calculations alone cannot explain dispositions and outcomes of young people's transitions from high school. The degree
to which these young people based their decisions on future working conditions and other intrinsic motivators can be interpreted as
reflecting their own agency. Consider Ron, a student apprenticing
as a motorcycle mechanic, who explains how his participation in
RAP is an almost natural extension of his leisure activities and interests:

RON: Hmm, the reason I chose [motorcycle mechanic] is because I race
motor cross bikes in the summer and I sled a lot in the winter. So, I thought
I knew enough about it and I might as well get paid to do something with
them ... And I do everything on my own motorbikes. I always figured being
a mechanic is something I already pretty much know so I might as well go
see if I can learn a bit more and help myself and help my buddies who are
at the track.

Apprentice car mechanics had the most enthusiastic attitudes toward their work. Even on the shop floor, young men and cars seem to be an irresistible combination. The German apprentices in particular felt excited about getting involved in a career that is such an integral part of the country's economic success and its citizens' lifestyle (a car is, after all, considered a German's "dearest child"):

WL: How did you decide to become car mechanics, what led to that?
KLAUS: Cars [general agreement] ...
MATTHIAS: fixing them up [*rumzuschrauben*] ...
WL: Always?
KLAUS: Since I've been seven ...
MATTHIAS: I think this is the best job for boys, because we all like to fix cars ...
STEFFEN: After all, it really is a dream job.
MATTHIAS: Because it has to do with cars, and later you can fix them up and stuff like that.
KLAUS: You learn a lot for your own free time, if you have a car yourself and you want to work with that, then you know that through your job already.

Becoming a car mechanic is a choice that is generally well accepted and even admired. Many of the car mechanics have friends lining up to have their cars fixed for free. This also means there is little need to justify the decision to enter this field. Apprentices in other occupations, however, focus more on the working conditions or what doing this specific work means to them. Apprentices in hairdressing are a group that fights its negative stereotype by highlighting the good work environment and the personality it takes to be a good hairdresser. For instance, Joelle and Liz single out the "fun" environment in which they get to work. But more importantly, they suggest that it takes a uniquely talented, creative personality to do well in their career:

JOELLE: Oh yeah, this profession is awesome for stuff like that. It's like not work. When you're having one of those days where you just laugh the whole day, because it's just ... It's not like, I'd say, your desk job; it's fun.
LIZ: You have to be an outgoing person as a hairstylist. If you're just a plain, ordinary old Joe, you're not going to get very far in life, because if somebody comes and goes "do whatever you want," and you're like [with tired, whiny voice] "oh, we're just going to give you ..." like zero cut, right. And it's like, you got to be fun, you got to be funky, you know.

In other words, the stereotype of hairdressing as an inferior career choice is stood on its head. To be successful, you have to be funky, creative, and outgoing. Or as Debbie, another Edmonton RAP student apprenticing in hairdressing puts it, doing hair is "more like an art."

What almost all apprentices do have in common when talking about their motivations and dispositions to enter the trades is the importance they place on doing what they consider "real," physical work. In turn, this real work is part of a real world, as opposed to the "not real world" of education (either high school or university) or the "not real work" done in offices. Although I discuss this theme in greater detail in chapter 6, its relevance to youth apprentices' career decisions warrants at least a brief discussion here.

Keith talks about his preference for doing physical work and how this preference influenced his decision making. However, he extends this preference beyond the actual workplace into the personal realm by arguing that learning a trade will also make him more self-sufficient in later life, as he will have learned how to "fix stuff at home."

KEITH: Um, I took apart a lot of stuff and I work with my hands better than I work with my head. Although you do need your head, but ... it's not as stressful as when you use your head. 'Cause, say, me being a lawyer, no way. There's no way I'm going to be a lawyer. And ... I'm not gonna be sitting in an office. I want to be moving around, I want to be getting stronger every day I work because I'm lifting stuff. I want to be able to fix stuff at home. I want to be able to be useful at my own home, like say ... "oh man, a breaker blew out ... oh, I know how to do that, I can fix it, I don't have to call anybody." So, I just want to know ... I don't know, that's my basic thought pattern. And the pay is good. [laughs]

Anne, a young Bremen woman who chose an apprenticeship in hairdressing over continuing her secondary education and entering a white-collar career explains her choice in similar terms:

ANNE: Actually, my parents were happy about my choice [to become a hairdresser], because it was always obvious that I'm not the type who wants to go to school for a long time. Not that I'm dumb or that I'm not interested in learning, but ... I'm not the type to sit around all day. Really, I have to do something that allows me to move around.

On the surface, the interview and focus group data suggest that academic-track high-school students are less concerned than youth apprentices about the income potential of their career plans. Most academic students say they want a job that provides satisfying work and has intrinsic value to them. While heavy physical work is not an attractive alternative, they also show a distaste for mind-numbing "cubicle work" that is similar to that expressed by youth apprentices:

ALISSA: That's what my dad does, too. He works for the government ... I actually went on a job shadow with him in Grade 9 and I still don't know what he does. He's some sort of a manager, he works with computers, but ... he told me, whatever you do, don't bother getting like ... don't get a cubicle job, because it's not very satisfying. And he's been there for coming close to 20 years ... I wouldn't want to just sit in a cubicle all day, doing the same thing over and over. He told me, whatever you do, don't ... don't get yourself into that kind of a position, 'cause ... you know. And it's the kind of thing, you get into a job like that and, the pay is OK, you work all right hours, you just don't bother to leave. Instead of going out and trying to find something that you'll find more satisfying. You don't bother to leave it, so you end up staying there for twenty years.

Maureen, an Edmonton high-school student planning to attend university probably says it best in her movie analogy:

MAUREEN: You know movies, I use this all the time, movies you see once and you're like "this is a great movie," but then you think about watching it again and you don't really want to. But then there's movies you could see a whole bunch of times. Whatever I do, it will be the movie I see a whole bunch of times.

Sonja, a Bremen *Gymnasium* student who plans to study biology at university, explains how it is much more important to have a job that is fun, as long as you do not become poor doing it:

SONJA: I mean, you don't want to live in poverty. You should have at least some money. But ... I would rather do something I like, that is fun. I know a few people here [at school] who want to study business or computing, because they think they can make a lot of money. That absolutely does not interest me, and that's why I don't want to study stuff like that. I'd rather have less money and be happy with a job I really like, than having a lot of money and a job I don't like.

These respondents' focus on the importance of having fun in a job, in contrast to making a lot of money, is representative of the conversations I had with academic high-school students in Edmonton. However, as the interviews and focus groups progressed, it became clear that extrinsic motivators do still play a very important role for academic-track students, even though this role may not be as readily and immediately acknowledged as it is by youth apprentices. For some, like Alissa, who had earlier in the focus group talked about her plans to study anthropology and sociology and the importance of being fulfilled in your job over having stability, the relationship between extrinsic and intrinsic rewards that a future career may offer is nevertheless recognized as a potential conflict:

ALISSA: I think that's probably one of the biggest qualifiers that I want, is a job that I don't want to run screaming from after working there for too many years. And ... I want to make money in my job, whatever I do, but I don't want it to be the main issue. I want to have enough to live comfortably, but I don't want to have to, you know, quit my job and go get higher pay for something I don't want to do. So, I think being happy is probably the biggest thing. Or being, you know, OK with my job.

Some of Alissa's German academic counterparts are concerned with finding a balance between having fun at work (*"es muss Spass machen"*) and making money and having some security and stability. Consider Barbara, who is most interested in a creative, artistic career. Although Barbara understands the volatility of the field she wants to enter (or maybe because she does), she also expresses more desire for a stable and well-paying career than did the other members of the focus group who had more traditional career ambitions:

BARBARA: Well, for me it is important that there is some stability, that I will have, in a way, a steady income. I won't have that as an independent artist. I would have to find my own contracts and would have to be able to hold my own in this competitive environment. And that scares me.

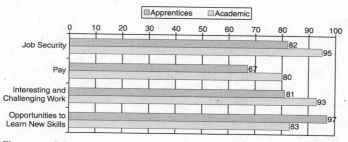

Figure 1.1 Select work values by type of program, Edmonton, and Bremen combined (percentages important and very important)*

*Respondents were asked: "Below are a number of reasons why people choose certain careers. How important are these for your own career goals?" They answered using a five-point scale, with 1 meaning "not important at all" and 5 meaning "very important." Responses of one to three were recoded as "not important"; responses of four and five were recoded as "important."

This tension between intrinsic and extrinsic rewards in their future careers is further confirmed by the quantitative data gathered through the background survey. Study participants were asked to rate (on a five-point scale, with one being "not important at all" and five being "very important") the importance of a number of extrinsic and intrinsic benefits to their future career goals. To simplify the presentation of the data and to account for the relatively small number of responses across the five categories, responses were collapsed into "important" and "not important," with the categories one to three coded as "not important" and categories four and five as "important."[1]

Figure 1.1 shows that academic-track students actually rated the two extrinsic benefits (job security and pay) as slightly more important than did youth apprentices. In contrast, youth apprentices expressed significantly more interest in careers offering opportunities to learn new skills. These responses may be somewhat surprising, since, in interviews and focus groups, youth apprentices placed more emphasis on having a steady income while academic-track students talked more about intrinsic rewards of their future careers. Two factors might explain these differences. First, academic-track high school students might be fairly confident in their higher income potential and therefore did not stress this is as much during interviews and focus groups. Second, youth apprentices have already made the transition into employment and actually receive the steady paycheques about which they speak. Receiving a steady income, as opposed to speculating about it, obviously has a more immediate effect on an individual's life course and his/her perception on the importance of this income. Similarly, youth apprentices' greater emphasis on the intrinsic benefit of learning new skills is most likely related to the fact that they are already working and that their position in the workplace is characterized by applied learning. In other words, learning new skills at work is the key element of being an apprentice.

When controlling for location (see figure 1.2), the different attitudes of youth apprentices and academic-track students observed in figure 1.1 remained essentially unchanged for either location. Percentage differences still show that academic-track students placed slightly more emphasis on job security, pay, and interesting work, but slightly less on opportunities to learn new skills. However, the Edmonton and Bremen sub-samples also showed differences.

The percentage differences in figure 1.2 show that youth apprentices in Edmonton were more likely than those in Bremen to stress job security and, particularly, pay. Although there was no discernable percentage difference for the academic sub-samples in terms of job security, Edmonton academic-track students were also more likely than those in Bremen to consider pay an important element of their future career. In terms of interesting work and opportunities to learn new skills, the relationship was reversed. Bremen apprentices and academic-track students rated these rewards higher than did the Edmonton participants. The greater emphasis placed on job security and pay by Edmonton youth apprentices contradicts the current economic realities in the two countries. While Alberta is experiencing a shortage of skilled workers in the trades, Germany is in a period of recession that has led to a decline in construction and industrial activity. How, then, might the cross-national differences in figure 1.2 be explained?

Both the novelty of RAP and its promotion as a non-academic pathway to a stable and well-paying career suggest that these issues are foremost on the minds of the young people entering RAP. The interview and focus group data I discussed earlier in this chapter certainly confirm this assumption. In contrast, the dual system in Germany has long been firmly entrenched in both the labour market and the educational system. Its benefits in terms of income and job security, although currently threatened by a recession, are neither in need of promotion nor are they questioned. The streamed

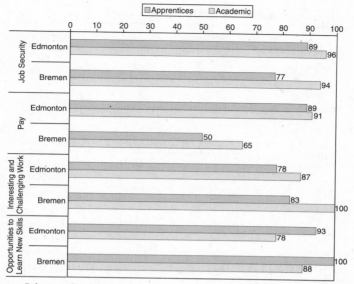

Figure 1.2 Select work values by type of program and location (Percentages important and very important)*
* See figure 1.1 note

secondary school system puts university out of immediate reach for most youth apprentices and unskilled labour is not a viable alternative in Germany's highly regulated labour market. The benefits of participating in the dual system (and the disadvantages of not participating) in terms of job security and income potential are well understood and may therefore not have been noted as important by the Bremen youth apprentices. Also, Bremen youth apprentices have already left the secondary school system and may therefore not see the need to define working in the trades as a rejection of high school's intellectual and academic purposes. Rather, Bremen youth apprentices see their apprenticeship as predominantly a form of learning. This finds expression in their greater emphasis on opportunities to learn new skills and challenging work compared to youth apprentices in Edmonton.

Despite the narratives of agency that have dominated the discussion of school-work transitions and educational and career dispositions so far, the socio-economic background data gathered through the questionnaire presented a less optimistic picture.

Table 1.1. Type of program by father's level of education, Edmonton

	High school or less		Non-university post-sec.		University		Total	
	No.	%	No.	%	No.	%	No.	%
RAP	7	64	8	44	6	46	21	50
Academic	4	36	10	56	7	54	21	50
Total	11	100	18	100	13	100	42	100

Table 1.2. Type of program by father's level of post-secondary education, Bremen

	Vocational		Academic		Total	
	No.	%	No.	%	No.	%
Apprentices	25	81	6	35	31	65
Academic	6	19	11	65	17	35
Total	31	100	17	100	48	100

STRUCTURAL REPRODUCTION: SURVEY FINDINGS

Parents' Education

Study participants in both Edmonton and Bremen were asked to provide information regarding their parents' educational attainment. Tables 1.1 to 1.4 will use father's educational and occupational attainment to illustrate the relationship between the participants' social background and whether they are in apprenticeships or academic-track programs. I chose to use fathers simply because the observed relationship was stronger. Nonetheless, similar but less pronounced relationships concerning mothers' educational and occupational attainment are evident in the data. Table 1.1 does suggest a relationship between parents' level of education and participation in either youth apprenticeships or academic-track programs in the Canadian sample. Edmonton participants whose fathers had a university education were much more likely to be in the academic group than were participants whose parents had a high-school diploma as their highest level of education. For example, only 36 per cent of those whose fathers had only a high-school education were in the academic group, in contrast to more than half of those with a more educated father.

The same relationship can be observed when looking at parents' post-secondary attainment. Table 1.2 shows the distribution of academic-track students and youth apprentices according to

Table 1.3. Type of program by father's occupation, Edmonton and Bremen combined

	NOC A		NOC B		NOC C&D		Total	
	No.	%	No.	%	No.	%	No.	%
Apprentices	4	21	32	63	18	82	54	59
Academic	15	79	19	37	4	18	38	41
Total	19	100	51	100	22	100	92	100

Table 1.4. Type of program by father's occupation and location

	Edmonton								Bremen							
	NOC A		NOC B		NOC C&D		Total		NOC A		NOC B		NOC C&D		Total	
	No.	%	No.	%	No.	%	No.	%	No.	%	No.	%	No.	%	No.	%
Apprentices	1	14	13	54	11	73	25	54	3	25	19	70	7	100	29	63
Academic	6	86	11	46	4	27	21	46	9	75	8	30	0	0	17	37
Total	7	100	24	100	15	100	46	100	12	100	27	100	7	100	46	100

whether their parents had completed vocational (i.e., apprenticeship training in the dual system, but also less common forms of school-based vocational education) or academic post-secondary (i.e., university or polytechnic, *Fachhochschule*) education. Bremen participants with fathers who were trained vocationally were themselves substantially more likely to be apprentices (81 per cent). The reverse was true for Bremen participants with university-educated fathers.

Parents' Occupation

The background questionnaire completed by all interview and focus group participants included an open-ended item about mothers' and fathers' occupations. Unfortunately, many answers were somewhat vague (e.g., "works in a warehouse"), but it was still possible to code most responses according to Canada's National Occupational Classification (NOC). Within the NOC, occupations are ordered into four skill levels: 1. Level A – professional occupations (e.g., lawyers, doctors, professors); 2. Level B – skilled occupations (e.g., assistant-type occupations and the skilled trades); 3. Level C – semi-skilled occupations (e.g., retail sales, clerical occupations, drivers); and 4. Level D – unskilled occupations (e.g., cashiers, cleaners, labourers).

Most respondents' parents – 54 per cent of all mothers and 55 per cent of all fathers – were in Level B occupations. This was par-

Table 1.5. Type of program by family income compared to national average, Edmonton and Bremen combined

	Below average and average		Above average		Total	
	No.	%	No.	%	No.	%
Apprentices	44	70	14	42	58	60
Academic	19	30	19	58	38	40
Total	63	100	33	100	96	100

ticularly the case for the German sample, which is not surprising given the country's credential-intensive labour market and the role of the dual system in training skilled workers. As with parental educational attainment, the relationship between parental occupational attainment and placement in vocational or academic tracks suggests socially reproductive tendencies in this sample.

As table 1.3 shows, participants with fathers working in low-skill occupations were substantially more likely to be apprentices than were participants with fathers working in NOC level A occupations. The reverse relationship was observed for students in the academic track.

When controlling for location (i.e., Edmonton or Bremen), we see the same pattern in both countries, but the relationship was even more obvious in the Bremen sample (table 1.4). Most remarkably, none of the Bremen participants whose fathers were employed in NOC level C&D occupations were part of the academic track.

Family Income

As with questions about parents' occupations, asking high-school students about family income often leads to unreliable information. To address this problem, study participants were told how much an average family earned and then asked to indicate whether they felt their family income was average, above average, or below average. Again, we see a relationship between family income (as estimated by the participants) and their participation in either youth apprenticeships or academic-track programs (table 1.5). Participants who estimated their family income as above average were more likely to be in the academic stream. There was no observable difference in this relationship between Bremen and Edmonton participants.

A purely quantitative portrait of the participants in this study thus provides ample evidence for the existence of processes of social and cultural reproduction. Furthermore, the data also show that some of these differences can be attributed to the different institutional arrangements in the education systems of both countries. Although one should be careful about generalizing from a relatively small and non-random sample, the observable differences between Edmonton and Bremen support the widely held belief that Germany's heavily streamed tripartite school system and the role of the dual system create more stratification than do comprehensive school systems like the one in Canada (cf., Kerckhoff 1995).

While some recent German studies have found a slight decline in the relationship between social origin and educational attainment (Henz and Maas 1995; Müller and Haun 1994), other research in Germany and Europe largely confirms that educational expansion in Germany, as in most other industrialized countries, has led to a number of unintended consequences, rather than the goal of equalizing life-course chances across social strata. For example, aggregate data continue to show that chances to attain high levels of education are circumscribed by social origin and that children with a higher socio-economic background have benefited from educational expansion more than any others (Friebel et al. 2000; Jonsson, Mills, and Müller 1996; Kerckhoff 1995; Shavit and Blossfeld 1993, 1996). Writing about the German experience, Mansel (1993: 38) suggests that: "Despite massive changes in production and employment systems (like, for instance, the move toward a service economy ...), and despite the (either real or at least anticipated) processes of individualization and the resulting de-structuring of life courses and increase in occupational alternatives, the structural relationship between parent generation – education system – occupational hierarchy and career potential has not opened up" (my translation from the German original).

Relying on their own massive longitudinal research project, which followed 1979 graduates from the three different German school streams in a northern German city, Friebel et al. (2000: 134) demonstrate streaming in secondary school and resulting educational attainment depend significantly on parents' educational status. For instance, while nearly 60 per cent of youth whose parents' educational status was considered "high" completed the highest, most academic school stream, only 11 per cent of youth whose parents had "low" levels of education did. Even more telling may be that none of the children of highly educated parents were found in the lowest, mostly vocational school stream. By 1997, nearly 20 years after their sample was first surveyed, this difference in attainment had essentially solidified, although members of the group characterized by low levels of parental education had gained some ground.

As discouraging as these findings may be, the situation in Canada is only marginally better. Andres et al. (1999), comparing results from five Canadian longitudinal school-work transitions studies started in 1973, 1975, 1985, 1989, and 1996 respectively (Anisef et al. 2000; Krahn and Mosher 1992; Looker 1993; Lowe, Krahn, and Bowlby 1997), found that the influence of class-based structural variables has indeed persisted over time. Both parents' educational level and occupational status have remained strong predictors of their children's occupational aspirations and expectations. Young people with university-educated parents are still more likely to attend university, while those young people not participating in any form of post-secondary education tend to come from families in which neither parent had attended university.

Two of the studies reviewed by Andres et al. will highlight these relationships. Following a group of 1973 Ontario high-school graduates, Anisef et al. (2000: 61) found that six years after graduation from high school, 53.2 per cent of the sample with a high SES background had completed university, compared to only 15.5 per cent of those with a low SES background. Similarly, following a cohort of high-school graduates in Edmonton over a nearly 20 year period, Krahn (2004) found that study participants with university-educated parents were more likely to complete academic programs in high school, had overall higher occupational and educational aspirations, were more likely to get a university degree themselves, and, as a consequence, were more likely to fulfill their high aspirations and to enter professional careers.

The quantitative evidence that participation in either youth apprenticeships or academic-track programs was still largely determined by SES makes a powerful argument for the reproduction of social inequality. Furthermore, the comparison between the Bremen and Edmonton sub-samples did suggest differences rooted in the structures of the education systems and labour markets of the two countries that highlight the importance of institutional structures on transition dispositions. Despite this overwhelming evidence of socially reproductive processes in school-work transitions, participants' narratives of rationality, choice, ambitions, and hopes cast a much more nuanced light on these reproductive and stratifying social processes. To obtain a more complete understanding of the interrelationship between structure and agency in school-work transitions, it is necessary to pay careful attention not only to what young people themselves say and believe but also to analyse the social and institutional contexts in which these decisions were made.

2

Institutional Context: "And It Was Kind of Hard to Get Information"

Across Canada, the federal government and most of the provinces and territories, as well as schools and the private sector have been involved in developing special programs to assist young people in making the transition into the workforce (Lehmann 2000). Human Resources and Skills Development Canada (HRSDC) has funded initiatives such as Youth Internship Canada, Youth Services Canada, and the Youth Information Initiative. High schools offer career, technology, and vocational programs and increasingly forge partnerships with the local business community. Co-operative education, internship, and youth apprenticeship programs have received growing attention as alternative forms of improving school-work transitions. Youth apprenticeship programs are designed to provide opportunities for high-school students to begin training in a skilled trade while at the same time completing high school.

THE ALBERTA REGISTERED APPRENTICESHIP PROGRAM (RAP)

A number of youth apprenticeship programs are in place in various provinces. Most programs offer apprenticeship training in the traditional trades that combines credit toward high-school completion with journeyperson certification. Compared to other provinces, Alberta has been the most persistent and successful in its pursuit of linking schools and industry in general and expanding its youth apprenticeship program in particular. This may be explained partly by Alberta's generally industry-friendly policy environment (Taylor

2001) but also by Alberta's already higher than average adult participation in apprenticeship training (Alberta Apprenticeship and Industry Training Board 2002) and a corresponding infrastructure on which to build its youth apprenticeship program. While the province has a long history of vocational education policy, the introduction of RAP can be traced to a number of reforms ranging from the mid 80s to the early 90s. These reforms were mostly prompted by concerns about projected labour shortages in certain occupational areas (e.g., the trades) and by a perception that vocational education needed to become more closely linked with the "real world" of work (Taylor and Lehmann 2002). In terms of its target audience, opinions differ on whether RAP should be specifically targeted at the middle majority of students – those neither predestined for higher post-secondary education nor at risk of dropping out or failing high school – or considered a stay-at-school program for at-risk students who would benefit from a more practice-oriented, applied alternative to the academic curriculum.

RAP is designed to allow full-time high-school students to begin an apprenticeship as early as Grade 11, earning credit toward a high-school diploma and a journeyperson certification at the same time. High-school students are eligible to enter any of the recognized trades in Alberta, provided that an employer is willing to take them on as apprentices. RAP apprentices receive one credit toward high-school graduation for each specified number of hours worked. The program is designed to allow a RAP student's worked hours to replace all course options necessary for high-school graduation, leaving him or her with only the required English, math, social studies, and science courses.

Once they've signed on with an employer, RAP apprentices are registered as proper apprentices with the Alberta Apprenticeship and Industry Training Board, but also maintain full-time student status at their high school. They are fully integrated into Alberta's adult apprenticeship system,[1] except that they have reduced hours in the workplace and they do not yet participate in any of the theoretical training of the program (which usually takes place in community colleges or technical institutes).

The program depends on flexible arrangements between schools, employers, and students to work out a mutually agreeable schedule. Depending on workplace demands, RAP apprentices may work and go to school at the same time. Alternatively, they may spend one semester exclusively at school, taking all their required courses, and the following semester exclusively at work, earning credit for their worked hours. RAP students who take the latter block release therefore need to take all four core courses in the same term. Generally, RAP students in one of the nine-to-five trades (e.g., construction or automobile mechanics) tend to work on block release, as their work schedules overlap with the school schedule. Those in occupations like hairdressing or in the hospitality industry (e.g., chefs) can build their hours around more flexible work schedules and often spend the morning at school and afternoons, evenings, or weekends at work.

On high-school graduation, RAP students have the option of continuing their apprenticeship training. Generally, they will have completed the equivalent of a first-year apprentice's work hours and receive advanced standing once they take up their apprenticeship training full-time. However, graduation from high school has been made a prerequisite to carry over worked hours into the post-high school remainder of the apprenticeship program. In other words, if a RAP student drops out of high school or fails to graduate, the Alberta Apprenticeship and Industry Training Board voids his or her accumulated work hours. This policy is considered an essential element of RAP's stay-at-school purpose.

Despite significant growth in enrolment since the first five students started in 1991, the 980 enrolled RAP apprentices at the end of 2001 (Alberta Apprenticeship and Industry Training Board 2002) – when this study was under way – still comprised less than one per cent of all high-school students in the province. The five most popular trades occupations in 2000 were welder, automotive service technician, heavy equipment technician, electrician, and hairstylist. The high enrolment in welding and heavy equipment mechanics is not surprising, given the prominence of the oil and gas industry in Alberta and the associated boom in construction. Automotive technician is also a perennial favourite among young men. More surprising, however, is the high level of enrolment in hairstyling, which indicates an increased interest of young women in RAP. Unfortunately, neither Alberta Education nor the Alberta Apprenticeship and Industry Training Board publish official data indicating the gender of RAP participants, but general apprenticeship statistics (Statistics Canada 1999) indicate that, despite the high levels of female participation in RAP as hairstylists, women have made very few inroads into the traditional male trades that form the backbone of the apprenticeship system, and that little to nothing is being done to address this gender imbalance (Lehmann and Taylor 2003).[2]

Currently no data are available to measure RAP's success in reducing high-school dropout rates or whether any at-risk students even enter the program. The existing data on RAP completion are not entirely promising. In 2005 only approximately 13 per cent of all individuals who had been enrolled in RAP in the 14 years since its inception had actually completed their apprenticeship and become certified, and a further 10 to 15 per cent were still active apprentices but not yet certified (Alberta Apprenticeship and Industry Training Board 2005). Given that certification is not mandatory in most trades and that construction in Alberta is currently booming, this is hardly surprising. It is also in stark contrast to the situation in Germany, where employment in trades occupations requires certification and both participation in and completion of apprenticeships is at a much higher level.

THE DUAL SYSTEM
IN GERMANY

Germany's dual system of vocational education may be one of the most thoroughly studied, observed, and evaluated vocational programs in the world. Undoubtedly, it has informed, in one way or another, a large range of vocational policy initiatives across North America, and a great number of vocational education bureaucrats have been eager visitors to German workplaces and vocational schools. Alberta's RAP is no exception (Lehmann 2000). The success of Germany's dual system is seen in its ability to help young people avoid periods of labour market floundering (perceived as characteristic of North American school-work transition processes) and in Germany's remarkably low youth unemployment rates. The dual system has also been credited with making Germany into a leading manufacturing economy on the strength of its highly skilled labour force. Comparing youth unemployment rates, Germany certainly seems to have an edge over Canada, particularly for the 15 to 19 age group, which, for the Canadian youth population, includes those who entered the labour market directly from high school without further post-secondary education or training (see

Table 2.1. Youth unemployment rates in Canada and Germany by age group, 1998

Age	Canada (%)	Germany (%)
15–19 years	20	7.6
20–24 years	12.6	9.9

Source: *OECD, Education at a Glance* (2000)

table 2.1). In Germany, labour force participation in this age group is dominated by young people in the apprenticeship system.

Despite all the attention given to the dual system over the years, however, its proper place within Germany's social, political, and cultural framework is rarely understood. Policy debates too often ignore or downplay the ways in which the dual system is built on Germany's tripartite secondary education system and its occupationally segregated labour market. In addition, comparisons of unemployment and participation figures are limited by the fact that the German dual system covers white-collar and service occupations, for which Canadians train in community colleges.

Educational Context:
Secondary Education in Germany

The provision of education in Germany is the responsibility of the individual federal states (*Länder*), thus paralleling the provincial responsibility for education in Canada.[3] One of the most significant characteristics of the German educational system, illustrated in figure 2.1, is its rigorous streaming at an early stage of a child's schooling, which has a crucial influence on a child's future educational and occupational destinations, including entrance into the dual system. Aptitude tests, and parental decision at the end of Grade 4 (when the student is 10 or 11 years old), determine where a student is placed in Germany's three secondary education streams.[4]

Parents can "override" what aptitude tests suggest and teachers recommend. Students can be placed in one of the higher school types (on probation), even though their test results would suggest otherwise. Similarly, parents can decide to place their child in one of the lower school types, although his or her elementary school performance would warrant attendance at a higher level. Although money is not an immediate issue in secondary-school placement (there is no tuition in any of the schools), some parents might be

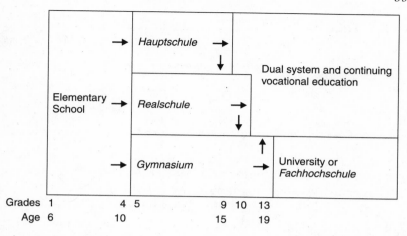

Figure 2.1 Basic structure of the education system of the Federal Republic of Germany
Notes:
This structure varies in the different *Länder*. For example, in some, the first two or three years of
Secondary Education Stage I (grades 5–7) constitute a non-streamed orientation stage.
Age refers to earliest possible entry.
At the secondary and post-secondary levels, other, marginal forms of schooling exist (e.g., full-time
vocational schools, which offer a transition year for mostly *Hauptschule* graduates unable to find an
apprenticeship position).

concerned about the long-term financial implications of their child
attending school until Grade 13 (at the upper-level school called
Gymnasium), as opposed to entering an apprenticeship and earning
an income after Grade 9 (at the lowest-level school, *Hauptschule*).

In the "lowest" stream, the secondary modern school (*Hauptschule*)
covers Grades 5 to 9 and has traditionally had the task of preparing
students for entry into apprenticeships in crafts and skilled trades.
This stream is very clearly a preparation for apprenticeships in
mostly blue-collar, retail sales, and lower-level clerical positions.
Emphasis, especially in the final years of the *Hauptschule*, is placed
on providing information and knowledge about the world of work
and occupations to facilitate students' career choices.

The "highest" stream, grammar school (*Gymnasium*) covers
Grades 5 to 13 and is the only secondary school stream that provides the qualifications to enter university. Gymnasium was traditionally reserved for Germany's elite and prepared only a small
minority for university entrance. In 1965 only about 15 per cent of
all thirteen- year-olds attended the *Gymnasium* and only about 8 per
cent of the appropriate age group obtained the *Abitur* (*Gymnasium*

Table 2.2: School leavers, by type of qualification, Germany, 1960–2002*

	No Qualification		Hauptschule		Realschule		Gymnasium (Abitur)	
	No.	%	No.	%	No.	%	No.	%
1960	132,000	20	354,600	53.7	117,200	17.7	56,700	8.6
1980	147,100	12.4	391,400	33.1	422,200	35.7	221,700	18.8
2002*	123,200	10.5	237,900	20.3	451,600	38.4	361,500	30.8

* Data for 1960–1990: Federal Republic of Germany only; 2002: Germany (United)

Source: *Bundesministerium für Bildung und Forschung (2004) Grund- und Strukturdaten 2003/2004*

graduation diploma, allowing university access) (Max Planck Institute for Human Development and Education 1983).

In the "middle" stream, the intermediate secondary school (*Realschule*) covers Grades 5 to 10. It is neither biased towards preparing a student for entering university (as is the *Gymnasium*) nor towards employment, although a great number of graduates seek apprenticeships in skilled trades and white-collar jobs in commerce and the service industry.

Until the early 1970s distribution across these three school types clearly favoured the lower-stream *Hauptschule*, with only a small minority of students in the upper-stream *Gymnasium* and a somewhat larger minority in *Realschule*. This traditional pattern of participation at the secondary level has undergone significant change since the late 1960s (see table 2.2). The so-called *Wirtschaftswunder* – Germany's rapid rise to one of the world's most dynamic and prosperous industrial states in the 1950s and 1960s – not only led to a newly found self-confidence but also to the recognition that Germany's scientific and technological potential had to be improved, as did the school's role in a socially expanded definition of citizenship. Rather than moving toward a comprehensive secondary-school system, as had been practised in the East German state (or in countries like Canada), the reform route taken in Germany was to expand the roles of the *Realschule* and *Gymnasium*. This was accomplished by building new schools and hiring new teachers throughout the country and by encouraging teachers and parents who had hitherto not considered these schools as viable options to send their children to the higher-level school streams. In recent decades the shift from the manufacturing to the service sector has further increased the attractiveness of the *Realschule* and *Gymnasium*. *Realschule* certificates allow young people to enter the middle echelons of public administration and of management in the private sector, while *Gymnasium* opens the door to universities and professional or knowledge-based careers.

All three types of secondary schools in Germany now have approximately even levels of enrolment, although these enrolment levels hide serious problems regarding who enrols in which type of school. While the upper-level *Gymnasium* has become the destination for middle-class students and the *Realschule* is the preferred destination for upwardly-mobile children from working- class families, the *Hauptschule* has increasingly become the "problem child" of the education system. In many urban areas the *Hauptschule* has become a "remainder school" for the children of foreign workers, immigrants, and members of marginal groups (Baumert et al. 1994). The social and educational devaluation of the *Hauptschule* manifests itself above all in the school climate, characterized by high rates of absenteeism and disciplinary problems. The discrepancy between what was intended and what has become reality is quite evident in the name *Hauptschule* itself, which translates into "main school." Despite its name, the *Hauptschule* no longer serves the broad masses or the average student, but draws its students from a class-specific stratum that has become increasingly narrow. Adding to the disadvantage of *Hauptschule* students is a form of *displacement competition,* caused by the increasing number of *Realschule* and *Gymnasium* graduates who are now competing for apprenticeship positions (Schober 1984). Lempert (1995) argues that students who would have been "good *Hauptschule* students" a few decades ago are now at least enrolled in the *Realschule.* Similarly, many *Gymnasium* graduates, rather than going to university, are entering apprenticeships that would have been taken up by *Realschule* graduates in the past. Official data for 2003 show that only 30 per cent of all apprentices had entered the dual system with a *Hauptschule* certificate as their highest level of educational attainment, while 37 per cent had graduated with a *Realschule* diploma and 14 per cent had a university entrance qualification, i.e., the *Abitur* (Bundesministerium für Bildung und Forschung 2005).[5] Employers have responded by raising the entrance requirements for many apprenticeships (Heidenreich 1998). This has further decreased the attractiveness of the *Hauptschule* and has had devastating effects on students' motivation, as they see their chances for gaining high-quality apprenticeship positions in the dual system ever more diminished.

Organizational Structures of the Dual System

Apprenticeship training in the dual system is of central importance for the vocational qualification of the working population and for Germany's social and economic structure. While the roots of apprenticeship training in Germany can be traced back to the guilds and trades of the Middle Ages, the term "dual system" is relatively new (Greinert 1994a). It was coined in 1964 by the German Commission for Education in its report on vocational training and education (*Gutachten über das berufliche Ausbildungs- und Schulwesen*) (Münch 1995). Duality in Germany's apprenticeship system is defined by the two different locations in which it takes place: the firm (workplace) and vocational schools.

Although apprenticeship training in Alberta and elsewhere in Canada is largely confined to traditional trades occupations – 49 in Alberta – the German dual system covers over 300 occupations, ranging from traditional trades to the types of modern service and administrative occupations that are usually part of the community college system in Canada (Bundesministerium für Bildung und Forschung 2004). This helps to explain the different roles apprenticeship training plays in the German and Canadian education systems and labour markets. In contrast to its marginal role in Canada, apprenticeship training in the dual system is the most important form of post-secondary education or training in Germany. In 2003 approximately 72 per cent of the German workforce held a certificate obtained through the dual system compared to only 8 per cent with a university degree (Bundesministerium für Bildung und Forschung 2005: 406–7). In contrast, only 1.4 per cent of the Canadian workforce were certified apprentices in 2001 (Statistics Canada 2003b). That apprenticeship training is the most important form of vocational education in Germany is not only expressed in the high participation rate but also confirmed in international comparisons of vocational qualifications of management personnel. Compared with their European or North American colleagues, more German executives and engineers have traditionally started their careers as apprentices in the dual system (Baumert et al. 1994).

Of the two main partners in the dual system, the workplace is recognized as more important by far. Training in a firm is characterized by its close link between working and learning. It is argued that such vocational training offers an advantage over school-based training, as vocational schools or colleges are rarely in a position to continuously update their machines and equipment. Furthermore, apprentices are said to learn how to work economically and responsibly, to respect and work with others, and to handle customers and suppliers. It is also argued that trainers in companies are better able to integrate new technical demands into training, and that graduates from an apprenticeship program can be productive immediately after completing their training (Bundesministerium für Bildung und Wissenschaft 1994).

Apprentices spend the majority of their time in the workplace and attend vocational schools only one to two days per week (or on longer block releases, depending on occupation). Under the Vocational Training Act, a company that is willing to train apprentices must fulfill certain requirements (Schlicht 1994). The apprenticeship must be in one of the regulated training occupations and all training must be under the supervision of accordingly qualified staff. The firm must create a training plan that meets the requirements of apprenticeship regulations and it must be considered suitable in terms of set-up and equipment. It must also demonstrate an appropriate ratio between apprenticeship positions offered and qualified skilled workers to supervise apprentices.

Employers decide whether to train at all, how many training places to offer, what applicants they will eventually hire and for which occupations they will offer training (Schlicht 1994). All these functions are basically carried out in the labour market. The government does not regulate training quotas, employers do not have to offer guarantees that apprentices will be kept on staff once they complete their apprenticeships, and fully trained apprentices are not obliged to remain with their employer. A company's investment in its apprentices therefore involves the risk that a freshly trained skilled worker will depart to another company. This potential for poaching is often cited by Canadian employers as a reason for not being more engaged in employee training. In contrast, a firmly entrenched culture of corporate involvement in vocational education guarantees a flow of trained and certified employees between companies that minimizes the losses associated with poaching. About one in five companies in Germany is actively engaged in vocational training, supplying the economy with a substantial pool of skilled labour. This means that, for many companies, losing employees trained in house can be compensated for by hiring staff that has been trained somewhere else. Smaller and medium-sized companies, whose investment in training represents a larger share of their overall budget and who may provide less attractive long-term employment, tend to lose out more heavily in this relationship. Nevertheless, many companies in Germany actually train apprentices beyond their projected employment needs (Bundesministerium für Bildung und Wissenschaft 1994). It may be argued that this reflects employers' recognition of their social and educational responsibilities, although in reality it hints at the use of apprentices as cheap labour. Nevertheless, Germany's credential-driven labour market with its strong occupational channelling and high involvement of firms in the acquisition of skills results in a relatively good fit between supplied and demanded skills. Up until the early 1990s close to 80 per cent of all former apprentices found employment within the occupational field for which they had been trained and many remained with the company that trained them (Büchtemann et al. 1994). More recent figures, however, show that labour-market problems do affect the success rates of apprentices in finding immediate employment, particularly with the firms that trained them. In its 2002 report on vocational education (*Berufsbildungsbericht*), the German ministry of education and research (*Bundesministerium für Bildung und Forschung*) documented that approximately 60 per cent of apprentices in the former West German *Länder* found employment in the company in which they apprenticed. This average hides significant differences between size of firm (bigger firms are more likely to keep apprentices once they complete their training) and industry. In the new *Länder* of the former East Germany, this average is 46 per cent, reflecting continuous economic problems (Bundesministerium für Bildung und Forschung 2002).

Vocational schooling is offered on a part-time basis and is, without a doubt, the less important partner in the dual system. The vocational school curriculum follows rather than leads what takes place at work. In the minds of apprentices and employers alike, the company has a higher priority than the vocational school (Koch and Reuling 1994). Nevertheless, vocational schools (*Berufschule*) are a compulsory component of the dual system. Apprentices attend vocational school one to two days a week or on a block release for a longer period of time. There is no tuition fee (vocational schools are public schools) and apprentices continue to receive income from their company while attending vocational school, even on a block release (Münch 1995: 51). Educational goals of the vocational schools include the extension of vocational skills and knowledge. Vocational schools have the task of teaching general and specialized subject matter while paying attention to the requirements of the students' vocational training. In addition to providing theoretical-technical knowledge associated with the occupation, vocational schools also fulfill the function of continuing young people's education for citizenship (Haag 1982: 44). Therefore, general subjects such as German or social studies form an integral part of the education they provide.

A final noteworthy element of the dual system's organizational structure is its rather complex competence and responsibility structure, which is in marked contrast to the loosely structured framework that guides apprenticeships in Canada and the belief in liberal ideals that limits Canadian governments' direct influence on labour markets. The German dual system is guided by a *corporatism* characterized by a high level of joint decision making, involving the federal, provincial, and local governments, employer groups, unions, and school representatives.

Although education is under the jurisdiction of the individual states (*Länder*), the federal government is responsible for overseeing the training in firms and defines the required duration of the training period, the description and designation of the job, the knowledge and capabilities associated with it, and its achievement criteria (Pritchard 1992). The *Länder* are responsible for the vocational schools and their curricula, the specific conditions for releasing apprentices from work to attend vocational school (e.g., block versus weekly attendance), and keeping vocational school curricula and other matters in tune with training conducted in enterprises. The chambers (*Kammer*) – employers' organizations on a regional level – are responsible for controlling whether companies and their trainers qualify to offer vocational training, promoting vocational training by providing counselling to enterprises and trainees, supervising the quality of the apprentices' training, organizing their final examinations and issuing certificates, and organizing continuing vocational training (Münch 1995). Finally, unions also play an important and co-determining role in Germany's apprenticeship system. All apprentices are members of their union and as

such are protected by collective agreements. All collective agreements include clauses specifically dealing with issues concerning
apprentices, and apprentices encountering problems during their
training can approach their union representatives for assistance.
Industry-wide collective bargaining in Germany is also said to lead
to relatively small wage differentials and similar working conditions
among companies in the same industry, which in turn reduces
poaching incentives (Rieble-Aubourg 1996).

This close level of cooperation and coordination is referred to as
the *Principle of Consensus*, and is seen as a crucial aspect of the success of the dual system (Schlicht 1994). Interests of both employers
and employees have been taken into account through legislation
specifying that employer and employee representatives be present
in equal numbers in all institutions and committees dealing with
vocational training (Münch 1995). Although this *Principle of Consensus* ensures that training regulations, once passed, are met with
universal approval, it also makes the process of change within the
system rather slow and cumbersome.

Participants in the Dual System

The structural development of training in the dual system does not
follow any comprehensive plans that regulate the number of
apprentices to be trained in the various occupations. Rather, it is
regulated by supply and demand in the labour market, with the
supply of training opportunities depending on the willingness of
individual firms to provide training. An individual does not have a
right to vocational training and a firm has no obligation to provide
apprenticeship positions. The decision to offer apprenticeship
positions is largely based on issues of profitability, expected returns
on the investment in the apprentice, and economic conditions and
trends.

Apprenticeships are allocated like any other employment relationship. A potential apprentice has to apply for an apprenticeship
position with a company and usually undergoes various screening
processes, such as interviews or tests. Once a candidate has been
selected, the prerequisite for beginning an apprenticeship with
a private or public enterprise is to formally enter a contract
(*Ausbildungsvertrag*) with the company. This contract states the
type of apprenticeship, its title, its length, what vocational school

is to be attended, and the pay and holidays for the apprentice. Apprentices are represented by unions, considered full-time employees, covered by social insurance programs, paid for attending part-time vocational schools, and protected against dismissal under the Vocational Training Act.

Participation patterns show certain social-demographic determinants. One of the features often discussed when comparing Germany's dual system to apprenticeship programs in North America is the young average age at which apprentices begin their training. German apprentices start their training at around age seventeen (Heidenreich 1998: 327; Münch 1995: 42), compared to Canadian apprentices (not RAP apprentices), who tend to begin apprenticeship training in their late 20s (Skof 2006; Sharpe 2003). Young foreigners have a significantly lower participation rate in vocational training than German-born youths, which reflects their relatively lower levels of secondary education, but possibly also discriminatory hiring practice. Women are over-represented in apprenticeships in service occupations and men in traditional trades and industrial occupations. As discussed above, one of the most significant factors determining not only participation but also the type and occupational area of apprenticeships is educational attainment at the secondary-school level. Educational attainment, in turn, is affected by social class, which returns us to the key question of how institutional arrangements are implicated in the reproduction of social inequality. Before I present data to address this question, I will analyse how different institutional features aid or hinder successful school-work transitions.

TRANSPARENCY AND FLEXIBILITY

Germany's labour market builds on an extensive range of federally regulated occupations, all of which have a clearly defined job content and prerequisite profile (e.g., the type of training or credential necessary to perform the job). Such arrangements send unmistakable signals to youth as to the type of education and training needed to enter an occupation. The dual system is intimately tied into this framework, as it provides the officially regulated training programs that will lead to certification in many of these occupations. In contrast, the labour market in Canada is characterized by segmentation into internal and external labour markets, with often

very opaque and firm-specific job requirements. For most careers –
with the exception of the professions and some trades for which
certification is mandatory – a specific type of credential is not necessary. What is required is an opportunity to break into an internal
labour market and to climb its career ladder. Consequently, educational credentials and occupations are not clearly linked, although
a relationship between higher levels of educational attainment and
social mobility still exists and is generally understood. A useful way
of understanding and conceptualizing these differences requires
taking a closer look at the relationship between *transparency* and
flexibility of education systems and labour markets.

Hamilton and Hurrelmann (1994: 331) define transparency as
"how well young people can see through the system to plot a course
from where they are in the present to a distant future goal." Transparency of structures is obviously related to the potential for
agency. Reflexive and active engagement requires that individuals
understand the context in which they have to make decisions and
in which they have to act, providing what Giddens has called ontological security (Giddens 1984). However, social structures that are
too rigid, despite an abundance of transparency, may restrict the
options available to individuals. Both Germany's hierarchical education system and its highly regulated labour market have been
described as having very transparent, yet also very rigid and inflexible structures (Geißler 1991). Through early streaming and
specialization in school, and by restricting access to most jobs to
those with official credentials, the German system sends very clear
signals to young people as to the transition paths that must be taken
to achieve specific career goals. Yet, once set on a path, change
becomes relatively difficult.

The other half of this duality, flexibility, can also be seen as a prerequisite for agency. Flexibility allows, if not requires, individuals to
consider alternative paths and to engage in reflexive risk-taking
that nonetheless leaves room to renegotiate or to retract. However,
too much flexibility may actually be problematic, opening up a
bewildering set of options, difficult to comprehend and navigate
without a proper understanding of a specific decision's consequences. Too much flexibility obscures transparency and limits the
capacity to understand and thus reflexively engage with the social
environment. School-work transitions in Canada, or more generally
the relationship between educational credentials and their applica-

bility in the labour market, have been described as being unconnected and opaque, to the particular detriment of youth who do not participate in higher post-secondary education (Lehmann 2000). As there are few clear, obvious connections between school achievement and the labour market, planning for the future and even high-school course selection are difficult and arbitrary (Hamilton and Hurrelman 1994: 338).

Flexibility over Transparency: The Canadian System

While programs like RAP increase flexibility and choice by adding an alternative to mainstream academic options, proponents of the program have also argued that it makes the labour market and career options more transparent at an earlier stage. High-school students receive information about RAP and careers in the trades through presentations in their schools made by representatives from *Careers: The Next Generation* (CNG), the industry-based foundation promoting RAP in Alberta. They also have access to training and labour-market information in their schools' libraries and resource centres. Individual students may be encouraged to look into the program by teachers or counsellors. Yet, for many RAP students, knowledge about the program, how it works, and what the requirements and the long-term career prospects are, remains rather elusive. Tim, who apprentices as a millwright in Edmonton, provides a good example of the rather confused and incomplete understanding of Alberta's apprenticeship system on which most RAP students base their decisions to enter the program:

TIM: It was kind of difficult at first, because talking to some of the people at school [teachers and counsellors] about it, they kind of were talking to me up at their level. And I did not really understand what they were talking about ...

WL: Ah, just tell me a little more about that. Did they try to discourage you to do this or did they try to encourage you?

TIM: No, they encouraged me to do it, it's just that I wasn't really sure on what to do because I had never done something like this before ... And it was kind of hard to get information from them.

WL: OK. Do you think that was because they didn't know themselves what RAP would mean because it's a fairly new program?

TIM: Yeah. That could be it.

This lack of understanding of apprenticeship structures and employment conditions needs to be considered when attributing agency to the choices and decisions of RAP participants. It appears that agency is most likely expressed by those who individually seek further information to inform their choices or who have access to credible role models (e.g., individuals with experience in the chosen occupation). Carl, an Edmonton RAP student, provides an example of what appears to be a very determined and informed decision-making process:

WL: To become an underwater welder ... First of all ... let's put it this way, I would assume that you are planning to finish your apprenticeship once you're done high school and get your ticket.

CARL: Yeah.

WL: How much longer will that take?

CARL: Uh, this summer, I'm writing my first year [exams]. And then the summer of Grade 12 I'll get my second year, and the year after I'll get my journeyman.

WL: So, you will get your journeyman certification a year after you complete high school?

CARL: Yeah.

WL: To become an underwater welder, do you have to take a lot of extra education?

CARL: Well, there is an engineering course. And by then I need to renew my scuba diving licence. And then there is basically a ten-month course for underwater welder.

WL: And who runs that? Do you know?

CARL: Well, there is a really good place in London. And then there is a couple of places ...

WL: Is that London, England?

CARL: Yeah ... and then there are a couple of places in Vancouver and Victoria. And then there are two places, [a local community college] has one ... They just started last year. I'm not sure how good it is, or whatever. And then [a technical college] in Calgary, they have one, too.

WL: Is it very difficult to get into these programs?

CARL: Uh no, not really. My company I'm working for right now, they will pay for my education, for the test and all that, for just like on-land welding. And the time I miss from work and school, if I get above 70 per cent on the test, they pay me for that time I missed.

In contrast, Stephen, an Edmonton RAP student apprenticing in landscaping, is almost completely unaware of the conditions and requirements of apprenticing, even though he had already been registered and working as an apprentice for some time when I spoke to him:

WL: OK. Let's talk a little bit about your decision to go into RAP. How did you find out about it?

STEPHEN: Well, in classrooms they were talking about it. So, yeah, that's how I found out about it.

WL: Who is they?

STEPHEN: Hmm, I forget ...

WL: OK. What did they tell you about it that interested you?

STEPHEN: About the credits. Work experience and everything ...

WL: Did you find your employer yourself, or did the school find it for you?

STEPHEN: Like ... what do you mean by that?

WL: Some of the other people I talked to say that Mr [workplace co-ordinator] contacted an employer for the placement. And other students have gone out and found an employer themselves and then came to Mr [workplace coordinator] and said "I want to work for that company."

STEPHEN: [pause] I don't know.

WL: You don't know?

STEPHEN: No.

WL: How did you decide on working for this specific company?

STEPHEN: I don't know.

WL: How did you know about them?

STEPHEN: [pause] like who?

WL: Your employer? How did you come together, you and your employer?

STEPHEN: [pause] I don't know ...

WL: Once you graduate from high school, how much longer before you will finish your apprenticeship?

STEPHEN: [pause] just probably during that year, I don't know. I'm not really sure yet ...

WL: And then once you're done with your apprenticeship, once you get your ticket, will you be working in the same field?

STEPHEN: Hmm, I don't know really. I'm not sure yet.

During the interview, it became clear that Stephen was actually apprenticing in his parents' landscaping business, which is probably

why he had such a problem making sense of my questions about
finding employment. Clearly, there is little to no evidence of agency,
or informed choice, in Stephen's account of deciding to become a
landscaping apprentice. This lack of understanding of essential institutional features of apprenticing is often compounded by the roles
that teachers, counsellors, and work placement co-ordinators play in
the decision-making process. These adults often assume the responsibility of placing RAP participants with employers. This appears to be
a valuable service to offer to interested students, but it also significantly limits the potential for choice and agency. Tim spoke earlier
about the difficulty of getting information about RAP and apprenticing from teachers and counsellors. Here he comments on how he
decided on both the occupation in which to apprentice and the
employer for whom he is working:

WL: How did you decide on a specific employer and on a specific trade?
TIM: Because the school found me the place ... where I'd be working. And
    they just ... The place where I'm working right now, they looked at what I
    was apprenticing for and they just put me in a certain spot in the building, in
    a department.

Other RAP apprentices told similar stories in which the final decision to apprentice in a specific occupation merely reflected where the
school was able to find an employer willing to take on the student:

WL: And how did you decide on heavy-duty mechanic?
MAX: Well, I actually wanted to do three things. Automotive mechanic, heavy-
    duty mechanic, or auto-body repair person. And the one that I decided on
    was heavy-duty mechanic.
WL: Why was that? Because an employer was found in that area, or did you
    make a decision?
MAX: That's were the employer was found.
WL: So, it could have gone either way, depending on who they found?
MAX: Yeah.

Understanding Labour Market Opportunities

Another aspect related to transparency in school-work transitions is
young people's understanding of labour market opportunities in
their chosen career fields. In terms of the larger, economic policy

implications of RAP, an awareness of employment opportunities also plays a crucial role in attracting young people into a career field that is currently experiencing serious labour market shortages. Particularly in Alberta, the recent oil and gas boom coupled with an aging workforce in the trades has caused serious concerns about a shortage of skilled workers. One of the selling features of programs such as RAP is their promise of employment upon completion. It appears that those students most satisfied with the progress of their apprenticeship, and those whose decision to enter RAP seemed to be based on an understanding of what it means to be an apprentice, are also most aware of the employment prospects their choice offers. Keith, an Edmonton electrician apprentice seems to understand how the current labour market in Alberta works in his favour:

WL: How difficult do you think it will be to find work as an electrician once you're done as a journeyman?

KEITH: Not hard at all. There's too many ... like in any newspaper, look under the trades, electrician, millwright, they're always there. Always. And it's a big list. They're looking for ya [laughs].

Like Keith, the following two RAP students are aware of the labour shortages in the skilled trades and are confident that tradespeople will always be in demand:

WL: Are you concerned at all about finding work once you have your ticket?

TED: Well, right now, welding is in high demand. Like, they got that statistics thing and they said welding here in Alberta will be in high demand probably for the next up to 100 years. Syncrude is good for another ... they just hit some big hole or something, I don't know, and they're good for another 100 years. There is going to be a demand for welders.

DEAN: Welders don't live past 50 ... In carpentry, people are always going to get houses or buildings or something, right. I can't really see a machine taking over my job.

Brent apprentices as a cook and already has two years of work experience. He was one of the most articulate, informed, and determined apprentices with whom I spoke. Here is what he has to say about employment prospects as a chef, but also about his future career plans:

BRENT: If you're a cook, you can find a job no matter how bad you are [laughs]. It's really high in demand. We're looking for cooks and dishwash-ers non-stop. Everybody wants cooks because it's one of these trades that people get into and they're going to get hired because there's a lot of things going on ... And I want to go around the States and get my schooling either in Europe or Paris or the States. And after that, I might even come back and get my international Gold Seal. And that's like the highest you can get in Canada, and that takes forever ... I'm not about to just sit in a no-name restaurant for thirty years and just sit and cook burgers, you know. I wanna be out doing hotels, world-class cuisine. Learning how to actually do, create the things they do.

Some RAP students confidently compare their own employ-ment opportunities to those of university graduates, despite an over-whelming public discourse that predicts ever higher levels of post-secondary education necessary for employment success in a post-industrial economy. Recall Riley and Nathan who ear-lier talked about the financial advantages of earning money while learning as an apprentice, compared to spending money as a university or college student. Here are their comments on employment prospects with a trades ticket, relative to a higher post-secondary credential:

WL: You know there is so much talk about needing more and more education these days. Do you think you will be held back without university in your career or life?

RILEY: Not really, because if you get a ticket, there is like ... once you're a journeyman, if you're like ... you can get a job anywhere. There is always ... like trades are in most demand right now. All the old people are retired and they have no one to fill them. Like up at Syncrude right now, they need sixty electricians, and they found only twenty to fill the jobs. So they're still looking for forty.

WL: So, you're pretty confident that there will be lots of work?

RILEY: There's like ... my company is trying to hire people, and there's just not enough people to meet the demand.

NATHAN: I think the emphasis in the last ... well, five years at least, on most kids has been to go to university and to go to college and get a degree in something, whereas they haven't been focusing a lot on the trades. And I think that's opened up a really big spot for anybody who wants to. I mean, it wasn't hard to find a job.

Not all RAP students, however, equate good employment opportunities with a fulfilling career. Tyler was enrolled as a RAP student, apprenticing as a heavy-equipment technician at the time of the interview, although he was toying with the idea of not completing his apprenticeship and possibly preparing for college or university instead. Consequently, his outlook was less optimistic than that of other RAP students:

WL: Do you get a sense that if you decide to stay in the field that there would be a lot of work?

TYLER: Yeah I think that there'd be a lot of work, for sure. But who knows if it'll be a lot of good work or just crap.

The overall sense of optimism about employment opportunities in the trades expressed by Edmonton RAP students is not uniformly mirrored by their colleagues in Bremen. Only the service occupation apprentices, like the chefs and hairdressers, are really confident that their line of work will always be in demand. Sven is one of the Bremen apprentices, training to be a hairdresser. Much like Brent in Edmonton, his extreme confidence about his future is coupled with very ambitious career plans:

SVEN: Look, when we know how to do something, that's something we got in our hands. Nobody can take that from us. And hair grows everywhere in the world. You could go off to Spain and cut hair on the beach for a couple of dollars ... Hair always grows ...

WL: Where do you see yourself in 10 years?

SVEN: I want to work for a while [in a salon] and then apply with a big company, because I'm young, I have ideas, and I know how the trend is going. Maybe I could develop products for this trend ... Can I dream a little, too? Then I'll be standing there and people are looking at me and say: "Here's a trendsetter." I do want people to know who I am.

For the apprentices in construction trades, the future doesn't seem quite as rosy:

WL: How easy or how difficult do you think it will be finding employment as a journeyman once you're done with your apprenticeship?

KAI: Here in Bremen, as an electrician, the chances aren't all that good.

MATTHIAS: No, companies just don't get enough work.

KAI: In our company, they just had to let five journeymen go. Earlier, they thought that they would need a lot of people, so they took on a lot of apprentices. Usually, our firm prefers to keep those they had as apprentices. But now, they only get temporary contracts, and after that, many have to leave. Not a lot is going on.

WL: Are you worried about that?

STEFFEN: Yeah, a bit. If you think about it sometimes, the recession in construction ...

Given Germany's current high levels of adult unemployment, these young people have every reason to be concerned about employment past their apprenticeships. This is noteworthy, since North American policy-makers often see German-style apprenticeships as a solution to school-work transition problems. However, the real problem often lies in the lack of labour-market opportunities. The relatively low levels of youth unemployment that are seen as a hallmark of the dual system thus mask employment problems apprentices encounter once they have completed their training. Companies like the one Kai talks about continue to train relatively high numbers of apprentices, despite a recession in the trades. While this may be a good practice, both in being prepared for an upswing in construction activity and in giving young people a chance to receive training even in bad economic times, there is also an element of exploiting these young people as cheap labour during their apprenticeship tenure. Nonetheless, the comments by Kai and his colleagues do reflect a rather thorough understanding of labour-market opportunities in their careers, which can be related to the high levels of transparency associated with Germany's dual system.

Transparency over Flexibility: The German System

In Germany, transparency is central to the close relationship between a streamed, tripartite secondary school system and an occupationally structured labour market. Transparency is maintained by an extensive and impressive network of federal employment centres (*Arbeitsamt*)[6] that engage in vocational counselling and assist in placement. In addition, students in any of the three secondary school types are required to participate in career exploration internships. Ilka, one of the Bremen academic high-school students, talks about the range of contacts and information services she has used to form dispositions about post-secondary plans:

ILKA: For me it was a number of things. We have a vocational counselling service here at school, and ... well, I was always sure that I wanted to do something with children, but I just didn't know what exactly. I did an internship in a day care and ... well, that wasn't enough for me, with the money and the demands, although I actually quite liked the age. And then I spoke with this woman, and she said "Why don't you study primary education, that is a fairly young age as well and you could bring in your skills and interests." Then I had information about the job sent to me, read through all that, and really liked it a lot. I told everybody about it and actually received a lot of support.

Despite its early streaming processes and the initially limiting impact on agency, the greater transparency of the German education system and labour market thus opens up *Handlungsspielraum* (room for agency). In other words, finding oneself in a certain location in the social structure (for instance in the upper-school stream, like Ilka), and having access to a multitude of well-established information sources creates an understanding of the range of options open to individuals. Although these options are limited by the initial streaming process, this limitation itself provides a framework in which knowledge about the structures and consequences of choices enables agency. Obviously, this range is greater for those graduating from the upper-school stream (*Gymnasium*). But even the far more limited range of occupational opportunities for graduates from the lower streams (*Hauptschule* and *Realschule*) appears to create conditions to enable agency, as the labour market sends very clear signals to individuals regarding the credentials needed to enter specific careers:

WL: Did any of you ever think about going to work right after school, without an apprenticeship? I mean, you could probably make more money right away. [all: no]
KAI: Yeah, but only shitty work ...
KARL: Yes, and no prospects for employment later.
KAI: If you're unemployed, what can you do then?
KARL: Yeah, doing an apprenticeship is absolutely necessary.
KAI: I'd agree.

Understanding of these structures is aided by a number of public agencies and institutional arrangements (like the *Arbeitsamt*), compulsory internships in secondary schools, counselling services in schools, and the general co-operation between education, industry, and unions in matters of vocational education. Moreover, the central importance and the long-standing tradition of these institutions, services, programs, and relationships further guarantees that most young people will have somebody to talk to who has gone the same route, either in their family or within their group of relatives, friends, and acquaintances, their schools, or their community. Consider, for instance, the following conversation with two young Bremen participants, both apprenticing to be chefs and explaining how their interest in this career arose:

HANS: Well, I got interested in this because both my parents work full time and I had no choice. I had to cook at home. And after a while it really was fun. And then I started getting interested in it as an occupation and started to look into it further. At first, I didn't really want to do it because of the hours you work as a chef. But then I thought, you'll probably get used to that, and I actually did get used to it pretty fast. And it really is a lot of fun.

WL: Where and how did you find out about this occupation?

HANS: At the *Arbeitsamt* and with relatives. One of my friends is also working as a chef.

WL: Did it help talking with others who also work in this area?

HANS: Yeah, that helped a lot, because I really had no idea what this is all about. That it is really quite exhausting, that you have to work a lot of overtime, and that you won't have a lot of free time left.

MARIA: As I said earlier, I did a number of different internships at school.

WL: All in different areas?

MARIA: Yeah, and of all the jobs I tried, I liked cooking the best.

WL: May I ask what the other occupations were?

MARIA: For example, I did an internship in a day care as a child care worker, and also one in retail. Working as a chef was the only one I really liked, I'd have to say.

WL: Without the internships, would you have considered becoming a chef at all?

MARIA: I don't think so.

Like Maria, a number of other Bremen apprentices decided about their occupation through internships at school. Thomas, a

Bremen automobile mechanic who had graduated from the *Hauptschule,* claims that he never cared much about cars. He only got interested in automotive mechanics after he realized, during his first internship in house painting, that he has a fear of heights. So he tried a second internship in a garage.

Internships for the purpose of career exploration play a far more important role in the curriculum of the two lower school streams (for instance, *Hauptschule* graduates like Thomas need to complete at least two internships). Even so, the *Gymnasium* requirement to complete one internship is still an important way to gather insights into potential careers:

SIMONE: Well, I did my internship with a lawyer, because I was undecided between law and medicine. But now, I'm really turned off the law profession. It seemed quite boring, always sitting at a desk, writing, and so on. I don't know. And that's why I now tend more toward going into medicine.

The vocational counselling services of the German *Arbeitsamt* also fulfills important functions in informing students about different occupations, increasing their understanding of requirements in specific careers, and assisting individuals with finding employers. Ellen, a hairdressing apprentice, talks about her experiences with the vocational counsellor at her local *Arbeitsamt.*

WL: Does anybody else have any experiences with counsellors at the *Arbeitsamt?*
ELLEN: Yeah, the person I visited was quite helpful ... but also because I already ... well, I only went there once. I already had a pretty good idea what I wanted to be, and then he was able to tell me about the prerequisites, how to apply, where the vocational schools are, and so on. He did tell me those types of things and printed a lot of information for me.

Ellen obviously had concrete ideas about what she wanted to do and was in need of more specific information about her career choice. Others, like Attila and Frank, both apprenticing in a metal trade, benefited from the services offered at their local *Arbeitsamt* in a multitude of ways:

ATTILA: Yeah, I watched a film [about workers in the metal trades], and I really liked that. How they were standing at the lathe.

WL: Did you also talk to a counsellor at the *Arbeitsamt*?
FRANK: Yes.
WL: Was that helpful?
FRANK: Yeah, it really was. Without him, I wouldn't have my apprenticeship right now. He sent me all that stuff. Like, he made some suggestions [about different kinds of occupations in the metal trades], and then he sent me all this information material about them. Because, I didn't know what all these different jobs were. And then I worked through all that material, and finally made my decision in the end.

Not all German participants were as happy about their experiences with the *Arbeitsamt*. Particularly those with higher levels of education found the services at the *Arbeitsamt* rather useless, as the following conversation between Simone and Silke, both students at a Bremen *Gymnasium*, attests:

SIMONE: OK, we all went to the career library at the *Arbeitsamt*, from the school here. But that was quite stupid. You could enter your interests and stuff into a computer, and then you would get a list with occupations. It had primary school teacher for math, and such crap on it. Stuff that doesn't interest me at all. It wasn't very good, or useful.
SILKE: Yeah, the computers she just talked about, I used them too. And it printed out that I should become a math teacher, or something in engineering. But I found that very funny, as I'm almost failing math [laughs].

Although Simone and Silke felt that the *Arbeitsamt* was not of much help to them, they did make use of some of its services. And in some roundabout ways, the "stupid" and "funny" results of the computer printouts probably did help confirm a set of dispositions toward career areas that they had already been forming. However, despite the greater transparency of the German system, its complement of institutional features and services, and its potential to create *Handlungsspielraum* (room for agency) for graduates from all three school streams, it can also be interpreted as constraining.

Institutional Context as Constraining

Despite the more transparent linkages between education and the labour market in Germany, its network of information centres, and its compulsory internships during secondary schooling, many young people still enter occupational paths based on largely untested assumptions and beliefs about different types of work. Connie is a young German woman who graduated from the German *Realschule* and now apprentices as a hairdresser. Here, Connie talks about her earlier plans to continue her schooling and to subsequently embark on a white-collar career, and about why she ultimately decided to abandon these plans to apprentice as a hairdresser:

WL: Did you originally have other career plans?

CONNIE: Yes, I actually wanted to be [*Speditionskauffrau*; administrative assistant in transportation] and I did apply in that area ... I did an internship with [company name] and they would have taken me on as an apprentice, and that was fine with me. But then I started thinking that I would like to do something more creative and I figured that hairdressing would be OK. Why not try that. At that point, I didn't think about money. You live with your parents. That's totally ... you have some delusions and you think, man, it'll all be great, you'll be really famous [laughs] ... you'll be standing on a stage cutting hair and ... Well, it wasn't like that. As I said, I started working in a salon, and right away, it was a total reality check. Now, I really have ... well, I think I'll finish the apprenticeship for sure, that's certain, I won't quit. But afterwards, I'll either continue with school or I'll do something totally different, maybe also try university or something. I'll have to see.

WL: Well, you almost answered my question. Do you regret your decision to become a hairdresser?

CONNIE: Well, if I had known how this job really works, I might have done something different ... My brother is now starting university ... he was actually the only one who right away told me "no, don't do that, you can't be a hairdresser." Yeah, now that he's at university, I'm starting to have my doubts ... I'm starting to think, is time going to run out? He is starting at university, and, well ... you're still doing an apprenticeship.

Connie's expectation to work creatively, to become famous and to cut hair on a stage, in front of an audience, is obviously nowhere near the everyday experiences of almost all hairdressers. To some extent, it can be argued that increased individualization, a decline in the deterministic force of social structure, and other conditions of late modernity as discussed by social theorists like Beck (1992) and Giddens (1990) have created conditions in Germany that are more akin to the Canadian experience. In other words, perhaps the

transparency inherent in a system that rather effectively reproduced social inequality by streaming young people into career
paths according to their social origin is being replaced by flexibility
and individualization, as the educational system has expanded and
opened up more alternatives, particularly for the lower middle
classes. However, as Beck's notion of risk society and Connie's story
above suggests, this increased flexibility does come with certain
risks. I discuss individualization and risk in chapter 4. For now, it is
important to highlight the inflexible, constraining, and reproductive capacities of Germany's education system.

Streaming

Despite its potential to create *Handlungsspielraum*, Germany's transparent yet inflexible dual system can often lead to transitions that
are hardly motivated by interest and disposition. In some cases, the
plethora of regulations and standards leads to situations in which
young people are forced into certain apprenticeships despite very
different dispositions. Bulcin, a young Turkish woman apprenticing as a hairdresser in Bremen, talks about her dislike of hair, even
though she has begrudgingly accepted the need to complete this
apprenticeship to fulfill her real career ambition of becoming a
make-up artist:

BULCIN: I want to become a make-up artist. I went to the *Arbeitsamt* and
    they told me that if you want to become a make-up artist, you have to
    apprentice as a hairdresser first and get two years work experience in a
    salon. OK, so I said I'll do the three-year apprenticeship, because then I'll
    have a ticket ... that's why. Other than that, I didn't want to become a
    hairdresser ... A friend of mine, she has a salon with her uncle. At first, I
    would go there for almost a year to see what they do. And all that fucking
    hair, lying everywhere. I thought that was the shits. I couldn't even touch
    hair.

Bulcin ultimately understood the advantage of doing the internship in order to fulfill her true career goal. Anja, who also apprentices as a hairdresser, is an example of somebody whose agency is
almost completely circumscribed by institutional and cultural factors. In Germany, entering the labour market as an unskilled
worker is a more severe disadvantage than in Canada. Completing

at least an apprenticeship is seen as a minimal requirement for success in the life course. For some, like Anja, the actual occupation in which one apprentices is almost no longer important:

WL: How did you decide on becoming a hairdresser?
ANJA: Because I couldn't get anything else.
WL: What did you try first, or what did you want to do at first?
ANJA: I honestly had no idea what to do. I sent off about 45 applications, everywhere ... like administrative assistant, and also hairdressing, and other stuff. And nobody responded, and the salon where I work now was the only employer who contacted me. And then I started right away.

Although Anja expressed her disillusionment with her schooling, she actually graduated from *Realschule*. Consequently, she is already in a better position to compete for an apprenticeship than those who graduated from the lowest school stream, the *Hauptschule*. In the earlier description of the dual system, I alluded to a process commonly known as displacement competition. Because of increasing levels of educational attainment made possible through expansion of the education system in the seventies, graduates from the *Hauptschule* have become disadvantaged for apprenticeship positions. Here is a sample of quotes from apprentices who graduated from the *Hauptschule*:

(Bremen Apprentices Focus Group, roofers):
OLIVER: Automotive mechanics, I once tried that out in an internship.
WL: And you didn't like it?
OLIVER: Well, I was told that it wouldn't work, you need to have *Realschule* to get into that. And that was that for me.

(Bremen Apprentices Focus Group, electricians):
TORSTEN: Initially, I wanted to apprentice as a *Mechatroniker* [a new occupation combining electronics and computing], but they wouldn't accept me with only *Hauptschule*.

(Bremen Apprentices Focus Group, metal workers):
WL: How difficult was it to find an apprenticeship position?
ATTILA: I wasted three years before I found one. After Grade 9, with my *Hauptschule* diploma, I wanted to start an apprenticeship. Couldn't find anything. Then I participated in [lists a number of federally sponsored

pre-apprenticeship programs for young people with trouble finding apprenticeships], still couldn't find anything.

Recent statistics show that graduates from the *Hauptschule* stream are no longer the majority in the dual system. Of all German apprentices in 1999, 36 per cent had graduated from the *Realschule*, versus 30 per cent from the *Hauptschule* (16 per cent did have *Abitur*). The remaining 18 per cent had entered the dual system either without secondary credentials or after participating in a variety of federally sponsored job preparation programs. This shift toward a preference for *Realschule* graduates is even more prominent in apprenticeships for more prestigious occupations, like automotive mechanics or all the upper-level service occupations (Bundesministerium für Bildung und Forschung 2000, 134). Most affected by these trends are young people from lower-class families and young non-Germans.

Sven, a *Hauptschule* graduate who is now apprenticing as a hairdresser, sums up his view of the disadvantaged position of *Hauptschule* students:

SVEN: It's really tough in our school system here. I mean, if you only have a *Hauptschule* diploma, the *Realschule* students already think of you as an asshole. And they are already shit in the eyes of the *Gymnasium* students. Really, as a *Hauptschule* student, you carry a heavy load around ... And why should those sitting at the top ... I mean, here he has to choose from ten people with *Hauptschule* and five with *Realschule*, and he has to hire four. Of course he'll take the four from the *Realschule*. He doesn't give a shit. People aren't interested in what you've done, they are only interested in your diploma, and that's the thing.

Collins (1979) and Murphy (1988, 1994) suggest that instead of reducing inequality, mass education has allowed the middle classes to solidify their privileged position, as ever higher educational credentials have become prerequisites for entry into certain career paths (particularly in the professions). Collins (1979) has referred to this as credential inflation, arguing that despite the expansion of education systems in industrialized nations, social inequality by and large remained unchanged, albeit at an overall higher level of educational attainment.

Although Sven's comments above are exclusively focused on the credential implications of streaming, they are also reminiscent of neo-Marxist views on education. For instance, Bowles and Gintis's (1976) *correspondence thesis* states that the social relations in the educational system structurally correspond to those of production, as the power relationships experienced at school socialize students to the discipline and fragmentation of the workplace. The school and learning environments experienced by students streamed into different programs or school types reinforce the internal organization of capitalist enterprises through their different emphasis on rule-following in vocational programs or independent thinking in academic programs.

Not surprisingly, research on streaming and school placement shows that working-class students are more likely to be streamed into less challenging programs in high school (Oakes 2005; Curtis, Livingstone, and Smaller 1992). Kerckhoff (1995) claims that highly stratified educational systems (e.g., Germany) produce a stronger association between socio-economic status of origin and educational attainment because of earlier streaming and sorting. Despite educational reforms and an opening up of higher education in the 70s, there is ample evidence that streaming in Germany continues to occur along class, gender, and ethnic dimensions (Alba, Handl, and Müller 1994; Damm-Rüger 1994; Gellert 1996).

Clearly, the often touted advantage of Germany's transparent education system needs to be considered in the light of these reproductive processes and inflexibilities. As documented in the earlier analysis of the quantitative data, participants in the dual system are more likely to come from a lower socio-economic background, whether measured by family income or parents' educational and occupational attainment. The qualitative findings above further add to this perception, as graduates from the *Hauptschule* stream also had the greatest difficulties in finding apprenticeship positions. Yet, despite these institutionally based disadvantages, the German youth apprentices' understanding of how the dual system functions, and of the options open to them within the system, in other words the system's transparency, also created conditions for informed decision making and, thus, agency (or what I earlier called *Handlungsspielraum*). In contrast, the flexibility of the Canadian labour market came at the cost of uncertain and confusing transitions. The latter applied not only to youth apprentices who had very little information about the institutional requirements of their apprenticeship, but also to academic-track high-school students who expressed uncertainty about where their studies might take them.

This lends support to Giddens' notion of structures (including institutional features) as both enabling and constraining (Giddens 1984). In terms of Giddens' structuration theory, the transparent sets of rules and relationships guiding the German system create a sense of ontological security that seemed missing for a substantial number of Edmonton youth apprentices who were relatively poorly informed about apprenticeship requirements and expectations beyond high school. Yet, although the streaming at the secondary level in Germany and the resulting preferences in the labour market send very clear signals to students from all three school types about the boundaries within which they can realistically form dispositions about career plans (i.e., *Handlungsspielraum*), it is obvious that for some there is very little room for choice.

3

Gender: "Men Work, Women Have Children"

The previous chapter focused on institutional features that both helped and hindered young people in their transitions from high school to further education and employment. Obviously, education systems and labour markets are key institutional features. Gender also emerged as a powerful aspect related to institutional features, in the sense that welfare-state arrangements, educational practices, employment and hiring preferences, and cultural factors variously affect young people's career dispositions.

Gender is implicated in all of the experiences discussed by the young men and women in this study. Gender is implicated in streaming processes from primary to secondary education in Germany and in vocational vs academic-track placement in Canadian high schools. Gender is an element of the discussions around attitudes toward schooling and resistance to theoretical, abstract, and academic learning, which I discuss in chapter 4. Gender is also part and parcel of the ways in which young people construct vocational identities, as I demonstrate in chapter 6. This chapter however, focuses on the ways in which institutional arrangements are directly implicated in gendered experiences and on how the young men and women in the study directly and indirectly reflect on the role of gender in school-work transition processes.

Although Davies (2004) argues that gender and ethnic inequalities in Canada have declined I found that, with respect to occupational aspirations and educational attainment, gender continues to exert an extremely powerful influence on the way young people expect their educational and occupational careers to unfold. Certainly young women now outperform young men at almost all

educational levels and in nearly all disciplines. Of all undergradu-
ate degrees awarded in 2001 in Canada, 60 per cent went to
women, with engineering, mathematics, and computing being the
only areas in which there were fewer women than men. Increasingly, this trend is also manifest at the level of graduate studies and
in professional programs. Sixty per cent of law degree recipients
and 55 per cent of medical degree recipients were women in 2001
(CAUT 2004). This success story in the education system must be
tempered, however, by the labour-market experiences of women.
Women are still more likely to be found in gender-typical occupations. Those who have broken into traditionally male careers
(such as law or medicine) tend to practise in less prestigious sub-
disciplines (e.g., family medicine rather than surgery or real-estate
law rather than corporate or criminal law). And women continue to
be nearly non-existent in the skilled trades.

Gender-stratification was also evident in this study. Although
there were substantially more women than men in the academic-
track sample, the vast majority of youth apprentices in the study were
male. The Edmonton sample included only five women, all of whom
apprenticed as hairdressers. Although I made efforts to include
young women apprenticing in traditionally male trades, not one was
in the schools selected for this study. I had a lead for one young
woman, but by the time data collection began, she had already dis-
continued her apprenticeship as an automotive mechanic.

Essentially the same picture emerged for the German youth
apprentices. Out of thirty-six participants, eleven were female.
Again, none of the female youth apprentices was in traditionally
male trades, although two were not in hairdressing but were
apprenticed as chefs. This reflects recent national apprenticeship
statistics. In 1997 in Canada only 2.5 per cent of building construction trades, 1.5 per cent of industrial and mechanical trades, and 2
per cent of motor vehicle and heavy equipment apprentices were
female (Statistics Canada 1999). In Germany, the figures are similar: only 2 per cent of motor vehicle, 1 per cent of metal trades, and
on average 1 per cent of building construction apprentices are
female (Bundesministerium für Bildung und Forschung 2004).

Efforts to increase female participation in male-dominated
trades in Germany, although they do exist, appear to have been relatively unsuccessful and many have even been abandoned in recent
years (personal conversation, vocational school teacher, Bremen,

30 May 2002). Similarly, there are few efforts in Alberta to increase female participation in traditional male trades, either in RAP or in apprenticeship training generally. There are no equality of opportunity programs or diversity initiatives (at least at the high-school level) that try to increase the participation of women in male-dominated apprenticeships. Generally, it is seen as sufficient to ensure that young women are aware of opportunities in the trades (Taylor and Lehmann 2002). More research is needed to investigate, for example, why so few women choose careers in the trades, to what extent this gender imbalance is related to gender-role socialization or hostile workplaces (see Gaskell 1992), and how cooperation with different partner groups (e.g., Women in the Trades, an Edmonton-based foundation promoting the employment of women in trades occupations) might redress these imbalances. Fenwick (2004), for instance, argues that issues of equity – including gender equity – in vocational education have become victims of neo-liberal preoccupations with efficiency, accountability, and competitiveness. Not only do young women encounter employer resistance in the labour market but also schools may back away from encouraging women to enter traditionally male youth apprenticeships. Too often, schools appear more concerned with the establishment and maintenance of amicable relationships with employers participating in these programs than with the promotion of gender equity and balance.

Maybe this "lack" of women in trades occupations need not be a problem, if we consider the increasing importance of a knowledge-based service economy. Certainly women's tremendous gains in educational attainment have them well-positioned to move into knowledge-intensive, professional-type employment. McDowell (2003) speaks of a crisis of masculinity, as young, particularly working-class, males encounter a changed labour market that no longer requires their skills and attitudes. Yet, for young women who are not university bound, their employment in the service industry is no less precarious and uncertain. Alberta is in the midst of a severe labour shortage in the skilled, manual trades and young men entering these careers currently have outstanding employment and income prospects. Young women are largely shut out of these opportunities and little is being done to correct this problem. And even those women who complete higher education eventually encounter nearly insurmountable barriers in their attempts to climb corporate ladders. Held back by what has become known as the glass ceiling, fewer than 20 per cent of top executives in North America are women. Not only do women encounter an authority gap as they begin to reach higher levels in an organizational hierarchy (Reskin and Padavic 1994), they are also faced with cultural dimensions of femininity and family that become powerful influences in career decisions and working lives (Evetts 2000).

GENDERED CAREER EXPECTATIONS

Although the young men and women in this study largely conformed to gender stereotypes in their educational and career goals, on first sight most of the young women did not appear to be guided by gendered expectations. Education and career clearly took precedence over getting married and raising a family for most of the young women, particularly those in the academic streams. Lisa and Nadine in Edmonton and Silke in Bremen, in separate interviews, sum up the feelings of most young women in the academic-track sample:

LISA: You work on your career and you think of yourself, because you'll get halfway through university and you'll meet that guy and he'll be like "well, I don't want you to work, I just want you to stay at home." And you'll be like "I don't want to stay home!" I think you should think of yourself first.

NADINE: Well I don't know, having a family, that's just way too far off. Like right now, I know this sounds kind of selfish, I want me all to myself. I want to have my own life and do whatever I want to do.

SILKE: I feel like this: I want to stand on my own two feet, not having to be dependent on anybody, not even my parents. And if I do marry, I don't want to depend on my husband. I might want to have two children in ten to fifteen years and have a regular life, so I can be there for my kids, but even then I want to work and earn money.

Similarly, in the quantitative findings derived from the background survey, the vast majority of the young women did not consider gender an important factor affecting the achievement of career goals (17 per cent of Bremen men and 15 per cent of Edmonton women rated gender as an important factor, compared to only 4 per cent of Bremen women). The following excerpt from a focus group with female *Gymnasium* students in Bremen shows the level of confidence associated with the young women's career expectations:

WL: [Are you] concerned that being a woman could hold you back?

SILKE: Not anymore, I don't think.

THERESA: For example, the daughter of my mother's boss, she was the only woman in her year studying mechanical engineering and physics, and she makes a shitload of money ... She pushed through. She did have to deal with sexism, dumb jokes, and stuff. But she just said, what the heck.

FARIDA: It depends on the person.

THERESA: Yes, it depends on your character. A woman with a weak character wouldn't choose something like that.

SIMONE: Yeah, she'd rather be a secretary.

FARIDA: And if you're lucky [unintelligible] ... with equal opportunity, you may actually be better off than men. You might actually have an advantage.

Any concerns regarding the gendered nature of work and career appear to be resolved through narratives of potential advantages (e.g., through equal opportunity legislation) and success through personal commitment, attitude, and ability.

These encouraging findings are reflected in other research on the gender and career ambitions showing that women have as high or higher ambitions as men (e.g., Krahn, Lowe, and Hughes 2007). Yet, upon closer investigation, traditional gender pressures and expectations prove to be persistently powerful, even for the most determined women in this study. Lisa's comment about being asked to stay at home reveals underlying concerns about her role as a woman and the gendered expectations she will eventually encounter. Jillian, another academic-track Edmonton participant, discussed her concerns about combining work and family more directly when I asked her if she could foresee any reason why individuals might not achieve their goals. It is important to remember that my initial question asked for any reason, not a gender-specific reason:

JILLIAN: Hmm, get pregnant. [laughs] ... Uh, my mom, she got pregnant when she first got married, when my dad was still in university. And she wanted to go into education and it was an unplanned pregnancy, like ... she was married, but it was an unplanned pregnancy. And so that kind of changed the course of her life. She didn't get to do what she wanted to do. She never ended up going to university. And so that's very important. And she stresses that kind of a point to me a lot, that the choices I make now could influence the rest of my life, and I got to be very careful in doing whatever it is I'm doing. And, you know, it might be fine being a kid, going

out partying and stuff, but you gotta keep your head on straight, because
you don't want to mess up now.

It is interesting to note how Jillian uses her mother's experiences
with an unplanned pregnancy as a powerful and immediate reminder
to make the right decisions, although an important gendered subtext
of this story remains hidden to her: the fact that her mother sacrificed
her education, while her father completed university and entered a
career in teaching.

Heinz et al. (1987) criticize school-work transition and career
decision-making research that tends to take youth as the basis for
analysis or theorizing, without considering how gender may be
implicated in this process. Their German longitudinal research,
following Grade 7 *Hauptschule* students through the remainder of
their *Hauptschule* education and into the labour market, found
a correspondence between traditional gender roles in society, a
gender-segmented labour market, and gender-stratified transition
processes into employment. Although their interviews with both
young men and young women about to enter employment and
apprenticeships in the dual system revealed a strong perception of
gender neutrality (e.g., neither boys nor girls believed in traditional ideas about the types of work a man or a woman should or
should not do), their eventual transitions largely followed traditional gender roles. Heinz et al. concluded that this essential ascrip-
tion into a gendered labour market and apprenticeship system is,
in hindsight, re-interpreted by individuals as the result of long-
standing dispositions, demonstrating how gender expectations have
been internalized and both conform to and reproduce a gender-
stratified labour market.

Similarly, Looker and Magee's (2000) analysis of longitudinal
data on Canadian youth's educational and occupational plans,
expectations, and attainment revealed that despite young women's
very ambitious career goals, they still expect to have primary
responsibility for childcare. Like the young women in this study,
the women surveyed by Looker and Magee (2000: 86) accepted the
idea that gender is not a barrier to their career, yet they had "not
released themselves from the expectation that they, and not the
men in their lives, are the ones responsible for the care of young
children." These expectations cut across class status and were iden-

tical regardless of how high or low the young women had set their career goals, just as I found with the young women in this study.

Not surprisingly, then, a more thorough analysis of female participants' narratives revealed that expectations regarding parenting and motherhood played an important role in the formation of their dispositions toward post-high school plans. Many of the young women with whom I spoke in interviews and focus groups (in the academic and apprenticeship sub-samples) brought up the issue of how having children and raising a family was an integral part of their decision-making process. Often, what was not said betrayed concerns about being women and having a career as much as what was expressed directly. Joelle, who apprentices as a hairdresser in RAP, explains how her decision to become a hairdresser was influenced by traditional beliefs about gender roles:

JOELLE: I wasn't sure what I wanted, going into like high school. So I'm like … I kind of took it [hairdressing in RAP] because, well, it's always a career, it's always something to fall back on if you want to stay home with your kids, something like that. You can always work part-time doing it. Or something like that. So there's always options there. Or you can work from home or things like that. It wasn't really a career move coming into high school, like that's what I was going to do for the rest of my life.

The relatively early integration of youth apprentices into the workforce and adult roles may reinforce traditional gender expectations and roles, in part because the social networks of these young women have started to shift away from friends at school to older colleagues at work. As these colleagues are more likely to be in a "family" stage in their life course, the apprentices themselves may start to anticipate these events in their own lives. Ellen, one of the Bremen hairdressing apprentices, explains her experiences with colleagues, or at least her understanding of the common life and family paths chosen by young women in her career field:

ELLEN: Many have children real fast. At first they want to achieve a lot, but once they're done with their apprenticeship, very quickly they have children. And then, well, they prefer to stay at home, because you cannot make a lot of money as a hairdresser anyways, no, and then it's better for the boyfriend or whoever to work, kids are being raised, and that's that. As our [vocational school] teacher always says: two keep working as hair-dressers, the rest have children.

Although Ellen relates women's decision to give up work to have and raise children partly to the low income potential associated with her career, expectations regarding parenthood cut across class lines and career goals. Joanne is an Edmonton academic-track high-school student who suggested that her career plan of becoming a physical therapist was as much motivated by an interest in the occupation as it was by her expectation that working in this field would help her balance work and family:

JOANNE: Yeah, I'm sort of struggling between wanting to stay home and be a mom and wanting to go to work. Because the whole, I love to cook, I don't want my kids in daycare – I've worked in a daycare, they're not nice places. And I want to be there when they grow up. I sort of struggle between that so I'm thinking if I am married and if it permits, I'll work part-time so that I can be there most of the time at least ... My mom stayed home with me. I never went to a daycare, not once. And it was great.

Although this was rare, some of the young women, like Dorothea, one of the Bremen academic-track *Gymnasium* students, talked about actively censoring their career ambitions to accommodate motherhood:

DOROTHEA: I decided against going to university, because it would simply take too long, and I might have to miss out on having a family. And I definitely feel that if I have children, I want to be there for them. And then I would give up my job, at least for some time....

In contrast, the male participants in both countries seemed to be either blissfully ignorant of these issues (concerns about balancing fatherhood and career were not once raised by the male participants) or did not see the need to treat them as anything affecting their own careers. The following excerpt from a focus group of apprentice car mechanics in Bremen demonstrates male attitudes:

WL: I already asked you about your career goals for the future. How about personal goals, like starting a family?
[people talk over each other]

MATTHIAS: Best not at all [laughs] ... uh, I don't know.

KLAUS: Let's say if you have a wife and she has a good job and makes good money, and you make good money, too, that's great, isn't it?

DETLEF: [laughs] Yeah, but that puts you into a different tax bracket and in the end, you'll actually get less.

KLAUS: ... with children!

DETLEF: If you are a single mother, you'll have nothing. I can guarantee you that.

THOMAS: But you're not going to be a single mother now, are you? [everybody laughs]

More seriously, contrast the following comments made by Murray and Maureen in a focus group with Edmonton academic-track high school students to witness the different ways in which gender affects how young people think about careers and their lives:

MAUREEN: I do want all these things [career and family], too, but I think the hardest part will be being able to find like a balance between the two, like not sacrificing too much of what you always wanted for yourself and then too much ... like not sacrificing anything that you would want to, like kids and the family and the acreage and anything like that. So, I don't know, I guess I still don't know.

MURRAY: I got mine all planned out. Well, I'm going to go to college or university, get my degrees and stuff like that. And then by the time I'm done that, I'll be 26, 28, somewhere around there. And then what I want to do is I want to have a nice stable job for four years, get some money underneath my belt and during those three or four years, when life is stable, I want to meet someone and then marry her after a couple of years, have two kids, the boy is two years older than the girl [everybody laughs] and I have everything planned out the way I want it to be.

Murray may be somewhat unusual in that he has already given such detailed thought to his life and having a family (cf., Friedman and Weissbrod 2005), but there is no concern or worry in Murray's mind that having a family is going to interfere with his career. The unspoken assumption, without a doubt, is that his wife will stay at home with the children. Not surprisingly, young women like Maureen talk about their lives, work, and family in less certain terms. Or, alternatively, the few young women who had decided to have children were prepared to give up their careers in return, at least for some time.

These findings are not new. Investigating the work-family attitudes of young men and women, Friedman and Weissbrod (2005) found that while young women were likely to have already decided about family roles (which could include not having children), young men were less likely to have given them serious thought. Evans (2002) found that although young German women generally saw themselves as having the same employment chances as men, they still expressed the view that at some point they would have to choose between work and family, and that child-rearing responsibilities were generally given preference. Analysing the relationship between work and family life for older generations in Germany, Krüger (2001: 416) found that, despite changing attitudes about the role of women in the home and at work, about 70 per cent of her sample continued to engage in work (or preparation for work) corresponding to gender stereotypes.

Overall, the situation is similar in Canada, despite the differences between the young women in Edmonton and Bremen in this study. While overall labour force participation and educational attainment of women has increased over time, employment of women is still concentrated in female job ghettos, with lower average earnings, fewer benefits, and limited career potential (see Krahn, Lowe, and Hughes 2007 for an overview of women's employment in Canada). As far as the relationship between parenting and work is concerned, Looker (1993), in a 1989 study of seventeen-year-old youth in three different Canadian locales (Hamilton, ON; Halifax, NS; and rural NS), found that when neither marriage nor children were being considered, women's preferences to work full-time were similar to those of men. However, when they were asked to consider their employment plans once they have children, she found a significant decrease in the number of women who planned to work, and the majority of those who still did so envisaged working on a part-time basis. These expectations of young women are confirmed by aggregate statistical evidence, which shows how having children reduces women's labour force participation (see, e.g., Statistics Canada 2000b).

Although it is impossible to generalize from the narratives of a relatively small number of women, it nevertheless appeared that the young women in Germany were more direct and concrete in the concerns they expressed and in the ways they discussed their plans to juggle family and work. The comments by Heidi, a Bremen *Gymnasium* student who hopes to become a teacher, appear to be typical of the beliefs of many German women:

HEIDI: That's just the way it is here: men work, women have children. And I can live with that, I think ... uh, if the man makes good money. That's why he doesn't have to take that into consideration when choosing a career.

What may be the reasons for these different attitudes in the two countries? One potential explanation lies in the different welfare-state arrangements and in how these differences might shape cultural expectations regarding the role of women in the home and at work.

GENDERED SCHOOL-WORK TRANSITIONS AND WELFARE REGIMES

These differences between young German and Canadian women regarding the formation of gender and career identities highlight the role of institutional features, particularly in the realm of welfare arrangements. Esping-Andersen's (1990) welfare regime typology is useful for discussing these differences. He argues that there are three highly diverse welfare regime types (liberal, conservative, and social-democratic), each organized around its own discrete logic of organization, stratification, and social integration. Canada is considered a *liberal* welfare state, in which the market is considered the best provider of individual welfare. Germany is seen as a *conservative* welfare state, in which benefits depend largely on employment-based contributions. The emphasis is on conservative family values and a traditional male breadwinner model, with a substantial set of policies and regulations that encourage mothers to stay at home (e.g., relatively extensive and generous maternity leaves and benefits). The differences in these welfare regimes support public perceptions and discourses that, in turn, affect how young women themselves perceive their role in the family and the economy. Both the persistence of a male breadwinner model and the relatively generous benefits accorded women who choose to leave the labour market to care for their children are institutional features that have profound impacts on the formation of young German women's dispositions toward balancing family and career. The German labour market, unlike Canada's, offers relatively few opportunities for part-time or other flexible work arrangements. Although stricter labour regulations and better employment protection should be considered an advantage for employees, they may have negative implications for women who seek a gradual return to the labour market. Furthermore, schooling in Germany revolves around a daily timetable that makes it nearly impossible for both parents to work, as children and youth begin their schooling day very early and often finish by one or two in the afternoon. As women are expected and indeed continue to be the primary caregiver for their children, their return to the labour market after having had children becomes very difficult or is, at the very least, much delayed, as Simone, a Bremen academic-track *Gymnasium* student explains:

SIMONE: As a woman, I think if you want to have children later on, obviously you'll be out of work for a while because you're the one who's pregnant, even if the husband takes paternity leave. So, you'll still have to find your way back into work ... that is something that can hold you back, because I definitely want to have children, but I also want to accomplish things in my life. And I don't know if I'll be able to get it all together ... I don't really want to have children when I'm thirty-five or forty ... that's too late.

For a substantial number of the young German women in the study, the anticipated conflict between employment and motherhood did become a deciding factor in their educational and occupational plans, as is shown here in an excerpt from a focus group with Bremen academic-track women. Katharina, who wants to enter business, and Heidi, who wants to be a teacher, discuss the importance of giving precedence to family over work:

KATHARINA: Well, I think family is important and in my opinion, all the money in the world won't make a person happy, if he [sic] doesn't have his [sic] family and his [sic] children around him [sic]. I think that women who say they want to have a career, they'll by unhappy in their lives, or disappointed ... I want my children to be around and hold my hand when I croak [all laugh], not some nurse, no way.

HEIDI: As a teacher, it is perfect. I can take three years of maternity leave, or I can wait until my children are at school, and then I can return. That's a big bonus and really confirmed my decision [to become a teacher].

These gendered findings highlight how cultural and institutional features that seem, at first sight, to be unrelated to school-work transitions still exert very powerful influences on young people's dispositions. Germany's specific welfare arrangements, with their continued reliance on a male breadwinner model and generous maternity leave benefits, have created conditions in which young women seem to have more readily accepted their primary role as stay-at-home mothers and the labour-market discrimination that goes with it.

Concerns about independence from others (like a husband) notwithstanding, few of the women interviewed were truly worried about how their future choices between employment and family might affect their quality of life. Yet, feminist critics of welfare-state arrangements have highlighted how specific institutional arrangements put women into positions of dependence and how the state's action or inaction may facilitate or hinder the level and quality of women's labour-market participation (O'Connor 1996; Orloff 1996). Liberal welfare regimes such as those in Canada often force women into labour-market participation not because they wish to work in their jobs, but out of economic necessity and because of a lack of adequate state provision. In conservative welfare regimes such as in Germany, women encounter opposite pressures to not work. In addition, (full) labour-market participation for women (or their ability to deal with the state) is restricted by the division of labour within families. Of importance are state provisions that facilitate access to the labour market, such as child care and other caring facilities, employment and pay equity, and flexible forms of parental leave.

Unlike the somewhat more optimistic assessment of structures creating conditions for agency (*Handlungsspielraum*) in Germany's heavily regulated education system and labour market that I proposed in chapter 2, women's role in Germany's welfare regime was clearly affected by a limited *Handlungsspielraum*. Dispositions of the young German women regarding school-work transitions were often based on how well they could be consolidated with the demands of having a family. Yet the same women who discussed issues of maternity as relevant to their career choices also suggested that gender is no longer a structural factor that could hold them back from achieving their goals. Or, as in the following comments by Katharina, who earlier talked about her preference for family

over career, they argue that the potential structural barriers they
encounter as women actually create incentives for more active decision making:

KATHARINA: I think it is different for boys, because ... I mean, they don't have
to give birth to children. I believe girls have to think about these issues earlier ... The boys can take their time, they'll find their way somehow. But us,
we have to get cracking, or else we'll go under [the others laugh].

Gender and social class are similarly experienced vis-à-vis social
structures and institutional arrangements. Young women reconstructed potential gender disadvantages into advantages or rejected
the possibility of career barriers. The working-class youth apprentices, as shown in chapter 2, also did not articulate the socially
reproductive nature of their participation in youth apprenticeships,
although some of the young men and women in Bremen acknowledge the negative impacts of their lower levels of secondary education. Male apprentices overwhelmingly list their interest in manual
work as the only reason for participating in youth apprenticeships,
while the women talk about their preferences for gender-typical
employment and life-course paths. The limiting and reproductive
aspects of class and gender thus remain hidden from them. It may
therefore be tempting to revert to a more determinist interpretation
that sees structural forces working behind individuals' backs and
essentially negating the agency they themselves expressed in their
career dispositions. However, the following chapters demonstrate
that this would be too narrow a view, as even reproductive processes
are infused with various forms of agency.

4

Social Context:
"It's Just What My Family Does"

The previous chapters have highlighted a key empirical and theoretical dilemma: despite individuals' narratives of independent decision making, career and educational dispositions were clearly affected by social status. Not surprisingly, the young people in this study overwhelmingly felt that career and educational success depended on motivation, talent, and hard work. In the questionnaire administered at the end of interviews and focus groups, participants were asked to rate the importance of various factors for achieving career goals. Structural factors were represented by family background, race or ethnicity, and gender. Individual factors included "having the right attitude," "being willing to make some sacrifices," and "being flexible." While these individual factors mimic a public discourse that suggests everything is possible if one just tries hard enough, they also allow us to investigate the extent to which young people buy into this ethos or are aware of the degrees to which achievement is circumscribed by factors of structural inequality. A final measure is reserved for the amount of importance youth apprentices and academic-track high-school students accord educational attainment.

Figure 4.1 shows that the views of youth apprentices and academic-track high-school students differ most about the importance of high levels of educational attainment. As is to be expected, academic-track high-school students were more likely to rate high levels of educational attainment as important for career success. This difference was more pronounced in the Bremen sub-sample, perhaps because training in the dual system has traditionally led to very stable and well-paying careers. Youth apprentices in Bremen may

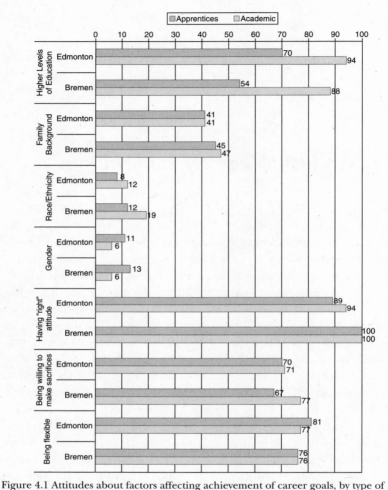

Figure 4.1 Attitudes about factors affecting achievement of career goals, by type of program and location (percentages important and very important)*

*Respondents answered question: "On a scale from 1 to 5, with five indicating very important, generally how important do you think are the following for achieving career goals?" Responses in categories one to three were recoded as "not important"; responses in categories four and five were recoded as "important."

therefore be more confident about success without higher levels of post-secondary education.

The ratings of the four sub-samples (Edmonton Apprentices, Edmonton Academic, Bremen Apprentices, Bremen Academic) differed relatively little on the influence of structural factors on the achievement of career goals. While family background was actually recognized by almost half of all participants as playing an important role in achieving career goals, only a very small minority of respondents considered race or gender as having any impact. Interestingly, the academic-track sub-samples were slightly more likely to rate race/ethnicity as a factor contributing to career success, while the youth apprentices were more likely to consider gender a contributing factor. What is most significant in figure 4.1, however, are the big differences between individual and structural factors, the former being seen as much more important for career success. All four sub-samples uniformly stressed the importance of being motivated, having the right attitude, and being flexible as important prerequisites for achieving one's career goals. These findings may be somewhat surprising, as one may expect a greater sense of class consciousness amongst the Bremen participants. After all, Canada is generally considered a less class-based society, and earlier findings in this study have highlighted the class-based stratification of Germany's education system. Yet this emphasis on individual effort over structural constraints regarding occupational success has also been confirmed by other research (Berger, Brandes, and Walden 2000).

Despite these rather individualistic attitudes, previously analysed quantitative data as well as a closer look at the interview and focus group data revealed a rather different story – a story that is best explained in a theoretical framework that borrows from the late Pierre Bourdieu's work on social and cultural reproduction.

HABITUS AND CULTURAL CAPITAL

Bourdieu's work is concerned with explaining processes of social reproduction without reverting to a simplistic form of structural determinism. The two most important concepts for understanding school-work transitions processes in Bourdieu's complex oeuvre are those of habitus and cultural capital, both of which can be applied to account for the formation of dispositions towards certain educational and occupational choices, given a set of structural parameters.

Cultural Capital

According to Bourdieu, capital is defined as the set of actually usable resources and powers an individual possesses. This can take the form of economic, cultural, social, and symbolic capital. Bourdieu defines capital as "accumulated labour (in its material- ized form or its 'incorporated,' embodied, form) which, when appropriated on a private, i.e., exclusive, basis by agents or groups of agents, enables them to appropriate social energy in the form of reified or living labour" (Bourdieu 1986: 241). Capital is best understood as resources determining social relations of power. These resources may be social, cultural, political, or even religious in origin (Swartz 1997: 75), and can be accumulated, converted, and strategically used to change or maintain social relations.

More concretely, economic capital refers to the financial resources at one's disposal, whereas social capital represents an individual's network of social resources (although, in Bourdieu's work, nothing is ever quite as simple as that). Cultural capital is a more complex phenomenon, central to Bourdieu's theory of repro- duction of inequality through education (Bourdieu and Passeron 1977). Cultural capital calls attention to the ways in which cultural resources rooted in social origin, such as language ability, knowl- edge, and tastes, are linked to educational and occupational aspira- tions and attainment. In this respect, Bourdieu is able to explain how elements of the school culture and curriculum favour the chil- dren of "cultured" middle- and upper-class families, while alienat- ing working-class children who do not see their experiences and knowledge reflected in curriculum.[1]

To measure this notion of cultural capital, participants were asked in the questionnaire whether they engaged in various cul- tural activities. These included both "high" and "low" culture, such as listening to classical versus pop music, going to the theatre versus going to the movies, reading books versus reading magazines, and playing an instrument versus playing sports. A cultural capital index, which was created by adding the number of high-culture activities in which respondents participated, showed that overall 78 per cent of all respondents participated in only few high culture activities and 22 per cent participated frequently in such activities.[2]

Table 4.1 provides evidence of the type of relationships we would expect: young people with low cultural capital were over- represented in the apprentice group and those with high levels of cultural capital were more likely to end up in the academic track. Table 4.2 shows that results for the Bremen and Edmonton sub- samples were similar.

Table 4.1. Type of program by levels of cultural capital, Edmonton and Bremen combined

	Low cultural capital		High cultural capital		Total	
	No.	%	No.	%	No.	%
Apprentices	54	68	9	39	63	61
Academic	26	32	14	61	40	39
Total	80	100	23	100	103	100

Table 4.2. Type of program by levels of cultural capital and location

	Edmonton						Bremen					
	Low cultural capital		High cultural capital		Total		Low cultural capital		High cultural capital		Total	
	No.	%	No.	%	No.	%	No.	%	No.	%	No.	%
Apprentices	21	62	6	37	27	54	33	72	3	43	36	68
Academic	13	38	10	63	23	46	13	28	14	57	17	32
Total	34	100	16	100	50	100	46	100	17	100	53	100

Table 4.3. Levels of cultural capital by gender, Edmonton and Bremen combined

	Low cultural capital		High cultural capital		Total	
	No.	%	No.	%	No.	%
Male	54	88	7	12	61	100
Female	26	62	16	38	42	100
Total	80	78	23	22	103	100

Gender emerged as an even more important variable, with women being much more likely to engage in "high" culture activities (see table 4.3).[3] Some of this relationship is a function of the higher proportion of females in the academic group. Gender, however, appears to have an independent effect, which was also apparent in the interviews and focus groups, and has elsewhere been documented as part of women's gains in educational attainment compared to boys (McDowell 2003; Weiner et al. 1997).[4]

Habitus

Habitus ensures the active presence of past experiences within individuals in the forms of schemes of perception, thought, and action. Bourdieu has defined habitus as "an acquired system of generative schemes objectively adjusted to the particular conditions in which it is constituted" (Bourdieu 1977: 95). In other words, habitus

"encapsulates the ways in which a person's beliefs, ideas and preferences are individually subjective but also influenced by the objective social networks and cultural traditions in which that person
lives" (Hodkinson and Sparkes 1997: 33). In a strict structural
sense, habitus creates dispositions to act, interpret experiences,
and think in a certain way. However, Grenfell and James (1998)
argue that Bourdieu's concept of habitus goes beyond a simple for-
mulation of biographical determinism as it is actualized through
individuals, both consciously and unconsciously.

As individuals' upbringing and social environment are the strongest contributors to the formation of habitus, using habitus allows
us to place school-work transition processes in a framework that can
account for the active formation of dispositions towards certain
educational and occupational choices, but with an understanding
of how these dispositions are rooted in social structure (Andres
1993; Hodkinson and Sparkes 1997).

In addition to the more direct cultural capital variables applied
above, the questionnaire included a set of items approximating a
measure of habitus. Respondents were asked to rate on a five-point
scale how important certain skills were in their homes. The skill sets
included manual and physical skills, artistic skills, intellectual skills,
and the ability to express oneself well and convincingly. This measure of habitus around class-specific skill sets and attitudes follows
Nash's (2003: 55) notion of socialized dispositions:

If it can be shown that the experience of a certain social group produces a
culture that disposes those brought up within that culture to develop
characteristic preferences, then actions which follow those preferences are
explained to the extent, and only to the extent, that those preferences can
be demonstrated to be responsible for their engagement in a practice.

My argument here is that a working-class family may place more
emphasis on being handy and able to fix things, whereas a middle-
class family may stress intellectual skills. This reinforces a class-
specific habitus that in turn affects individuals' tendency to think
about their vocational and educational abilities and interests in
these terms.[5] Hence, it appeared as a very useful and context-
specific way of measuring one aspect of habitus. Without a doubt,
there are innumerable other (and possibly better) ways in which
habitus and its various aspects could have been measured. The

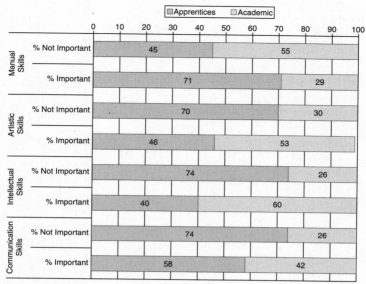

Figure 4.2 Program type by skills used in the home, Edmonton and Bremen combined*
*Respondents were asked: "On a scale from one to five, with five indicating very important, how important do you think are the following skills in your family?" Values of one to three were recoded as "not important"; responses of four and five were recoded as "important."

value of these skills in the home, however, seemed to serve as a useful proxy to measure habitus as a way in which individuals were socialized into developing certain career and educational dispositions. The nature of these measures already indicates their close relationship to forms of cultural capital.

Not surprisingly, participation in either the apprenticeship or academic streams was affected by these measures of habitus. Figure 4.2 shows that apprentices were more likely to have grown up in homes in which manual skills were considered important and less likely to have grown up in homes in which being artistic, intellectual, or articulate were considered important skills. The reverse, of course, is true for participants in the academic streams.

When taking location into account (see figure 4.3), the percentage difference suggest that a preference for manual skills in the home is a stronger predictor for participation in youth apprenticeships in Bremen. Similarly, a preference for artistic skills in the homes of young people in Bremen was more likely to influence participation in the academic track. These findings suggest that at least for this group of young people, habitus and cultural capital played

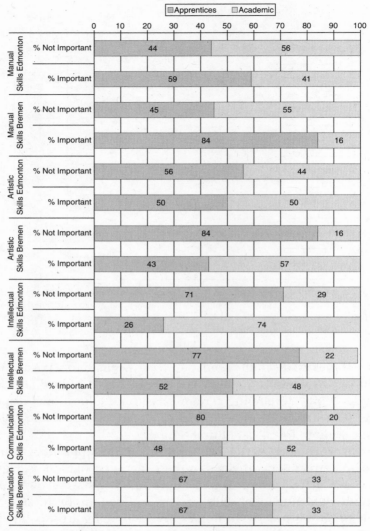

Figure 4.3 Program type by skills used in the home and location*
* See figure 4.2 note

important roles not only during the rigorous, early streaming in
Germany's school system but also in the formation of vocational
and educational preferences throughout secondary education.

Percentage differences in figure 4.3 also suggest that preferences
in the home for being intellectual and articulate were more important for participation in academic programs in Edmonton. This

may at first appear contradictory to the other findings of cross-national differences. This, too, may be explained by the differences in the two school systems. Like their academic peers, Edmonton youth apprentices are still part of the high-school system. As I show in more detail below, participation in youth apprenticeships is seen as a way to oppose the "theoretical" or "intellectual" elements of high school by pursuing more "practical" and "applied" forms of learning. In contrast, the German youth apprentices have already left the secondary-school system and are more likely to re-define intellectual skills in terms of work-related problem solving.

If habitus is indeed "history turned into nature," as Bourdieu (1977: 78) argues and the quantitative findings above suggest, then we should also find that individuals' narratives regarding their upbringing, their social environment, and the things they do with their families contribute to their overall dispositions toward a career. Tim, who apprentices as a millwright in RAP and whose father is employed in the trades, describes his relationship with the type of career he has chosen in rather vivid, almost deterministic terms:

TIM: I've been working with my dad [in construction] for five years ... I've always enjoyed working in a trade. *It's just what my family does* and I just seem to enjoy working with my hands rather than working with my mind all the time (my emphasis) ...

WL: Do you find that with your family at home, doing things with your hands was always quite important?

TIM: My family's been like that for all their lives and *I just had to grow into it*, I guess (my emphasis).

Although Tim clearly enjoys his work and expresses satisfaction with his decision to join RAP, there is a sense of fatalism in his suggestion that he "had to grow into" manual work, as this is what his family has done all their lives. In Bourdieu's terms, Tim's comments are evidence of an embodiment of structure; his disposition toward a career in the trades is the result of "a past which survives in the present and tends to perpetuate itself into the future" (Bourdieu 1977: 82).

Similarly, Dean and Ted, both apprentices in RAP, talk about the social (or maybe occupational) environment in which they grew up and which obviously shaped their dispositions toward work:

DEAN: No, nobody in my family ever went to college or university. My brother is the first one who graduated high school last year. [unintelligible] we're a whole trades family.

TED: Nobody in my family went [to university] ... trades, that's about it. If you do anything, it's always a trade ...

WL: Were you at any point ever interested at aiming for university?

TED: No. I knew probably in Grade 9 I was never going to university. I was just going for a trade in something ... [mostly unintelligible] Don't care for [books] ... no motivation [unintelligible].

NICK: Yeah, that's how I was. Like seeing it get done, not hearing about how it gets done.

TED: That's how I am. You can tell me how to do something and I'll forget. I can watch you and I can do it, no problem.

NICK: I actually have to do it myself to learn ...

DEAN: I've always been good with my hands ... I've never been book smart at all, I'm [unintelligible] when it comes to doing like writing work. But if you put me in like a shop, I can build just about anything ... [unintelligible] I'm good with my hands, I'm not good with my head.

This conversation illustrates how habitus and cultural capital intersect to create a remarkably strong set of dispositions toward education and work. And although interview participants such as Ted, Dean, and Nick may not be conscious of the way in which their social class and their upbringing contribute to their specific sets of dispositions toward manual work, they are able to justify their preference for this type of career as opposed to considering university as an option. This intersection between habitus, cultural capital, and dispositions toward work was remarkably similar for the German apprentices. Consider, for instance, the following conversation between Matthias, Thomas, and Steffen, all of whom are apprenticing as car mechanics:

WL: I just want to talk about your families a little more. Almost all of you have been fixing up cars with your dads and developed an interest that way. In your families, was there also any pressure to do well at school or to do bookish things, like reading, writing, and so on? ...

MATTHIAS: For me it was more manual, trades work.

THOMAS: They [my parents] said it doesn't matter if you're stupid, as long as you work.

STEFFEN: I think the way my dad did it was really quite good. He put out his hand and I was supposed to give him whatever tools he needed. If you don't think, then you'll get the wrench whacked over your head, if it's the wrong one.

Rudy is apprenticing as a roofer in Bremen. His explanation of why he started his apprenticeship, despite being warned about the job by experienced workers in the occupation during an internship, is even more telling:

WL: Did anybody warn you about the job?
BERT: Yes, the journeymen themselves. They said, don't do it, it's hard work and so on. But, I don't know.
RUDY: Yeah, I got that too, in my internship. Before I started my apprenticeship, they all said "train for something different, not this job. It's no good."
WL: Why did you do it anyway?
RUDY: Well, because ... I looked at my [*Hauptschule*] diploma and marks, and thought to myself ... in my family, almost everybody works in construction, and then I thought, why shouldn't I do it myself?

Not all of the students I interviewed are as clear on this issue. Debbie entered RAP as a hairdressing apprentice, although she agrees that her parents initially had hopes for her to go to university instead:

WL: Did [your parents] ever, at any point, when you were younger, want you to go to university or work towards university?
DEBBIE: Yeah.
WL: Was that their hope for you at one point?
DEBBIE: Of course, every parent wants that, right? They really wanted me to go to the university.
WL: Had they been to university themselves?
DEBBIE: No, they haven't.
WL: And, were you ever really wanting to go to university throughout school, up to now?
WL: No, I wasn't.
WL: Never?
DEBBIE: No.
WL: How come not?
DEBBIE: I'm not sure. I'm not sure at all.

Her comments on why she never considered university as an option are a vivid reminder of habitus as encapsulating the ways in which a person's dispositions are "influenced by the objective social networks and cultural traditions in which that person lives" (Hodkinson and Sparkes 1997: 33). As both of Debbie's parents have relatively low levels of educational attainment and are engaged in manual labour, Debbie's lack of interest in university is the result of a habitus that, according to Swartz (1997: 105), provides a "practical and taken-for-granted acceptance of the fundamental conditions of existence."

Just as a working-class home creates a very powerful set of dispositions toward a manual career, the families of the most confident academic-track students were characterized by an emphasis on doing well at school and aiming for university. Alissa, an Edmonton high school student with plans to study in the social sciences, talked earlier about her parents' role in "planting the seed and opening her eyes" to the possibility of going to university. Although she insists that the final decision to go to university will be her own, this decision will nevertheless be based on a very powerful set of dispositions, habitually enforced through a home which is characterized by her parents' relatively high level of occupational attainment:

ALISSA: Um ... ever since I was little, throughout the whole thing, it's always been "you're going to go to university" or you're gonna at least go to college ...

WL: From your parents?

ALISSA: Yeah, from my parents a lot. And like even my grandma, she put away some money for me and when she passes away I'm getting that. And it's only to be used for tuition. But, it's always been, you know, "you're gonna go to university" and that's never been an issue for me.

The fact that going to university has "never been an issue" for her suggests that her range of post-secondary options is as much constrained as that of working-class children choosing to go into youth apprenticeships. Part of this set of dispositions is certainly an expression of the North American ethic of social mobility through educational attainment. This ethic is not lost on the young people in the study, as the following comments from Rhonda, an Edmonton hairdressing apprentice, show:

WL: Do you think if you want to go to university it helps if you have parents that have been to university?

RHONDA: I would think so. I look at some of my friends and they spend their life doing homework, because their parents put that on them. That they have to have these certain marks because they have to go to university. And it's just ... education is everything.

Rhonda's comments regarding the differences between students with and without university-educated parents point to Bourdieu's second important theoretical concept for the study of school work transitions: cultural capital.

However, these relationships between habitus, socio-economic status, and dispositions are not necessarily as straightforward and deterministic as the above comments suggest. Consider, for instance, how Nadine, an Edmonton academic-track high-school student with plans to study biology at university, interprets them:

NADINE: I think it pretty much has a positive influence, no matter what your family background, because ... say if you lived in the slums and your parents had no education and you grew up in a box, it would make you ... I don't know, it would give you greater perseverance and determination to overcome anything that comes at you.

It is important to note here that Nadine has a "vested interest" in feeling this way, as her socio-economic background should effectively prevent her from success in higher education. Nadine has been raised by a single mother who did not graduate from high school and who works as a housekeeper in a hotel. If habitus was understood as a completely determinist principle that reproduces social relations via socio-economic status, Nadine's decision to study at university would be doomed from the outset. Either that or, if she succeeds, the concept of habitus could be discarded as inadequate for explaining social inequality.

Many critics of Bourdieu have taken the second stance (e.g., Jenkins 1992). For instance, Brown (1987) criticizes Bourdieu's concept of habitus and its implication in cultural reproduction through the education system (Bourdieu and Passeron 1977) as representing "little more than a bundle of values and attributes which predispose children unequally to master the middle-class culture taught in school" (Brown 1987: 30). He goes on to suggest that: "If differences in the habitus of working-class children and the way in which the structure and organization of the educational system acts to reinforce or transform it had been clearly specified, the idea of habitus might have offered a way of overcoming approaches relying either on the process of educational or on cultural differentiation" (ibid.: 29).

However, I propose that Nadine's story provides a compelling example of how cultural capital and habitus affect dispositions toward post-secondary education:

NADINE: I guess I wouldn't really have a role model either, except for, you know ... my mom's kind of what I don't want to be. She's a ...

JILLIAN: anti-role model?

NADINE: No, she's not quite that, but she's been housekeeping all her life and I actually took the same job for a while and I realized how hard that can be, too. She even told me, she's like "don't get stuck in this" ... Um, I guess the lesson I learned from my mother, uh, was not to be dependent, you know, to make sure that you can take care of yourself. So, part of the reason why I want to go to university is so I will always be able to take care of myself ... I [did feel] pressure from my family. It always seemed like it didn't really matter to them what I did, like they were trying to say, you know, that it doesn't really matter what you do, but it really does matter to them. I don't know, it's just ... I'm the youngest of five children and of that only two have graduated so far from high school, and they just have huge expectations for me. And that's OK, that's fine, because, [going to university], that's the same thing I want for myself.

Obviously, Nadine's plans are a response to her understanding of her mother's situation and life chances, as well as her own social position. Yet, her case defies the straightforward logic of habitus and cultural capital reproducing class positions, although I would insist that habitus is still instrumental in her post-secondary education plans. Unlike the more deterministic way in which habitus created sets of dispositions that essentially predisposed Debbie toward non-academic post-secondary training and Alissa toward university, Nadine's habitus and dispositions are as much shaped by her family's lower SES as they are by their hopes and expectations. Her mother's hopes for her to do better and her expectations for her to go to university, it seems, have been strong and consistent influences, shaping habitus and dispositions in a complex and non-deterministic

fashion. Nadine's experiences are thus more exemplary of dispositions understood as an open system. Bourdieu (Bourdieu and
Wacquant 1992: 133) himself argues that:

Habitus is not the fate that some people read into it. Being the product of
history, it is an *open system of dispositions* that is constantly subjected to
experiences, and therefore constantly affected by them in a way that either
reinforces or modifies its structures ... Having said this, I must immediately
add that there is a probability, inscribed in the social destiny associated
with definite social conditions, that experiences will confirm habitus,
because most people are statistically bound to encounter circumstances
that tend to agree with those that originally fashioned their habitus.
(emphasis in original)

Although the overall quantitative trend in my sample confirmed
social reproduction, it appears that Nadine is about to "break
through" the "prescribed," reproductive ways in which habitus has
shaped most of her siblings' life courses so far. Yet, this form of
agency does come at the cost of risk and uncertainty.

RISK AND UNCERTAINTY

Nadine's comments highlight discrepancies between habitus and
dispositions, as Nadine's habitus should indeed prevent her from
success in higher post-secondary education. Not surprisingly,
Nadine is aware of this dilemma:

NADINE: I think if I did have a parent who went to university it'd be a lot more
comfortable, because they'd know what you need to do. Like, I had to figure out completely on my own what I need to do, like applications and figuring out my student loans and everything like that. I just think it would be
way easier if I had someone who knew what it's like.

Nadine's decision to attend university is an expression of what
Evans and Heinz (1995) have called *strategic risk taking*, as university
is a choice that is, from a structurally determinist perspective, in
conflict with her social origin. This understanding of strategic risk
is related to Beck's (1992) notions of reflexive individualization in
what he calls a risk society. Beck argues that in a risk society the dissolution of traditional structural elements of industrial society,

such as class, gender, or ethnicity, has led to more uncertain, fragmented, and ultimately individualized (as opposed to structurally
determined) transition processes. Similarly, Furlong and Cartmel
(1997) suggest that we have moved from a Fordist social structure
to a post-Fordist society.[6] While Fordism was characterized by
school-work transitions that were generally short, stable, and predictable, and led to relatively standardized and homogenous life
experiences, transitions in a post-Fordist society have become more
protracted, increasingly fragmented, and less predictable.

Drawing on Beck's concepts, and relying on evidence from a
Dutch youth transitions study, du Bois-Reymond (1998) makes the
distinction between choice and normal biographies. The latter are
characterized by traditional, pre-determined, sequential stages of
development into adulthood, while the former are characterized by
increased options, negotiation, and tension between choice and
coercion. The increasing range of alternatives offered in late
modernity, which leads to choice biographies, requires a reflexive
engagement of individuals with these options, i.e., strategic risk taking. Evans and Heinz admit, however, that in cases where structural
constraints, such as the lack of material or social resources, impede
strategic risk taking, passive individualization ultimately may result
in harmful "wait-and-see" transition patterns. Thus, institutional
and market agencies continue to have structuring effects on the
choices and activities of young people. Furthermore, the authors
acknowledge that "risk is unevenly distributed according to location in the social structure, with young people in positions of disadvantage losing out heavily" (Evans and Heinz 1995: 10).

This would explain how Nadine's plans are characterized by
more uncertainty and represent a greater risk to her than they do
for somebody with a higher SES. Nadine's feeling of uncertainty is
in contrast to the far more relaxed and anticipatory attitude of
academic-track high-school students with university-educated parents, as the following two focus group excerpts attest:

ALISSA: It's kind of comforting to have a parent, like my dad went in. But, he
went to university how many years ago now? [laughs] I think things have
probably changed a bit since then ...

SILKE: I ... my dad, he studied medicine. He talks a lot about it. It always
sounds like a lot of fun, when he talks about it.

Trent, one of the Edmonton academic-track students, is a near-textbook example of a student from a working-class background who has been pushed by his father (who has worked in construction all his life) to consider university as a way out of the hard labour he himself experiences:

WL: You said earlier that your father is in construction. Did he at any point suggest you go into that area?

TRENT: No. He hates ... like when I went to work with him, and he works like a dog, probably ten hours a day. He's done that for about twenty years, you know. And I look how hard he works and I appreciate what he does, but he always tells me "no, you're not doing this!" ... You know, my whole life he's told me not to get into this, so I don't even bother.

Yet, as with Nadine, this drive for upward mobility comes at a cost of higher risk and uncertainty. Trent's plan is to go to university after completing high school, but he has no plans yet as to what he wants to study. He is also rather concerned about what it means to be at university and where it eventually might lead him. Lacking a frame of reference or role models in his immediate social environment, the decision to go to university seems as much a burden as it is liberation from the hard manual labour of his father:

TRENT: Yeah, I can honestly say I don't know what to expect from university, because I don't really know anyone who has ever been there ... I just don't want to pick the wrong thing, like I don't want to end up taking five years of extra school and then when you go to the job market, then all of sudden there is nothing there for you ... For some reason, I get a little scared thinking about the workload. People say that they are dropping out, like the mass of people that are dropping out, that quit in their first year.

WL: You mean at university?

TRENT: Yeah. That just kind of scares me a little bit, but ... as long as you work as hard as you possibly can, then that should be all right. But that's what scares me, just the workload and the mass of people that drop out in their first year, you know ...

WL: [Do you think] it might be more difficult for somebody like yourself whose parents haven't been to university to go and be successful there?

TRENT: Oh yeah, because they can't tell you what it's like.

Don is similar to Trent in that his father works as a painter in the trades but wants him to do better. Don faces the problem of not performing well enough in high school to go directly to university, as his parents had hoped. Instead, he has opted to take engineering-related courses at a local technical school. Unlike Trent, whose father's comments have left him convinced that he definitely does not want to follow in his footsteps, Don expresses an interest in the trades but isn't acting on it, which suggests that his father's influence is fairly significant:

DON: Well, [my parents] wanted me to go straight to university, but the marks aren't there ...

WL: Particularly your dad being in the trade, has he ever talked to you about possibly going into the trade?

DON: He told me not [with emphasis] to go into the trade. It's too hard work, it's too much physical work; not to do it ...

WL: So, would you say that your parents, or particularly your dad, have always pushed you towards academic stuff?

DON: Yeah, all the time.

WL: Do you think the fact that your parents themselves haven't been in an academic career, that makes it harder to think about that?

DON: Yes, because they don't really know what it's like, what the difference is. They just think this is better, take it. That's about it.

WL: So you think they're mostly concerned about your welfare, your well-being? Do you agree with them?

DON: [somewhat hesitant] It makes sense ...

WL: You said earlier that being a mechanic, a car mechanic maybe, interested you ...

DON: I love working on cars, even though it is tiring, but it doesn't really matter.

WL: So is that anything you still keep as a possibility, in the back of your mind?

DON: Kind of [laughs] ...

WL: If you were pretty certain that you want to be a car mechanic, do you think your dad would try to convince you not to do that?

DON: Yeah, for sure [laughs]. I talked to him about it. He said it's not a good idea.

Here then is a situation in which habitus, dispositions, and expectations are clearly in conflict. Don's interest in cars and manual work is as much a reflection of his habitus as going to university is not. Yet there is a strong push from his parents to choose a different future, one they themselves could not have. And the path to this future is seen as achievable through educational attainment.[7]

High-school students such as Nadine, Trent, and Don are cases of what has been discussed as *structured individualization* (Roberts, Clark, and Wallace 1994; Rudd and Evans 1998) or *bounded agency* (Evans 2002). Both these terms imply that agency, and the outcomes of agency, continue to be circumscribed by the individuals' location in the social structure. Evans (2002: 248) has described bounded agency as follows:

A temporally embedded process of social engagement in which past habits and routines are contextualized and future possibilities envisaged within the contingencies of the present moment, to arrive at a metaphor for socially situated agency, influenced but not determined by structures and emphasizing internalized understandings and frameworks as well as external actions.

Evans has arrived at a definition of agency, derived from a specific reading of Beck's individualization thesis, that is very reminiscent of Bourdieu's notion of habitus (Lehmann 2004). Study participants' narratives show forms of agency (or individualization) that are strongly framed by social origin, or habitus. The likelihood of success at university is probably still lower, and the level of risk involved certainly higher, for students with a lower SES. Contrasting the narratives of independent decision making with the survey findings certainly provides evidence of such bounded agency. However, what is interesting in this discussion of risk and uncertainty is that the narratives of at least some of the students whose post-secondary plans would lead to upward social mobility (e.g., Trent and Don) actually reveal a relative lack of agency. For both Trent and Don, the most important motivating factor to attend university appears to be their parents' wishes that they do so. In contrast, although the decisions of most youth apprentices to enter a trade may best be described as socially reproductive, they often speak passionately of their pride in the physical, manual labour they perform and how their participation is a result of a real personal interest in this type of work. Once again, we are faced with the dilemma of consolidating narratives of agency with structural evidence of reproduction.

Apart from these individual explanations of uncertainty, institutional factors may also play an important role. For instance, in comparison to Edmonton high-school students such as Trent and Don, who are planning to study at university, but who are somewhat concerned about their lack of understanding of what this entails, their German equivalents seem less concerned with these issues. This may be because they are attending classes in the highest school stream (*Gymnasium*), which has as its aim preparation for university entry. In other words, the institutional environment is clearly geared toward a certain transition path. The focus of curriculum is on university preparation, teachers emphasize university preparation, and most friends probably plan to attend university. Consider, for instance, the following conversation between Sandra and Simone, both Bremen *Gymnasium* students who have very ambitious career plans (lawyer and doctor, respectively), but whose parents have not been to university:

SANDRA: Well in my case, nobody in my family went to university. But I think if I manage to do well here at the *Gymnasium* and finish with a good *Abitur*, I mean, if I don't have any big problems, then I do want to go to university. Then, I think, it won't get a lot more difficult ...

SIMONE: I don't know anybody who is at university right now or has been. My parents didn't go. I don't know. I think that you'll have to do a whole lot on your own, that you won't have teachers, like here at school, who will tell you, "do this or do that." That's why I'm not sure if I'll be able to do it all on my own.

WL: Do you think it makes it more difficult if you don't have anybody in your family who has had those experiences, who could support you a bit?

SIMONE: I don't think it makes a difference, because they [those who have parents who have gone to university] didn't experience university themselves; they were only told about it. That's why I think it doesn't make a difference.

Perhaps Sandra and Simone appear to be far less concerned about uncertainty and perceive going to university as less of a risk than their Edmonton counterparts because of the greater level of transparency in the German education system. Students at the *Gymnasium* level have become so much a part of a school culture that is based on preparation for university that their understanding of what being at university entails might be far greater than that of similar

Edmonton high-school students. This in turn takes away much of the mystique and uncertainty surrounding university life. This suggests that schools, school culture, curriculum, and interaction with teachers play an important role in reinforcing or transforming habitus and dispositions.

ROLE OF THE SCHOOLS

In the previous section, I explained how cultural capital and SES interact to form habitus and dispositions within the family realm that ultimately affect career decision making and may contribute to social reproduction. Schools and the education system form another important field in which habitual dispositions may be cemented, or possibly altered. In *Reproduction in Education, Society and Culture*, Bourdieu (with Passeron) analyses how the education system perpetuates and legitimizes social inequality (Bourdieu and Passeron 1977). Middle- and upper-middle-class ideologies dominate curriculum, making it easier for children who grow up with this form of cultural capital to succeed in school, while the value of working-class knowledge and experiences is generally rejected. Students rich in cultural capital are better able to understand the value of an education, are more in tune with what is taught, and are in turn rewarded through better grades and generally better and more supportive relationships with their teachers. Working-class children find little in the curriculum that reflects their own experiences and tend to become increasingly alienated from the school culture, which leads to less success, vocational streaming, or even dropping out. This relationship is, of course, intimately related to the career decision-making process, as educational success and encouragement provide the foundation for the consideration of post-secondary destinations. In this context, RAP, as a high-school program, offers an interesting theoretical conundrum: is it a program that actually validates working-class knowledge in the education system, or is it a mechanism that formalizes social inequality and cultural reproduction by removing young people more interested in manual knowledge from the academic mainstream?

Relationship with Curriculum

Many of the RAP students with whom I spoke revealed an attitude toward school that can at best be described as indifferent. They usually had no problems talking about their lack of success at school. For many of these students, success at school was only important insofar as graduating with a high school diploma is a requirement for continuing their apprenticeship training: .

BRAD: I'm not that good at school. I get passing grades, but ... it's just not something ... somewhere I want to be. I gotta be doing something with my hands.

WL: Did your parents push you to do well at school?

BRAD: No, my dad says, if I get a 50, and that's as good as I can do and I tried my hardest, then that's good enough.

Reflecting Bourdieu's concepts of habitus and cultural capital, Dean, Ted, Doug, and Nick talk about their lack of interest in school curriculum and how this extends to their leisure activities:

WL: Do any of you at home do "bookish" things?

DEAN: Magazines.

TED: I read the TV guide. Sports and news.

DOUG: I read the books to my Nintendo games.

NICK: I read books and magazines ... [everybody talking at the same time, agreeing that they are not big readers] stuff that I like.

TED: You don't see me get down and read like a twenty-page ... or uh, 200 page novel. That's just not for me.

WL: Do you have to do it for school?

TED: They try to, but I don't do it. I just get somebody else's answers. I hate it, it's horrible. I hate reading books ... Read the back, and if I can't do it that way, hopefully it has a movie, I'll watch the movie.

As the following focus group excerpt shows, the streamed education system in Germany has the potential to exacerbate young people's feeling of alienation from education:

ATTILA: Almost all of us went to the *Hauptschule*, and right from the start, we didn't really give a shit about learning [laughs].

BERND: That's right.

UWE: Ten years at school, you know, that's enough.

This, of course, is in marked contrast to academic students. For them, success in high school and an acceptance of the high-school culture is essential, not only for their chances to be accepted to the post-secondary program of their choice, but also to confirm their identity:

LISA: [In] school, it's not so much teaching you, like ... "yeah, you got to memorize, like all these kings from like 1,600 years ago." [But] they're teaching you how to learn, how to use your mind. And if they didn't teach you how to learn, how would you go out in the real world and like survive, if you didn't know how to learn. Like going to a job with computers, they had to teach you how to ... use that computer or whatever. But if you had not gone to school and learned how to commit that to memory or whatever, you could not learn how to work that computer. So, even at school they are setting you up for the real world [others laugh] ... You know it's true.
[others agree; somebody: "yeah, it's very true"]
WL: So, you would say you certainly learn important things at school?
LISA: Not just ... important, yes, but also relevant to the real world ...
MAX: I'd have to say that's right on the button.

It would be unfair to suggest that all youth apprentices in my sample rejected school, just as it would be wrong to say that all academic students saw the value in everything they learned in school. Thus, you find apprentices like Peter in Edmonton who likes Shakespeare and enjoys reading *Macbeth*, and academic students like Farida in Germany who claims that "there is a reason why they say you learn for teachers, not for life." Yet there is an overwhelming sense among youth apprentices that the school system is not validating their interests and skills, which in turn contributes to a vicious cycle of low achievement and little interest in core educational subjects.

These qualitative findings are further confirmed by responses to questions about attitudes toward education asked in the questionnaire. The youth apprentices in the sample indeed preferred the applied form of learning they experience at work and were likely to agree that they do not enjoy school as much as work (see figure 4.4). Taking location into account, there were no discernible differences between the Edmonton and Bremen sub-samples (data not shown). This suggests that the streamed German education system and Canada's composite high-school system lead to similar attitudes in respect to the different values of work and education.

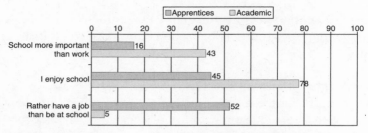

Figure 4.4 Attitudes about school, by program type (percentages agree and strongly disagree)*

*Respondents were asked: "For each of the following statements about your high-school education, please indicate how strongly you agree or disagree?" They answered using a five-point scale, with "1" meaning "strongly disagree" and "5" meaning "strongly agree." Responses of one to three were recoded as "disagree"; responses four and five were recoded as "agree."

Relationship with Teachers

Compounding youth apprentices' negative attitude toward schooling is a persistent undercurrent of resentment against (some) teachers that could contribute to a student's decision to choose RAP as an alternative to the more academic mainstream. Bonnie, an Edmonton RAP student apprenticing as a hairdresser, talks about her experiences with teachers at high school, where the only teacher who believed in her was her cosmetology teacher:

BONNIE: Other teachers just look down on me. They always thought that I was like that stupid girl that couldn't do anything more. So, they're just like [puts on patronizing voice] "oh, it's good that you are taking hairdressing." Last year was really bad, because pretty much a lot of my teachers told me … because I wanted to upgrade to English 30, that's what you need to get into university, and most teachers told me, no, you don't want to do that. And then I did pass with a 51 [proud voice]. And I worked my ass off to get that. You have no clue how hard I worked. I just wanted to prove to them, you sit there, you look down on me, like I'm an idiot. Well, I proved you wrong.

WL: Do you think students who want to go to university have a better relationship with their teachers?

BONNIE: Yeah, because the teacher knows they have to have those sorts of marks to get into the university. So they look at that student, and they look at … let's say a person in mechanics who knows what they're going to be, of course they're going to work. More or less, they look at the student who's going to university, because they don't think the other student is going there. There's that stereotype again. They're stupid, they can't go to university, let's not waste our time.

This impression that teachers selectively encourage students is echoed by German youth apprentices. Before starting his apprenticeship as a car mechanic, Steffen attended *Gymnasium* for one year (i.e., Grade 11), with the intention of gaining his *Abitur* and eventually studying law. But he dropped out at the end of Grade 11:

WL: I just wanted to ask you again, was it a difficult decision to drop out of the *Gymnasium*, or were you happy to leave?
STEFFEN: I was really happy to leave the *Gymnasium*.
THOMAS: [To Steffen] How many years did you do?
STEFFEN: Just one, Grade 11, but if you don't have any interest and you fall asleep in class, then it's no use. I have problems with school anyways. I can follow along and all, but for me, that's not a life.
WL: How did the teachers react?
STEFFEN: They want to get rid of you. In Grade 11, they really want to get rid of you. That's when they separate the wheat from the chaff, the good from the bad.
WL: There were no teachers who tried to ...
STEFFEN: [interrupts] Yeah, I had a whole bunch of friends, well they're still my friends, and they didn't make it either and eventually left. A whole lot, I think a third from that year has already left.

While youth apprentices talk about relationships with teachers (at least teachers in the core academic subjects) negatively, high-school students in the academic mainstream paint a decidedly different picture. Alissa perceives her teachers as caring and supportive of her plans for higher education:

ALISSA: Yeah, the teachers around here seem to care an awful lot about the students. They ... and a lot of teachers have been like forcefully telling us, "no, you're going to that [university] open house, I'm sorry, I don't care, I'm not giving you that [unintelligible]." So, they're really quite concerned about a lot of us. And they're concerned about what we are going to be doing later on. Like I had a lot of teachers like asking what's going to happen with me next year, which is really good, to hear that they care.

This ideal of mutual respect between teacher and student, expressed by a number of the academic-track students, is rather different from how youth apprentices perceive this relationship. We have already heard from Bonnie, who complained about her teachers' attitude toward her abilities ("They always thought that I was like that stupid girl that couldn't do anything more [than go into hairdressing]"). The majority of Edmonton youth apprentices suggested that their teachers in the academic core subjects not only had no interest in what they did, but generally did not even know about their involvement with RAP. Of course, this relationship of ignorance and disrespect cuts both ways, as the following comments by Nathan and Riley, both Edmonton apprentices in RAP, show:

NATHAN: I mean, at school the teachers tell you to do something, and you're saying, "well, what are you going to get me for it" ...

RILEY: I don't know, at school, if teachers say "do this" and you're just like "yeah, whatever." You sit there, OK you may have to see the principal, the principal will be like "blah, blah, blah, you did something bad" you know ... They say you get into trouble, they say [puts on whiny voice] "don't do it again, you're bad," and I'm like "OK, yeah, yeah, whatever."

Comments by RAP students such as Nathan and Riley, of course, bring to mind a different view of culturally determined reproduction, namely that of resistance theory as popularized in Paul Willis's (1977) *Learning to Labour*.

RESISTANCE

Notions of active working-class resistance as the basis for social reproduction in the education system originated with Paul Willis's landmark 1977 study *Learning to Labour*. In this ethnographic study of a small group of working-class "lads" in a school in a poor area of Birmingham, Willis proposes that the lads' rebellious, anti-school behaviour is a reflection of working-class resentment toward the middle-class values embedded in the educational system. However, the unintended consequence of their resistance is ultimately a reproduction of their own class position, as their aim is to leave school as soon as possible and to enter the working-class world of manual labour. Willis rejects claims that structural forces exclude working-class youth from achieving higher educational attainment and thus social mobility. Instead, he suggests that the lower level of educational attainment of working-class youth is not so much a result of an inability to compete at school, but of an unwillingness to compete, rooted in a deep class-cultural antagonism. Working-class youth are seen as actively and purposely resisting middle-class notions of mobility through higher education. Instead, they embrace working-class values associated with participation in the workforce. Pride in their working-class background and anticipation of the "real world of employment" lead them to oppose mainstream school culture, in which they see expressed resentment toward manual, working-class labour. Thus, an important element of resistance theory is its insistence on purposive, active, oppositional behaviour. School resentment and rejection is not seen as simply disappointment with the school system or fatalism about the future. Ultimately, however, this active resistance to the middle-class school culture reproduced the lads' position in the existing class culture.

The results of this study can be added to Canadian research (Davies 1995; Tanner 1990) that has found no evidence of the type of rebellious, counter-cultural behaviour described in *Learning to Labour*. Willis (1977: 56) came much closer to the Canadian reality, however, when he wrote about working-class students' rejection of the theoretical aspects of education: "The rejection of school work by 'the lads' and the omnipresent feeling that they know better is also paralleled by a massive feeling on the shop floor, and in the working class generally, that practice is more important than theory ... The shop floor abounds with apocryphal stories about the idiocy of purely theoretical knowledge. Practical ability always comes first and is a *condition* of other kinds of knowledge" (emphasis in original).

Much like Willis's lads, the youth apprentices with whom I spoke overwhelmingly embrace the practical, applied knowledge they learn at the workplace and, to various degrees, reject the theoretical and, to them, generally useless knowledge associated with academic subjects at school:

NATHAN: School is a lot of theory; well pretty much school is theory. Whereas a job is hands-on; you know, you're not sitting there with a math book, figuring out some paragraph and what the answer is. At work,

you're given a problem and you're physically solving it yourself. You're finding out, ok, I tried this, this doesn't work. I tried this, this doesn't work. I
tried this, it works. And you don't have to do six more problems, worded a
different way, to make sure you know. Once you've gotten it right ...

RILEY: you move on ...

NATHAN: you move on, because next time you come to it, you've done it
    physically. It's right there in front of you. It's almost impossible to forget
    that.

This preference for applied, practical knowledge over theoretical
knowledge clearly crosses borders, as this sentiment was frequently
echoed by German apprentices:

WL: Do you think *Realschule* or *Hauptschule* prepared you properly to make
    the transition to the working world?

KAI: No, as far as working is concerned, I don't think so.

SEBASTIAN: A bunch of things we learned then, we don't need at all today.

TORSTEN: I don't need any of it today, nothing.

Rather consistently, youth apprentices reject the theoretical
nature of school and prefer the hands-on character of work. However, most still recognize some value in certain academic subjects,
but only if they can see their potential applicability in the workplace. Thus, certain aspects of mathematics, physics, or chemistry
may be acceptable, whereas English and social studies hold very little value for most apprentices:

RILEY: Physics and math is pretty much all. English, phew, social, phew. You
    don't have to know the background of an engine. Where it came from,
    who invented it. It doesn't matter. You have to fix it. Like you're wiring
    something; [puts on pedantic teacher voice] "this is copper wire that Mr.
    Charlie Bobb invented in the 1950s; let's write an essay on him." You don't
    do any of that.

NATHAN: It doesn't matter where the copper wire came from, it doesn't mat-
    ter who discovered it. It's plain and simple; it's copper wire and you gotta
    do this with it. And that's the result. It doesn't matter, anything else.

Riley's and Nathan's comments, or the realization of Dean,
another Edmonton RAP student apprenticing as a carpenter, that in
the five months he has worked as a RAP apprentice he has not

needed to use any language or social skills, flies in the face of the employability skills discourse that stresses the importance of so-called transferable (i.e., more academic) skills over specific technical skills. This discourse generally looks at the education system as the arena in which young people are to become equipped with transferable skills such as communication, teamwork, literacy, and numeracy (Krahn, Lowe, and Lehmann 2002). But many of the apprentices with whom I spoke see the relationship reversed. Employability skills, or at least discipline and perseverance, are acquired in the workplace and are transferred back to school, at least in theory.

Not all RAP students share this negative view of high school as impractical and irrelevant for the real world. Ron, who apprentices as a motorcycle mechanic in Edmonton, has a more positive outlook on the importance of a general education, and not just as it relates to the workplace. Unlike most of the other youth apprentices in the sample, Ron acknowledges the value of learning in itself:

RON: [School's] always been pretty important to me. Because, where do you go without school? You gonna end up making fries for the rest of your life because you don't have a good high school diploma? And you gotta have good grades to get a post-secondary education, that's at least valuable ... I think everything you learn at school is something you can use in the future. Even if it doesn't relate to your future job or what you want to do, because it's more so the accepting of knowledge and taking it in and learning how to comprehend all that stuff.

Perhaps not surprisingly, Ron is one of the few youth apprentices with a relatively high socio-economic background. His father is university-educated and self-employed. Ron himself talked earlier in the interview about how he is still considering going to university after high school (actually, his father has hopes that he will study business and eventually take over the family company) and how his involvement in RAP as a motorcycle mechanic is mostly the result of his love for motorcycles and the fact that he has been involved in racing them for some time.

Kai is one of the Bremen apprentices who defends education against the more pragmatic attitudes of the other members in a focus group of electrician apprentices. Although he himself gradu-

ated from the *Hauptschule*, his father is a university-educated engi-
neer. This may explain Kai's more positive attitude about the value
of a general education for an informed citizenry:

WL: What are the most important topics here at the vocational school?
[general agreement: the technical, occupationally specific classes]
KAI: And math is maybe the most important, I think. Math is part of all the
  other classes.
MARKUS: Yeah, but what do you need social studies for, or German?
KAI: [German], so that you can use language, that you know how to write
  . somehow. I think that's gotta be expected, that you can write [the others
  laugh]. Yeah, I know, there are enough people out there who can't write.
  Even our age ... Yes, that's general knowledge, you have to ... I also think
  social studies is important. Everybody should know at least a little bit how
  government works and so on. I think that's just part of what you need to
  know, also that you can keep up with what's going on. And I think they
  should actually offer a little more in social studies here, because I think it's
  dumb if I don't even know who to vote for in the next election. If I had to
  vote now, who should I vote for, if you have no idea about what's going on.
SEBASTIAN: They're all bullshitting you anyway.

The key difference from the working-class lads profiled in *Learning
to Labour* is that none of the youth apprentices to whom I spoke
rejected school outright or provided any evidence of engaging in
the type of deviant behaviour described by Willis. Instead, school
and what you learn there, while not necessarily seen as important in
its own right, is at least recognized as the means to an end, namely
to graduate and receive your diploma. This finding is more in line
with Brown's (1987: 3) critique of Willis' culturalist explanation of
working-class student experiences at school. While Willis focuses on
the behaviour of a small group of male, working-class students,[8]
Brown argues for a different understanding of the experiences of
what he calls "ordinary kids": "The way the ordinary kids responded
to school was as much a working-class cultural response as the one
which led to its rejection. The ordinary kids' willingness to make an
effort in school, albeit limited, was part of an authentic attempt to
maintain command of their own lives; to maintain a sense of personal dignity and respect in circumstances where they were not academically successful; and, on their own terms, to enhance their
chances of making a working-class career when they left school."

Perhaps the comments offered by students like Nathan and Riley are closer to what Hargreaves (1967) suggested ten years prior to Willis, namely that the development of a counter-school culture is a consequence of educational failure, not its cause. According to Hargreaves, streaming and different treatment of working-class students by teachers leads to an inability to succeed in terms of middle-class definitions of educational achievement, which in turn is compensated for by the development of an anti-school attitude. This brings Hargreaves's explanation much closer to neo-Marxist, more determinist views of the role of education in the reproduction of class positions, such as Bowles and Gintis's (1976) seminal work on the correspondence between the organization of schooling and employment in capitalist society.

In the twenty-five years since Willis's book was published, the economy, labour markets, and education systems have undergone dramatic changes in all Western, industrialized societies. Willis's lads, one must assume, could still rely to some degree on a labour market with a reasonable number of unskilled and low-skilled employment opportunities. But such opportunities have largely vanished in our post-industrial, knowledge-based economy. McDowell (2003) argues that these labour-market changes disproportionately affect young, under-educated males.

Arguing from the perspective of changing employment relationships in a post-industrial labour market, Brown (1995) suggests that Bourdieu and others have exaggerated the inevitability of middle-class reproduction and that, despite statistical evidence that children from managerial and professional backgrounds do better, it is not a foregone conclusion. The discourse of "flexible organizations" is said to have important implications for the way cultural capital is deployed in the labour market, as middle-class families can no longer rely on the bureaucratization of education, recruitment, and employment.

I would suggest that Brown may actually have the relationship reversed. He sees a loosening of the relationship between cultural capital, educational structures and curriculum, and occupational attainment due to the changing nature of the post-industrial employment contract. I believe that the very developments he credits for devaluing cultural capital are actually increasing its importance in the workplace. Increasingly, the prerequisite for success in a post-industrial labour market is seen in more general education, not more specialized education. An ability to learn, the capacity to absorb new ideas, and a talent for working well with others are regularly cited as the most important skills in more flexible, de-bureaucratized organizations. These are skills usually associated with higher levels of education and are thus still intimately tied to cultural capital.

Brown (1995) also talks about truncated organizational careers and the greater risk associated with the post-industrial employment contract. Again, recent statistical evidence (see Statistics Canada 2003a; Taillon and Paju 1999) suggests that these trends have actually increased, rather than diminished, the importance of cultural capital. Ever rising levels of education are needed as a safeguard against labour-market uncertainty, and the resulting credential inflation increases the value of higher degrees from more prestigious institutions.

My observation that none of the study participants rejected the idea of receiving a high-school education and that nobody had seriously considered dropping out is obviously related to young people's realization of these relationships. Such a realization reflects a public discourse that demands ever higher levels of education for an even moderately successful vocational biography. The "stay-in-school-or-you-are-screwed-for-the-rest-of-your-life" rhetoric has certainly sunk in with these young people, as the following focus group excerpt attests:

WL: Had any of you ever thought of dropping out of high school?
DOUG: I haven't.
NICK: It's not worth it, really. After you do, then you're screwed for life.

Many students reported anecdotal evidence about what happened to those who actually did drop out. A common theme, as expressed here by Bonnie, one of the Edmonton RAP students, was that of drug addiction and prostitution as alternatives to high-school completion and solid, middle-class careers:

BONNIE: My best friend, she's like a complete drug addict, she's slept with guys for things. My other friends, I was in class with them, there's four girls, one stayed a coke addict and selling coke, the other one's – and she didn't graduate from high school, she was like sent away – the other one's, from what I hear, walking the street sometimes. The other one's a complete

addict. Like, these are my friends I grew up with, that didn't finish high
school. And then there's me, and I don't do any of that stuff.

While youth apprentices favour practical, applied knowledge
over abstract, theoretical knowledge, really deviant or rebellious
behaviour is perceived as self-destructive. In both countries, youth
apprentices, just like their academic counterparts, have accepted
the dominant discourse in which educational credentials are the
foundation for occupational success.

Despite the significant differences in the institutional and cultural environments in which the young people in Edmonton and
Bremen embark on their school-work transitions, their accounts of
agency and the underlying narratives of reproduction were strik-
ingly similar. Does this suggest that socio-cultural factors are more
important than institutional factors in school-work transition processes? This would certainly have important policy implications and
seriously put in question our current emphasis on human capital
solutions to labour market and educational problems. From a more
theoretical perspective, the data also highlight a key dilemma
regarding the relationship between individual choice (or agency)
and structural constraint. Are we to discount narratives of agency if
the result of this agency is socially reproductive? And should we
automatically label plans that suggest social mobility as acts of
agency? To answer these questions, one must further deconstruct
individual narratives to understand the strategies young people
employ to assert agency even within a constraining social, cultural,
and institutional context.

5

The Role of Policy:
"We're Supposed To Be Learning"

Going to work and going to school are two different things.

Debbie, Edmonton RAP student

I'm still scrubbing the floors ...

Bonnie, Edmonton RAP student

Proponents of youth apprenticeships point to their function of creating useful institutional structures for transitions (Evans, Taylor and Heinz 1993) and of providing youth not entering post-secondary schooling with meaningful career alternatives, thus ultimately promoting greater equality in the labour market (Alberta Apprenticeship and Industry Training Board 1996; Buechtemann, Schupp, and Soloff 1994; Economic Council of Canada 1992; Evans, Taylor, and Heinz 1993; Hamilton 1990). Such programs, however, have also been charged with streaming lower-class students into dead-end career options that do very little to facilitate long-term success in the labour market and may actually reinforce existing social inequalities (Geißler 1991; Kantor 1994). A brief summary of the preceding chapters indicates that both positions can be supported with data from this study.

Young people entering the Canadian labour market without any secondary credentials are most disadvantaged in terms of employment, employment stability, and income. Income potential increases with educational attainment (table 5.1) just as unemployment decreases (table 5.2). Furthermore, table 5.2 reveals that as levels of educational attainment increase, one becomes less subject to economic fluctuations. Proponents of youth apprenticeships in

Table 5.1 Canadian population 15 years and over and average earnings by highest degree, certificate, or diploma, 2001 Canadian census

Highest level of schooling	Less than high school	High school	Trades diploma or certificate	College diploma or certificate	University
Average earnings (Canadian average: $31,757)	$21,230	$25,477	$32,743	$32,736	$48,648

Source: *Statistics Canada, 2001 Census of Canada* (2001)

Table 5.2 Unemployment rate in Canada by educational attainment

	All levels of education	Less than high school	High school	College or trade	University
1991	10.3	15.3	10.3	8.3	5.3
1992	11.2	16.9	10.9	9.5	5.7
1993	11.4	16.9	11.6	9.8	6.0
1994	10.4	16.1	10.1	9.1	5.6
1995	9.4	15.0	9.6	8.0	5.2
1996	9.6	15.4	9.8	8.2	5.5
1997	9.1	15.6	9.2	7.4	5.1
1998	8.3	14.4	8.6	6.6	4.6
1999	7.6	13.4	7.8	5.9	4.4
2000	6.8	12.4	7.0	5.2	4.0

Source: Adapted from *Statistics Canada and Council of Ministers of Education, Canada* (2003, 393)

Canada are thus able to point to labour market advantages of participation, particularly if the targeted group is students who may be at risk of dropping out of high school or of not receiving any additional formal education beyond their high-school diploma.

Yet this study also offers ample evidence that participation in youth apprenticeships is implicated in socially reproductive processes. The young people in RAP or the German dual system were more likely to come from working-class or lower SES families, as defined by parents' education and occupational attainment, as well as family income. There is further evidence that educational and labour market structures reinforce processes of social reproduction. Both the quantitative and qualitative data presented support arguments that Germany's highly streamed education system and credential-driven labour market lead to more stratified school-work transitions. Yet the transparency of Germany's education system and labour market also creates opportunities for informed decision making and has, at least traditionally, opened possibilities for rewarding and well-respected careers in skilled employment. Although not the focus of this book, gender was shown to remain a critical factor in how people form dispositions toward future education and employment. The low involvement of young women in skilled trades training is detrimental to filling existing labour shortages, and the lack of efforts to increase women's participation in trades apprenticeships also means that young women are denied access to careers that currently offer high employment and income potential. Finally, the relationship between social context and decision making discussed throughout the book highlight individuals' active engagement in processes of social reproduction. Narratives of vocational preferences and accelerated maturity (see chapter 6) must be tempered by the recognition that these educational and vocational choices were rooted in a very strong class habitus and were often made, at least in Canada, with a minimum of insight into and understanding of the program (RAP) and related career options.

All of these issues have bearing on who enters programs such as RAP, why, and with what expectations; they also shed light on what such programs could offer these young people to make participation truly meaningful, not only as an educational and learning experience but also as a preparation for future employment. The quotations introducing this chapter highlight the importance of having such policy insights. For instance, it is important to ask whether youth apprentices such as Nick are actively engaged in decisions that truly reflect their own preferences and dispositions toward their careers and life courses. Do youth apprenticeships increase the potential for agency by offering a non-academic alternative to more practically oriented students, thus allowing them to get a head start on gaining a positive vocational identity? Or are we seeing, as might be the case in Ted's experience, a streaming process that formalizes a class-based reproductive process by removing lower-achieving, working-class high school students from the academic mainstream? And, following Bonnie's observations, how exactly are individuals experiencing youth apprenticeships and what are the implications of these experiences for creating meaningful educational alternatives?

POLICY CONTEXT

To start this discussion of the findings in the light of policy, their policy context must be considered. Policy-makers have been driven

Table 5.3 Unemployment rates in Canada by age and gender, December 2003 (seasonally adjusted)

Age	Both sexes	Male	Female
All ages (15+)	7.4%	7.7%	6.9%
Youth (15-24)	14%	16.5%	11.4%
Adults (25+)	6.1%	6.1%	6.0%

Source: Statistics Canada, *Labour Force Historical Review 2003* (2004)

by solving the dual challenge of facilitating school-work transitions and addressing critical labour shortages. In Canada, high levels of youth unemployment are being recognized as structural rather than cyclical problems, as youth unemployment rates remain significantly higher than adult unemployment rates (Betcherman and Leckie 1997; Statistics Canada 2004). The recession in the early nineties had a particularly severe impact on youth employment without any significant recovery trends throughout most of that decade (Krahn 1996). Table 5.3 indicates that young people aged fifteen to twenty-four are faced with unemployment rates twice as high as those for adults of twenty-five years and older.

Even though Canada has recently witnessed record low unemployment rates, the youth unemployment rate continues to be roughly double that of the overall rate. For instance, in February 2006 Statistics Canada placed the unemployment rate in Canada at a thirty-year record-breaking low of 6.7 per cent, while the youth unemployment rate in the same month was still at 11.4 per cent (Statistics Canada 2006). Most affected by unemployment or precarious employment are those in the labour market with the lowest level of educational attainment, regardless of age. This generally reflects changes in school-work transitions in industrialized nations, which have seen the employment prospects of underqualified men and women dwindle and high educational credentials become ever more important. A report on the transition from initial education to working life by Human Resources Development Canada (1998: 1) summarizes the transition experiences of Canadian youth as more challenging, varied, and open-ended than in the past. Transition processes are seen to be influenced by "the high rate of youth unemployment, the changing nature of the Canadian economy and job market, rising expectations of young people for postsecondary education, the concern for adolescents at risk of leaving school without the necessary skills, and the degree to which formal educational

programs at the secondary and postsecondary levels are adequately preparing young people for the world of work in the 21st
century."

Either explicitly or implicitly, most of the school-work transitions
literature agrees that transition processes have become more complex and less predictable. Whereas youth twenty years ago could rely
on more stable patterns of transition, youth today are dealing with
higher degrees of risk, uncertainty, and a need for more individualized decision-making (Furlong and Cartmel 1997; Livingstone 2004;
Lowe and Krahn 1999).

Yet while school-work transitions for young people have become
increasingly difficult, we continue to hear concerns about shortages of
skilled workers in the trades (e.g., Alberta Apprenticeship and Industry Training Board 1996; Statistics Canada 2003b). Policy-makers,
employers, and the media regularly portray the long-term prospects
for the Canadian economy as crippled by a demand for skilled labour
that far outpaces supply (e.g., Alberta Chamber of Resources and
Construction Owners of Alberta 1990; Bertin 2000). "Trades scrambling as labour shortage looms," states a front- page headline in the
Edmonton Journal (Finlayson 2003). One response from industry
groups to projected skills shortages has been to extend their reach
into the education system and to become more involved in the development of curriculum, at least vocational curriculum (Lehmann and
Taylor 2003). In Alberta, for instance, policy discussions throughout
the 1990s emphasized the importance of work education to economic
prosperity in Alberta (Alberta Education 1991, 1994, 1996).

Youth apprenticeship programs represent the "deepest" form of
partnership between schools and employers, as youth apprentices
receive high-school credit for the time spent working with their
employer (Taylor and Lehmann 2002). Proponents of youth
apprenticeships argue that participation opens possibilities to more
rewarding careers, provides satisfying career alternatives, and generally improves a young person's range of choices and career
options (Careers: The Next Generation 1998). Apprenticeship
training is considered a solution to a Catch-22 situation faced by
many young people: getting the work experience needed to gain
entry to stable jobs. It allows young people to gain such experience
while at the same time fulfilling the requirements needed to graduate from high school. It is expected that by linking the workplace
and the classroom, youth apprenticeship programs can ease young

people's transition to the workplace, encourage high-school completion by increasing the relevancy of classroom learning, help young people develop skills for employability and self-employment, and provide greater opportunities for youth to experience a variety of career options. Since employers also stand to benefit from a new generation of young, skilled workers who might otherwise bypass the trades as a career alternative, youth apprenticeships appear as a win-win solution to the dual challenge of youth transition problems and skilled labour shortages.

The 1990s saw a large number of apprenticeship-type educational programs appear across Canada. Although most high-school based youth apprenticeship programs focus on training in traditional, manual trades – for example, the Ontario Youth Apprenticeship Program (OYAP) – other programs, particularly in the Atlantic provinces, include work placements in service and semi-professional occupations. For instance, the New Brunswick Youth Apprenticeship Program (YAP) permits high-school students in Grade 10, after participation in career development and career exploration activities, to enrol concurrently in a secondary-school program leading to a high-school diploma and to become involved in career preparation in their chosen occupational area. While this program is less linked to traditional trades training and does not automatically grant credit toward journeyperson certification, it guarantees participants a community college seat in a related field and preferred status at the University of New Brunswick.

Although not a youth apprenticeship program per se, the Nova Scotia School-to-Work Transition (NSSWT) project is of interest to those concerned with school-work transition programs as it is one of the few initiatives that have been thoroughly evaluated (Thiessen and Looker 1999). Like RAP, this program was offered to students in Grades 11 and 12 and involved an in-school component and a work experience component. The objectives of the program were to provide generic and specific skills that would increase students' likelihood of making a successful transition to a rewarding career, and to provide realistic expectations about their future jobs while at the same time improving partnerships between schools and employers. Students were placed in "assistant" type positions (e.g., assisting veterinarians, lawyers, teachers, and mechanics). These placements gave students access to a much wider range of occupations than those covered by traditional apprenticed trades.

The outcomes of this project proved to be mixed, at best. While participating students generally evaluated their experience positively and as having better prepared them for their subsequent transitions, their high school performance eventually fell behind that of other students. As the program's design tried to encourage students from varied backgrounds to enter the program, this difference in school performance cannot be entirely attributed to self-selection. The program also fell short of establishing sufficiently close relationships between schools and the local business community to truly effect long-lasting structural changes. Some concern was also expressed about a lack of integration between the development of strictly workplace-related skills and skills required to succeed in post-secondary education (ibid.: 264–8). Still, the program was considered to be useful in that it made high-school experiences more relevant to participants. It also encouraged students to consider a variety of post-secondary pathways, provided participants with necessary work experience in their chosen career fields, and presented reflective learning opportunities that allowed participants to identify their strengths and weaknesses both in the workplace and in school (ibid.: 262–4).

Many of the policy issues and debates are situated within a human capital approach, which is premised on the assumption of a free labour market – a market in which people compete for jobs on the basis of their abilities, skills, and experience (Becker 1993). Individuals, therefore, will invest in their skills and abilities to increase their human capital and thus their market value. Human capital models presuppose individual agency and treat people's learning capacity as a resource like other natural resources in the production process that, when effectively used, is profitable to individuals, enterprises, the economy, and society as a whole. Work-entry problems of youth therefore are seen to arise from deficiencies in their own human capital. Consequently, school-work transition problems must be resolved individually by investing more rationally in one's human capital, and institutionally by reforming education such that it provides better linkages between schools and the labour market. Alberta's RAP is just such a program designed to provide better linkages with the labour market, particularly for those young people who might otherwise enter the workforce as unskilled labour.

A strong counter-discourse argues that although educational attainment has generally increased in most Western industrialized countries, access to the means of improving one's human capital and subsequent payoff in the labour market remain strongly related to structural factors such as class (e.g., Andres et al. 1999; Davies 2004), gender (e.g., Damm-Rüger 1994; Gaskell 1992) and ethnicity (e.g., Alba, Handl and Müller 1994; Michelson 1990). Several national school-work transition studies in Canada have shown little evidence of a decline of structural factors in predicting young people's occupational aspirations and expectations (de Broucker and Lavallée 1998; Fortin 1987; Guppy 1984). Despite the massive expansion of the Canadian post-secondary education system in the past several decades, and a resulting wider range of educational attainment within each socio-economic category, SES is still the strongest determinant of educational attainment. Whether measured by high-school dropout rates, achievement on standardized tests, or university attendance, working- and lower-class youth do not fare as well as youth from middle- and upper-class backgrounds (Davies 2004: 174).

This raises the important question of whether programs like RAP create meaningful alternatives that will result in positive educational and occupational outcomes, or whether they constitute another way of streaming working-class students out of paths toward middle-class career mobility.

IS RAP FULFILLING ITS POLICY POTENTIAL?

Labour Market Shortage

Alberta's RAP, too, represents a policy response to the twofold problem of high levels of youth unemployment in the late eighties and early nineties and an unfulfilled demand for workers in the skilled trades. Unfortunately, relatively few data are available to determine whether the introduction of RAP has reduced the demand for skilled workers. Skof (2006) has shown that enrolment in apprenticeships across Canada actually declined throughout the 1990s. Although enrolment has recovered in recent years, completion has not. Furthermore, the average age of newly registered apprentices in 2003 in Canada was the late twenties. These data suggest that programs such as RAP or OYAP have had no discernible impact on apprenticeship enrolments per se or on the age structure of apprentices. Given Alberta's red-hot economy, apprenticeship fig-

ures for Alberta are actually somewhat different and more promising (Alberta Apprenticeship and Industry Training Board 2005).
Alberta actually reports an 87 per cent increase in apprenticeship
registration since 1994. As for RAP, enrolment increased from 29
students in 1992 to 1,070 in 2004, although this remarkable
increase still represents only a very small minority of Alberta high-
school students. Overall, over 5,000 high-school students have participated in RAP since its inception in 1991, 660 of whom have gone
on to become certified in their trade and 1,700 of whom were continuing their training in 2005. Furthermore, although the average
age of Alberta apprentices at the time they begin their first apprenticeship is twenty-five, the most common age is actually nineteeen.
The RAP numbers are hardly watershed figures in terms of addressing labour market shortages, but the program's increasing popular-
ity suggests that it is becoming an alternative for an ever higher
number of students. The data discussed throughout the book make
it possible to comment on the ability of a program such as RAP to
facilitate the school-work transitions of non-university-bound high-
school students.

Alternative for Non-academic Students

RAP was targeted at the so-called middle-majority of students –
those neither likely to choose higher post-secondary education, nor
at risk of dropping out or failing high school. Some argue that RAP
should also be considered a stay-at-school program. If the latter
were the case, the real target group should be at-risk students who
would benefit from a more practice-oriented, applied alternative to
the academic curriculum.

It is difficult to measure the direct impact of a program like RAP
on high-school completion, and to the best of my knowledge, no
such evaluation has been completed. However, a 2001 satisfaction
study commissioned by Alberta Education and the Alberta Apprenticeship and Industry Training Board found that a majority of surveyed RAP participants felt that their participation had provided
an incentive to stay and do well in school. The same survey also
found that an even bigger majority of RAP apprentices had never
actually dropped out or considered dropping out of high school
(HarGroup Management Consultants Inc. 2001). Similarly, the
socio-demographic profile of the participants certainly showed that

most tend to come from the middle majority. None of the RAP participants to whom I spoke ever considered dropping out of high school (although some did agree that the program made it easier for them to stay at school), and most were reasonably successful at school prior to starting RAP. As a matter of fact, satisfactory standing in high school is generally seen as a prerequisite for participation in the program. None of the participants, therefore, could truly be labelled "at-risk" students. If the target group for RAP is students in the middle majority, the findings show that the program does reach this group. If, on the other hand, it is to be a program that also aims at facilitating transitions into employment for more disadvantaged students, it would be safe to argue that these students are not reached. The participation patterns reflect the tension between the perceptions of RAP as a school-work transitions program concerned with high levels of youth unemployment and as a program that more broadly addresses labour market demand in the skilled trades.

This focus on relatively well-achieving high-school students is also congruent with a broader public discourse that aims at raising the status of careers in the trades. A program such as RAP depends on the willingness of employers to take on high-school students as apprentices, and the continuation of partnerships between schools and employers seems to rest on the schools' abilities to provide employers with "good" students (Lehmann and Taylor 2003). One of the participants in the study who had started RAP but who was not kept on by his employer past the initial probation period told about the employer hiring three high-school students on probation, with the intention of keeping only one as an apprentice. Obviously, this type of selection process raises some concerns about the potential of RAP for offering an alternative to those students most in need of school-work transitions assistance.

Tanner, Krahn, and Hartnagel (1995), in a study of Edmonton high-school dropouts, confirm findings from other research that alienation from, boredom with, and rejection of the education system has led many young people to leave school early and to seek meaning in the adult world of employment. Although none of the RAP participants had ever seriously considered dropping out, the following excerpts from two different focus group discussions show how the program does provide an alternative to students who are weary of going to school:

DEAN: It might be a little more tempting to drop out before you had the RAP program than after. Because after you've been with the RAP program, you know what's out there for you. You know that there's work for you every day, and there's money for you every two weeks and that you can do it for however long, until you start to slow down. Whereas at school, if you never get into the RAP program, then you might just get so sick of school and not want to do it anymore.

NATHAN: That's half the reason I took the RAP program. I was getting bored with school. I had no initiative to be here, I had no want to be here, to do anything. I mean, in reality, for me school was becoming a joke. And I decided that, listen, I'm doing nothing here. I mean I might as well do something with myself. At least do something that's doing something for me. And that was going out and getting a job. And I thought, why not go out, if I'm getting a job, why not let it have more than one benefit to myself. I'm getting paid, I'm getting the equivalent of a 30-level course, I'm getting credits. I mean, how can I complain with something like that?

These comments suggest that RAP participants realize at least two of the advantages its proponents associate with the program: restoring an interest in education and facilitating transitions into the workplace. A third advantage, related to the first, is that by restoring an interest in education, students will be able to improve their marks and thus further increase their chances for a successful transition into post-secondary education. To a large degree, this is also related to RAP students' realization that, to continue their apprenticeship, they need to do well and graduate from high school:

WL: Do you find that being in RAP motivates you more to push hard?

CURTIS: Oh yeah, because I know that next semester, I don't have school. I just have to go to work and do what I do best, so ...

WL: What would happen if you don't do well in any of those [four core subjects]?

CURTIS: Then I have to be removed from the RAP program, but I don't intend on doing that.

WL: So, that's a real motivation there?

CURTIS: Absolutely.

But restored interest in school also comes with a cost. Curtis was actually not coping well with the dual responsibility of going to work and doing well at school. At the time of the interview, he was at risk of failing a number of his courses. Given that many teachers in the core subjects are not aware of RAP students' participation in the workplace, students like Curtis might find themselves in a very precarious situation. Others, like Keith, one of the youngest RAP students to whom I spoke, struggled with the demands of putting in a hard day at work and going to school:

WL: Do you think being in RAP has made you more motivated to work hard at school?

KEITH: No, it makes me a lot more tired when I get home. I just want to sleep. I want to go to bed at nine o'clock, because I wake up so early.

Nevertheless, Debbie, an Edmonton hairdressing apprentice, is representative of many of the Edmonton RAP students with whom I spoke, who saw the program as a "life saver." Here is her response to my question about what she might have done in high school if RAP were not an option:

DEBBIE: I honestly don't know. I don't know at all. Ever since I went into this RAP program, everything's been really good for me.

Facilitating School-Work Transitions: Creating Transparency

The issue of transparency and flexibility in school-work transition processes has been discussed at length in chapter 2. Although apprenticeship training has existed as a viable non-academic form of post-secondary education for a long time, it has not traditionally been an alternative known to many high-school students. Proponents of programs such as RAP have argued that they make the labour market and career options more transparent at an earlier stage. Yet, as I show in chapter 2, for many RAP students, knowledge about the program, how it works, and what the requirements and the long-term career prospects are, remains rather elusive. This lack of understanding of essential institutional features of apprenticing is often compounded by the roles that teachers, counsellors, and work placement co-ordinators play in the decision-making process. They themselves might be uncertain about the program and apprenticeship training in general, and they often assume the responsibility of placing RAP participants with employers. This limits the active engagement of apprentices in this important transition and can also lead to limited knowledge about the program and its implications. In contrast, I have shown how German apprentices' understanding of how the dual system functions and of the options open to them within the system – in other words the system's transparency – also created conditions for informed decision making. Unfortunately, this high level of transparency in Germany is based on early, rigorous streaming in the secondary-school systems, which in turn severely limits the options available to many young people, particularly those graduating from the lowest school stream (*Hauptschule*).

This raises some very important questions regarding the different functions of programs such as Germany's dual system or Alberta's RAP: the explicit function of creating transparent school-work transition pathways or alternatives and the latent function of reproducing social inequality. For instance, Kantor (1994: 446) claims that "the arguments for apprenticeship are based on flawed assumptions about the nature of the youth labour market and the connections between school and work as well as on unsettling assumptions about the purposes of public education." While those in favour of apprenticeships argue that offering alternatives for youth not entering post-secondary programs will make education more democratic, Kantor insists that apprenticeships may actually lead to a qualification of questionable value and more dead-end jobs. The initial optimism that youth apprenticeships promote more stable and better-paid careers needs to be tempered by recognizing what the data actually say when graduates from apprenticeship programs are compared with college or university graduates. Vocational credentials, such as those received through apprenticeships, provide a form of insurance against unemployment and poverty in comparison to what one would have experienced without any secondary credentials. However, there is no denying that unemployment rates remain much lower, employment security is more stable, and income potential is much higher for those with higher post-secondary credentials. This gap is evident immediately after graduation and only grows wider throughout the life course. For instance, a 1997 survey of the labour market outcomes of 1995 graduates from trades/vocational, career/technical, and university programs shows that, two years after graduation, 15.4 per cent of graduates from trade/vocational programs were unemployed, compared with only 9.5 per cent from career/technical programs, and 8.9 per cent from universities (Taillon and Paju 1999). Critics of apprenticeship training have argued that, instead of equalizing opportunities for the least advantaged or creating an equilibrium between labour supply and demand, youth apprenticeships will only add another dimension of inequality to an already unequal system, by streaming students from less advantaged backgrounds into lower paying and less stable jobs (Kantor 1994: 162).

Proponents of RAP argue that the latter need not be the case as participating students do not forgo high-school completion and thus retain the option of considering university. As a matter of fact, participation in such programs is said to make the academic content of high school more relevant for these students and actually increase the likelihood of future enrolment in higher education. Vocational education reforms and the introduction of programs such as RAP in North America are part of the discourse of *new vocationalism*, which promotes a more progressive approach to vocational education by eschewing traditional academic-vocational divisions (Benson 1997; Grubb 1996). The integration of vocational practice is meant to make academic knowledge more meaningful and accessible to the majority of students. In other words, such programs are seen as essentially empowering in that they make learning more relevant to students and thus improve the possibilities of an individual's success, both in the education system and the labour market. A central question, therefore, concerns the extent to which RAP achieves this goal.

Integrating Workplace Experience and Academic Learning

Hamilton and Hurrelman (1993) argue that what makes youth apprenticeship programs (and other workplace-based learning programs) attractive is that learning is integrated into everyday processes of the workplace, rather than constituting a "total pedagogic interaction," as is the case with school-based learning.

Such an integrated view of vocational education is congruent with the discourse of *new vocationalism*, a more "progressive" approach to vocational education that rejects academic-vocational divisions and promotes the idea that all workers need to be "knowledge workers." Instead of focusing on narrowly defined occupational preparation and the goals of immediate employment, the vision is for vocational education to become broader and better connected to academic content, and more critical of workplace practices and systems of employment (Grubb 1996: 3). This emphasis on an expanded concept of skills aims to overcome more narrow and conservative ideals of education centred on set content or curriculum. Similarly, Benson (1997: 202) argues for an integration of academic and vocational learning with the ultimate objective of actually acquiring "more, not less academic knowledge" by "embodying the pedagogical strengths of vocational education into the presentation of theoretical concepts."

Of particular importance in these debates is an emphasis on transferable, key, or employability skills. Central to these skills are critical thinking, problem solving, communication, teamwork, and leadership skills.[1] One should be strongly suspicious about the increasingly commonplace view that the development of employability skills should be the responsibility of schools rather than of employers (Lehmann and Taylor 2003). Yet it is still fair to ask how programs such as RAP, which have the development of such skills as one of their core functions, measure up to their own standards. Any connections that RAP participants experience between work and school are obviously related to curriculum, implementation, and integration. In terms of curriculum, none of the RAP students in the study was aware of a learning plan to guide and regulate what they do in the workplace:

BONNIE: I'm still scrubbing the floors ... [angry, but laughing] I'm still not getting clients, just because of where we're located. We don't have many walk-ins. And if a walk-in comes through the door, the other apprentice gets them, because she's just been there longer, it's just seniority.
WL: As apprentices, do you have something like a learning plan, or do you just learn as you go along?
[pause]
LIZ: Yeah, you just kind of watch and learn. Watch what they do and you just kind of pick it up.

Furthermore, while most students seem to be aware of the importance given to employability skills, I have already shown that they largely rejected their transferable or academic-theoretical element and focused either on job-specific or more traditional workplace skills associated with punctuality, cleanliness, and discipline. Recall

Riley and Nathan, who emphatically discussed the importance of being able to fix an engine, as opposed to the altogether "useless" knowledge of, for example, who invented the technology (see chapter 4). More often, participants in both Edmonton and Bremen felt that the transfer of what they considered important skills – work ethic, punctuality, and discipline – was not from school to work, but from work back to school. Ron, an Edmonton RAP student, describes what his apprenticeship has taught him:

RON: Hmm, if anything, it's a harder work ethic. Because you can apply that to school and really bury down and get homework done when you need to get it done or study when you have to get that done.

Although the evidence presented earlier in this chapter shows how RAP does indeed encourage students to stay at school and to see more relevance in what they are required to learn, what has also emerged from these findings is a rather uncritical acceptance of the program's educational and ideological functions. The policy discourse on RAP has been exclusively focused on providing linkages to the workplace and has lacked discussions about its educational purposes (Lehmann and Taylor 2003). Despite its ideological roots in new vocationalism, the program has yet to achieve its educational potential. At the moment, there is an almost exclusively one-sided adjustment (the student adjusting to the culture and discipline of the workplace), lacking any form of integration into curriculum. But it is exactly this integration that would be extremely useful for dealing with new conflicts, understanding new social relations, and being aware of one's rights in the workplace (Hamilton and Hurrelman 1993: 205–6).

There are currently no courses that allow RAP students to discuss with other students and teachers their experiences in the workplace:

DEBBIE: [No] one ever really talks to me about the work I do, here at school.
WL: You don't talk to any of your teachers or counsellors about what happens at work and the things you do at work?
DEBBIE: No, just Mr [work experience co-ordinator], actually. That's the only person I talk to about it.
WL: And what kind of things would you talk about?
DEBBIE: Like, sometimes, I'll be walking down the hall and he'll see me and say "How is work?" Just that kind of stuff.

WL: In the two, three months at work, have you learned anything, any values,
    any skills that you think will be useful for you at school?
DEBBIE: [pause – laughs nervously] Going to work and going to school are
    two different things. They are two different things. I can't really say.
WL: So, you don't see them very connected at this point?
DEBBIE: No.

The claim that work experience makes academic content more
meaningful and motivates students to work harder is therefore exclusively based on RAP participants' own realization of this relationship. It
is consequently difficult to argue that the program constitutes an
effective integration of vocational and academic learning. Some students are able to make this connection in that they feel more motivated to do well at school and to complete the core courses needed to
remain in RAP. But other students' attitudes toward education and
high school were far less affected by their participation:

WL: Do you think in the last year and a half that you have been in RAP, did your
    grades go up, go down, stay the same?
TYLER: Pretty much stayed the same.
WL: Do you think that being in RAP has motivated you to work harder in
    school than if you weren't in it?
TYLER: No.
WL: Do you think being in RAP has made it more difficult?
TYLER: Made school more difficult?
WL: Yeah.
TYLER: No, just the same. Same old stuff.
WL: Why not?
TYLER: Why not what?
WL: Why didn't it become more difficult?
TYLER: Well because school is school. It's the same, no matter what.

Rather than achieving an integration of academic and practical
learning, most students see in their RAP participation a chance to
escape from the academic requirements of mainstream high
school. Given that some students spend up to seven consecutive
months of the year exclusively in the workplace (summer plus one
semester), programs such as RAP may actually have the potential to
exacerbate the segregation of vocational and academic learning
(Lehmann and Taylor 2003). It is precisely this segregation of

school and work, and the reduced amount of time spent at the school, that attracts some students to the program:

TED: It was more or less, I guess, that I didn't have to go to school for a full year. I just had to go half a year [laughs] and that sounded kind of interesting to me. Actually, you work half a year and you go to school half a year. So, that's the best part.

DEAN: Yeah, that's the best part of it.

Although RAP has a built-in mechanism to encourage high-school completion – continuation of an apprenticeship is essentially impossible without high-school completion, and all accumulated working hours become void – few of the RAP students complete high school with the credits needed to consider other forms of post-secondary education. The educational experiences associated with participation in the program are thus more likely to reflect concerns raised by Bowles and Gintis (1976) in the mid 1970s and, more recently, by Jeannie Oakes (2005), rather than follow the tenets of new vocationalism. Oakes (2005) has highlighted the different learning that takes place in vocational and academic streams and concludes that this form of streaming and the resulting differences in curriculum and educational methods reflect and help perpetuate class (and racial) inequalities. Oakes found that students in higher-level tracks were exposed to material of academic and challenging content, allowed to work independently, and encouraged to engage in critical thinking, problem solving, self-direction, and creativity. In the lower tracks, material content remained very basic and unchallenging and the focus was on conformity, rule following, getting along with others, discipline, punctuality, cleanliness, and the development of rudimentary study habits. Clearly the work experiences of RAP students, focusing on discipline, punctuality, and cleanliness, largely reflect the educational practices Oakes witnessed in lower streams. Bowles and Gintis (1976) have argued that these different experiences mean that students become socialized into their respective, unequal future roles in the workplace and the social structure.

Related to this problem of streaming and socialization through vocational education is the aforementioned lack of learning objectives in RAP. What participants do at work does not seem to be regulated by any lesson or learning plans that the school may have discussed with employers. This makes it particularly difficult for

youth apprentices to come to terms with their new roles as employees and workers. Tim, who apprentices as a millwright in Edmonton, is talking about relationships with co-workers at his workplace.
Earlier in the interview, he suggested that older workers have little
patience with somebody as young as him and that he tends to get
along better with his younger colleagues:

WL: Yeah, how does that work out for you? Being at work where most of the
people you work with are a lot older than the people you're with at school
or that you usually hang out with?

TIM: It's a lot different, because the young people, they kind of know what it's
like to go through that phase. But some of the older people look at you different. Because you're such a young kid and they think that you shouldn't
be in there or something.

WL: Oh, is that right? You get the sense that ...

TIM: Where I work, some people give you a lot of attitude.

WL: Really. Is that difficult to overcome? Does that change over time?

TIM: Well, I've been working there for ... just about a year now, and I haven't
really seen a change ...

TIM: [the younger workers] ... we try and help each other out. Like if we have
questions or we're having problems with something, we'll like talk about
and see if we can figure this thing out before we actually go to our boss or
something. Because, there's times when we go to our boss and ask questions and he looks at us like "You should know what to do." He looks at
you like you're dumb.

WL: Even though you're just learning.

TIM: Yeah. We're supposed to be learning, but sometimes, like, he'll take out
his anger on us. It's ... sometimes it's just hard to put up with. But it's
something you got to put up with, 'cause you're just learning.

Tim's last comments are of particular interest. He argues that
you have to "put up with, 'cause you're just learning." But this
reverses the expectations; should you not expect more lenience
because you are learning? Or is Tim actually suggesting that you
have to learn to put up with exploitative social relations at work? If
this is what he means, and I believe it is, the school system's failure
to integrate workplace experiences into curriculum and to inform
students not only about their responsibilities but also about their
rights in the workplace, becomes even more critical. The following

comments by Riley, who apprentices as a millwright, support this argument:

WL: Were you treated like an adult [when you started work] ...?

RILEY: I don't know, you're pretty much the little toby that runs around, cleans their stuff. I don't know, pretty much, they ask you to do something, you do it ... like, as fast as you can, as good as you can ... be nice to them. Instead of cleaning something and leaving it on the bench, you take it back to him and say "here's your parts, where would you like them?" And they'll tell you where to put them. There are some people who just clean them and set them on the bench; "yeah, your parts are back there on the bench, they're clean." Then, they're like "yeah, whatever, you can clean all my other stuff too then." If you like try to help them, organize everything, make everything nice for them, then it shows them that you have initiative to actually do good. And then you'll get ahead and actually work on something, instead of sitting there, mopping the floor, washing stuff. Some people, all they do is wash the company trucks, because they had no initiative. They sweep the floor, you know, put no real effort into it. If you sweep the floor, put some effort into it, make it look like you care about what you're doing, then they'll be like "oh, this guy actually cares, he's doing something ... anything he does, no matter if it's a good job he likes to do, or a shitty job like taking out the garbage. He still puts the same effort into it."

This uncritical acceptance of power relations at work raises serious concerns about the value of a program that is essentially part of the students' high school education and should therefore have some pedagogical value. However, students are not usually given a chance to discuss and reflect on these workplace social relations at school. Neither are they always aware of their rights at work.

In contrast, the vocational schools that German apprentices attend include courses in social studies that inform students about labour laws and their rights in the workplace. This also gives apprentices a chance to talk to each other and compare their experiences. Vocational school teachers are in regular contact with employers about the welfare of apprentices, rather than having as their main concern the maintenance of amicable relationships between the school and the workplace. A group of Bremen apprentice hairdressers explains:

CONNIE: I think it is very important, the way the dual system here works. For the first one and a half years we were at vocational school two days per week, and now in the last one and a half years only one day. But I think that's quite good, because it brings in a little more variety.

JULIA: Also, you can talk to others about what you do.

ANNE: You also start making new friends.

JULIA: I don't know, in the beginning I found it very helpful that I was able to compare what I do with the others. I would say "hey, I've been washing hair for three weeks, doing perms, colouring hair, stuff like that; do you do more, or what's up?"

SUSANNE: For example, our social studies teacher really pays attention that everything goes as it should during our apprenticeships.

CONNIE: Yes, he gives really good advice. He gives you information about everything, about all the rights we have. That's really very helpful.

SUSANNE: He helps when you have trouble at work. For example, I had a real problem, that I was owed money, with a lawyer and everything. And he went ahead and wrote a letter for me.

Given the co-determining roles of unions in Germany's dual system, apprentices are also covered by collective agreements and are members of and have access to the union's services. In Alberta, workplaces are either not unionized at all, or the unions regard youth apprentices with suspicion, since they are concerned about how the employment of these young people might affect their more senior members (Taylor and Lehmann 2002).

The Future of Germany's Dual System

It is somewhat ironic that youth apprenticeships have attracted considerable interest in North America in the past decade, just as the future of the dual system is increasingly being questioned in Germany. I believe that it is important that policy-makers in North America are aware of these debates in Germany as they are relevant to North American school-work transition problems.

In the past, academic education and vocational education prepared young people for different jobs in different segments of an organization. This differentiation between vocational and academic education has been regarded as a key advantage of the German post-secondary educational system as it opens career alternatives for young people with different academic aspirations and capabilities. However, differentiation between academic and vocational demands has become increasingly fluid. Changing skill requirements in the workplace caused by new technologies and different organizational structures are said to emphasize individuality, problem-solving skills, and other skills more traditionally associated with academic careers. In contrast, training in Germany's dual system has been described as outdated and archaic, narrowly skill-based, and more concerned with antiquated virtues of discipline, punctuality, and cleanliness than with the more broadly defined demands of new workplaces (Geißler 1994).

Furthermore, streaming at the secondary education level as well as associated channelling into different career tracks is perceived as being at odds with the changing aspirations of young people in a more open and fluid society (Büchtemann, Schupp, and Soloff 1994). The reform and expansion of the education system since the late sixties have led to more participation in higher education and what I earlier referred to as *displacement competition*. This not only means that graduates from the lowest secondary education stream (*Hauptschule*) are losing apprenticeship positions to graduates from the two higher streams but also that employers can increasingly draw on university-educated people to fill middle-level positions which were traditionally part of the career path for graduates from the dual system (Heidenreich 1998: 331). Not only does this recruiting strategy compromise the attractiveness of vocational training, it also undermines German employers' own position as defenders of the status quo in workplace-based vocational education.

This disadvantage for *Hauptschule* graduates intensifies during periods of high unemployment, as has been the case in Germany in recent years. It has been argued that the supply of apprenticeship positions is too dependent on short-term labour market requirements and that this dependence seriously limits the "Freedom of Occupational Choice" guaranteed in Germany's constitution (*Grundgesetz*) (Oppel 1994). According to educational statistics collected by Germany's federal government, there were 711,400 applicants for apprenticeships in 2002 compared with 586,100 apprenticeship positions offered by employers (Bundesministerium für Bildung und Forschung 2004: 137). These numbers do not take into account mismatches between sought and offered positions or regional differences. For instance, the new *Länder* of former East Germany, lacking a viable economy, strong industries, and a training infrastructure, provide a very different picture from the economically stable *Länder* in former West Germany. In 1995, the last year statistics were collected separately, there was a surplus of apprenticeship positions in the former West Germany, while 191,700 applicants competed for 120,100 offered positions in the former East German *Länder* (Bundesministerium für Bildung und Forschung 2004: 137). Furthermore, although the demand for apprenticeships has outpaced supply, many offered apprenticeship positions remain unfilled every year. This mismatch may well reflect the position taken by critics of the dual system, who argue that apprenticeships in the dual system are based on outmoded vocational principles and no longer reflect the career aspirations of many young people (Geißler 1994; Heidenreich 1998; Heinz 2003).

Greinert (1994b) argues that a rational strategy to save the dual system must consider at least two dimensions: first, revision of wage agreements in the private and public sector and lowering the wage privileges of academic positions; second, the establishment of integrated educational paths in the form of doubly qualifying programs within a form of dual system. Graduates from an apprenticeship program would be allowed (usually limited) access to universities and polytechnics. University-based programs/courses could be integrated to complement vocational training, allowing for an upgrading of skills and qualifications and eventually leading to better chances of promotion, without the individual having to attend university for a complete four- to five-year academic program. It is argued that if young people have the choice between entering *Gymnasium* and only receiving an academic university entrance qualification or entering a program in a dual system and receiving both a vocational training and university entrance qualification, educational choices could be significantly changed (ibid.: 370). While this last point is actually reflected in Canadian youth apprenticeship programs, Greinert acknowledges that in Germany this would lead to the dissolution of the traditional *Gymnasium* and the whole streaming process – a prospect that currently doesn't appear to be a realistic option.[2]

Policy Suggestions

Redressing some of the problems with RAP that have been highlighted in this study appears, at first sight, to be fairly straightforward. Students could be provided with a venue in which to debrief their workplace experiences with teachers and fellow students. Given the relatively low enrolment rates in the program in individual schools, this may not be possible at the student's own school. However, school boards could facilitate meetings at regular intervals (e.g., once a month or every two weeks) at a central or rotating location. These classroom meetings could be facilitated by a qualified teacher or counsellor who would also provide specific information on responsibilities and rights in the workplace, labour laws and regulations, apprenticeship regulations, unions, and workplace safety. Youth apprentices have some very concrete and immediate learning needs that are very different from those of their academic-track peers, and that cannot be adequately dealt with in the mainstream curriculum. My interviews with German youth apprentices, who do have these types of meetings and courses at their vocational schools, showed how important it was for them to find out what other apprentices were doing at work, how one's own workplace compared to others, and how one's treatment in the workplace compared to that of others. Without this understanding of workplace rules and regulations, youth apprentices are open to forms of exploitation against which they have no recourse or which they may not even recognize.

Although youth apprentices in RAP are formally indentured with the Alberta Apprenticeship and Industry Training Board, my interviews showed that few had any idea what being an apprentice really meant. Again, before entering an apprenticeship through RAP, interested students could receive much better information about what their participation will entail. Furthermore, schools and employers (together with the relevant provincial apprenticeship or industry training board) could draw up more detailed learning plans for the time students spend in the workplace. This would help teachers and work experience co-ordinators supervise and follow students' progress at work, and would formalize employers' commitment to entering into a work and learning/teaching relationship with students.

Policy-makers could also address a number of gaps in programs such as RAP. It appears that unions have not been involved in RAP, neither in its design nor in its implementation. Partly, this is the labour movement's own fault, as it appears to have decided to remove itself from many of the negotiations and policy debates

(Taylor and Lehmann 2002). However, the industry-driven nature of the program leaves little doubt as to which workplace partner is in the driver's seat. If unions were to participate more fully, a more critical perspective on workplace social relations could be fostered from the outset.

There appears to be little effort to increase participation in RAP by women, members of ethnic minorities, and disabled individuals (Taylor and Lehmann 2002). I was unable to find and interview any young women apprenticing in traditionally male occupations. Much more research is needed to investigate why, for example, so few women choose careers in the trades, and to what extent this gender imbalance is related to gender role socialization or hostile workplaces (see Gaskell 1992). In addition, the demand of employers to receive students in good academic standing also means that students at risk of failing in high school are unlikely to gain entry into the program, even though such programs are presented as a way of helping students with academic performance problems. Cooperation with different partner groups (e.g., Women in the Trades, an Edmonton-based foundation promoting the employment of women in trades occupations) and employers could make programs such as RAP more inclusive.

Integrating such suggestions into educational practice requires a far more radical rethinking of the role of vocational education and work experiences in Canada than might at first be thought. Critiquing the hidden political and ideological practices of processing, labelling, and stratifying vocational students, Kincheloe (1999: 183) suggests that a truly progressive form of vocational education "helps students make sense of the economic, social and cultural relations that influence their workplace performance and sense of possibility for the future." Vocational programs could include issues of social justice that would give these young people not only manual skills but also social skills to understand the conditions and contradictions of capitalist production and reproduction (Shilling 1987: 407). In reality, however, schools generally do not have teaching staff familiar with employment laws. More crucially, the success of programs such as RAP depends on the cooperation of employers and their willingness to take on students as apprentices. Unlike Germany, Alberta has no culture of training young people in the workplace. Apprenticeship training makes up only a small portion of post-secondary education, and in most instances, starting apprentices are in their mid 20s. As a consequence, schools, at least at this relatively early stage in the development of RAP, are more concerned about maintaining amicable relationships with the few employers interested in offering apprenticeship positions than they are with the development of a curriculum critical of employment practices. Informal conversations with teachers and other school staff involved with the program served to highlight the importance of developing a positive reputation with employers. This in turn influenced the selection of participants, as the schools did not want to apprentice students who might tarnish the school's reputation.

These issues create an interesting and complex set of educational contradictions. Teachers and counsellors were sincerely concerned with the well-being of participating students. The students themselves largely viewed their participation in RAP as a positive and meaningful experience. Yet this experience was also clearly limited by exploitative workplace practices and by a lack of integration into academic learning. Without an awareness of these contradictions, the potential for providing truly empowering educational experiences that also facilitate the transition into employment remains critically limited.

6

The Role of Theory:
Choosing to Labour?

I don't really want to do an office job, because I'd rather be out actually
doing work.

Nick, Edmonton RAP student

I really wanna get out of [school] and just start my life, start a career, get
going.

Brent, Edmonton RAP student

THE INTERPLAY OF STRUCTURAL DETERMINISM AND
INDIVIDUAL CHOICE IN SCHOOL-WORK TRANSITIONS

Policy debates are rarely informed by any theoretical understanding
of how the implication of programs is constrained by institutional
structures and how the programs contribute to the maintenance of
various forms of social inequality. In most instances, policy debates
and programs are situated in what might best be described a social
vacuum. Even though programs such as RAP are variously debated
as helping at-risk students or focusing on the middle majority, the
conditions of being a member of these groups is rarely discussed or
understood. Yet the scholarly literature on school-work transitions
has long been concerned with the interplay of structural determinants and personal choice or agency on individuals' transition
pathways. Not surprisingly, the previous chapters have revealed a
complex and often contradictory relationship between structural
constraints and individuals' own perception of their agency. Analysis of the survey data showed that participation in either youth
apprenticeships or academic-track programs was strongly deter-

mined by socio-economic background and cultural capital. Specifically, young people from lower SES families reported lower levels of cultural capital and were more likely to participate in youth apprenticeships. Despite this evidence of structural reproduction of inequality, the subsequent analysis of interview and focus group data provided a much more nuanced picture. Both youth apprentices and academic-track students spoke about their choices, their decision-making processes, their ambitions, and their plans for the future in ways that suggested reflexivity and informed agency. Particularly the youth apprentices (in both countries) described their decisions to enter the trades as the result of rational choice calculations and vocational preferences.

These findings are neither new nor surprising. Rudd and Evans (1998: 41) summarize the dilemma created by such findings regarding structural reproduction and individual narratives of agency:

An important methodological and epistemological discrepancy arises here. This is based around the possibility that there is a tension between an individual young person's responses to such questions [of agency] and evidence provided from broader social and economic trends and patterns. In other words, a young person will typically be optimistic and will say that he or she is in control of his or her life course and that occupational success is largely based on individual effort, whilst there may be a whole mass of data and theory ... which suggests that many young people, especially from particular social groups or "trajectories", have only limited chances of "success" (conventionally defined) in the labour market. This is just a particular manifestation of a classic problem for social and educational researchers: there is a possible discrepancy between individual/subjective viewpoints and larger-scale social and structural patterns and trends.

These discrepancies are explained through concepts like structured individualization (Roberts, Clark, and Wallace 1994; Rudd and Evans 1998) and bounded agency (Evans 2002), both situated within a late modernity theoretical perspective (Beck 1992; Giddens 1990) and aimed at overcoming the dualism of structure and agency. Yet both these concepts tend to theorize an imbalance between the effects of structure and agency, based on an individual's location in the social structure. Evans and Heinz (1995) have argued that the lack of material resources (i.e., lower-class status) impedes the degree to which individuals can engage in strategic risk taking, which is considered a necessary element of life course success in late modernity. In other words, social status continues to determine to what degree individualization will be structured and agency bound. Both the quantitative and qualitative data discussed in this book further confirm, at first sight, these notions of structured individualization and bounded agency. The vast majority of participants have embarked, or are about to embark, on school-work transition paths that can be considered socially reproductive. Working-class participants were more likely to participate in youth apprenticeships, while middle-class participants were more likely to plan on studying at university.

In this study, many of the academic-track high-school students with university-educated parents spoke with great enthusiasm and excitement about going to university. Some also spoke with great respect about their parents as role models. Anthony, an Edmonton student planning on following his father (and older sister) into engineering, spoke about how much his dad enjoys his work and how he envisions a similar life for himself. Lisa, an Edmonton student who wants to be a teacher like both her parents, even talked about how great it would be to work alongside her mother. None of the academic-track high-school students with highly-educated parents ever seriously considered career alternatives like an apprenticeship. Similarly, most youth apprentices had parents who themselves work in skilled trades or other forms of manual labour. Hardly any of the youth apprentices saw higher post-secondary education as a possible alternative for them, because their marks at school put university out of their reach, their participation in youth apprenticeships restricted their access to academic-level courses, or they did not see any value in a university education. Although their decisions were not entirely structurally determined or void of agency, both the academic-track students and the youth apprentices whose transition plans reproduced their social status formed dispositions from a habitually limited range of possibilities.

The cross-national comparison further confirms these findings. As with the Edmonton participants, the dispositions toward school-work transitions of the Bremen participants were informed by class habitus. We saw how most Bremen youth apprentices came from working-class backgrounds, in which parents (mostly fathers) had also participated in apprenticeship training, often in the same or similar occupations. We heard from youth apprentices like Steffen, who is training to be an auto mechanic like his father, and who talked about spending many hours, as a child, working on cars with his dad. We also heard from Julia, a young working-class Bremen woman who had actually started Grade 11 at the *Gymnasium*, who performed reasonably well at school, and whose parents, siblings, and teachers expected her to complete *Gymnasium* with her *Abitur* in hand. Yet, she decided to quit school and start an apprenticeship as a hairdresser, because she felt this career to be more in line with her family background and social environment.

However, there were some apparent differences. Structural and institutional factors in Germany appeared to have more pronounced socially reproductive effects. Although sample sizes were far too small to make generalized statements about these cross-national differences, the data can nonetheless be interpreted in the light of other research that supports the findings from this study: parents' educational and occupational attainment more strongly influenced school-work transition outcomes for the Bremen participants, compared with those in Edmonton; similarly, for the Bremen sub-sample, the types of skills valued and fostered at home (e.g., intellectual versus manual skills) were more significantly related to participation in either apprenticeships or academic-track programs.

Not all educational and occupational plans followed this predictable pattern of social reproduction. For instance, although the cross-national findings suggest that the institutional features of Germany's education system and labour market are very habitus-confirming, they also have habitus-modifying effects. Recall Sandra, the Bremen *Gymnasium* student who had completed an internship at a hair salon, even though she is planning to attend university. Since neither of her parents has participated in higher education, employment as a hairdresser might be seen as more congruent with her habitus. Although she enjoyed working in a hair salon, she also insisted that her time at the *Gymnasium* would have been wasted if she did not go to university. In Sandra's case, the exclusively academic institutional culture of the *Gymnasium* may have "overridden" social status.

Another interesting case is that of Nadine, the Edmonton academic-track high-school student whose mother works as a cleaner in hotels. Although confident about her current plans to study biology at university, she expressed concern about her lack of financial resources and not having immediate role models to assist her with the transition to university. Her decision to attend university can therefore be interpreted as structurally bound, as financial concerns, a lack of role models, and a lack of cultural capital put her in a more precarious, uncertain, and risky position. Her resolve to attend university, however, is also related to an understanding of her underprivileged situation and her aim to do better than her parents and her siblings. She clearly indicates that what she considers her mom's "failure" encouraged her to aim higher. Thus, Nadine's choice to attend university, or her agency, is the result of dispositions that are simultaneously informed by and transcend her social origin.

Other examples of participants in similar situations demonstrated how ambiguity and uncertainty in dealing with present situations often arise out of the discontinuity between individuals' social background and their educational and occupational goals. This was evident for Trent and Don, two Edmonton academic-track students whose parents are engaged in manual labour but nevertheless pushed their sons toward university. Trent and Don's concern and uncertainty about what it means to go to university gave evidence of a habitus that clashed with the demands of the present situation (whether to enroll at university and what program to choose), but also significantly affected the future, projective dimension of their agency. Trent has so far been unable to distance himself from the confines of his past experiences. His lack of cultural capital, in turn, negatively affects his capacity to successfully engage in strategic risk taking. In contrast, Don is already somewhat reluctant to accept studying at university as his best choice. In fact, Don seems much more interested in working with cars and had also considered becoming a car mechanic. For now, however, Don has given in to his father, who has strongly advised him, out of his own experience as a house painter, against work in the trades.

Unlike their fellow academic-track students with university-educated parents who were quite certain about what to study and what to expect at university, the capacity of students such as Trent and Don for successful strategic risk taking was significantly circumscribed by their habitus. While Nadine's own reflexive engagement with her underprivileged social status created dispositions to do well, Trent and Don found themselves somewhat at odds with their parents' hopes and wishes. Although Trent did not doubt or question the benefit of going to university, his lack of cultural capital made him uncertain about what to study, what life at university will be like, and whether he will indeed be successful at university. Research into the relationship between social class and university suggest that Trent and Don have every reason to be worried. Studies have shown that the middle-class culture and expectations of university forces working-class students into positions of cultural outsiders with problems connecting to their wealthy peers and integrating into university life, which ultimately lead to crises in competency and fears of academic inadequacy (Granfield 1991; Aries and Seider 2005). Sennett and Cobb (1972) have referred to these processes as part of the "hidden injuries of class."

Thus, if we conceive of the relationship between structure and agency as more integrated and mutually constituted, issues of social reproduction become decidedly messier. For instance, can we always assume that dispositions and choices that lead to social reproduction are less agentic? And within this socially reproductive category, should we make any normative distinctions between those who reproduce their advanced social positions and those whose decisions maintain a tradition of manual labour? Are only decisions that lead to upward social mobility truly agentic, as they suggest successful strategic risk-taking and a distancing from the habitual element of agency? Trent and Don's experiences show that it would be misguided to automatically presume that career plans indicating upward social mobility are the result of a more agentic engagement with one's habitus and social environment. Trent and Don's plans to attend university were not only accompanied by uncertainty (Trent) and misgivings (Don) but also showed far less evidence of reflexive agency compared to most of the study participants whose choices would be considered socially reproductive. Although the outcome of their transitions from high school are reproductive, academic-track students were not propelled into these choices and most actively sought information about different career options or fields of study. In most cases, the narratives of youth apprentices were full of agency, expressed as preferences for and interest in manual or physical work, anticipation of future employment possibilities, or simply as a way of gaining a head start in a promising career. Often, these narratives of essentially reproductive decisions were characterized by far more agency than was evident with participants whose plans suggested upward social mobility, as the example of Trent and Don showed. As the youth apprentices, unlike their academic-track peers, had already made some level of commitment to a future after high school – the Bremen apprentices more so than the ones in Edmonton – their agency can be interpreted as an active form of biography construction.

AGENCY AS BIOGRAPHY CONSTRUCTION AND RATIONALIZATION

The last year of high school is a very important period in school-work transitions, as students begin to consider seriously life after high school, narrow their options, and reinforce dispositions toward specific career destinations, while also preparing for exams and eventually graduation. Edmonton youth apprentices in RAP are in a unique situation, compared to their schoolmates, as they have already embarked on a career path and have thus dealt with a range of choices still ahead for most other students. That they have already ventured into the adult labour market, but also still attend high school, puts them in an interesting position in which they continue to evaluate their initial choice to enter a possible career in the trades. RAP students are confronted with an education system that consistently emphasizes the value of higher, academic education. They interact with family, teachers, and peers who may not always be supportive or understanding of their choice.

Constructing Choice

In previous chapters, I have shown how a set of biographical circumstances (e.g., family and upbringing) interacts with a social context (e.g., school system and curriculum) to create relatively consistent and powerful dispositions toward career and educational plans. Youth with firm commitments to attend university were found to come from families in which parents had higher levels of post-secondary education, or at least stressed the importance of education with their children. The same young people received further encouragement in school systems that favour those entering with higher levels of cultural capital. In contrast, many youth apprentices grew up in an environment rich in manual work traditions and marked by a distrust of or indifference to higher education. While their academic mainstream schoolmates were encouraged by teachers and counsellors to do well academically and to aim for university or college, most youth apprentices were noticed (mostly by vocational teachers) for their manual talents and felt ignored by teachers in academic subjects. Some of the RAP students had given thought to this *de facto* streaming and to the possibility that their choice to enter the program may be considered inferior by their fellow students:

WL: Why do you think not more people take advantage of a program like this?
...
NATHAN: I think the reason more people aren't going after this is that they think it's more like a lower-class type job, because it's labour. It is a lot of physical work, and they're thinking that people who are doing that don't have the brains.
WL: Do you get that kind of attitude from people?
NATHAN: Hmm ... yeah I do actually. Some people do, they think, ah, you're a tradesperson, you know, you're not that smart. That's why you're doing it.

However, none of the youth apprentices to whom I spoke claimed to care about this perception. Yet, there remains an unspoken sense that their decisions need to be justified more than those of students who plan to go to university. Luis, a first year RAP student apprenticing as a chef, speaks for most youth apprentices:

WL: Now that you've chosen to apprentice as a chef, you don't get the sense that people look down on you?
LUIS: Sometimes they say it's not as ... you know, it puts me down one less than them. Like, it's not a really smart job, you're like an idiot, is how they treat ... Some don't treat me, but they ... sometimes it seems like that, that I'm less than them.
WL: How do you feel about that?
LUIS: It doesn't bother me, like. It did affect me once, but my manager told me, even if you like it, no matter what it is, as long as you like it, forget about everybody else. It doesn't matter what they think. It's what you want. If you like being a garbage man, then be a garbage man. No one's going to stop you. So, you know, it made me think, it doesn't matter what they want to be, I just be what I want to be.

The following conversation with four young women who entered
RAP as hairdressing apprentices is characteristic of the ways in
which their decision to become hairdressers is both justified and
reconsidered:

BONNIE: I want to do a whole bunch of things. I want to get my own business, I want to become a massage therapist and I want to do hair. I want to
make some money, OK! [laughs]. Just there's a lot of courses that I still
have to do to raise my marks, to be able to go to university to take business. So, right now I just worry about my hairdressing. I do that, see how
that goes. If I really still like it and I find that the money is OK, then I'll keep
with it. If I find that I want to become something *more*, I might take massage
therapy. I know that's a big responsibility, but I like money, so ...

WL: You made an interesting comment. You said "if I would like to do something *more*." Did anybody ever tell you that you could do more with your
life than hairdressing?

BONNIE: No, everybody's just like, "you don't have high enough marks to do
something" ...

WL: So people aren't looking down on your choice?

JOELLE: They think ... we're stereotyped as stupid people ...

WL: Does that bother you?

JOELLE: It's because we don't go like to university or something like that. So,
it's kind of like ... well, you're not going to university, so you're not going to
make anything out of your life. Or something like along that line. Like, I
mean, even from your friends. I know ... there's lots of people I know who
are going to post-secondary kind of things, and they don't mean to do that,
but you still, every once in a while, you kind of ... you still kind of get that
sense.

WL: Does that hurt you?

LIZ: No [emphatically]! Because you know one of these days we are going to
turn around and ... we don't want to be better than them, but we're going
to prove everybody wrong. Like I'm going to go and upgrade my marks
and take nursing within two years. Just because I don't do it just out of high
school, that doesn't mean I'm not smart enough, or I can't do it and I don't
want to do it. Because I want to do it and I will do it.

Youth apprentices often engage in a form of biography construction that reaffirms habitual states and earlier decisions. Decisions
are often recast as having been based on already existing interests
and on the pleasure and enjoyment the work promised to entail.

Work experience gained since starting their apprenticeships is largely described as fulfilling this promise, as having been "fun:"

DEAN: I've always been fascinated with like watching things get done. Like, you sit there and you watch them pour concrete foundations for your house, and watch them frame it, and you watch them put the plywood on and drywall it. I just love watching getting things done.

JOELLE: Oh yeah, this profession [hairdressing] is awesome for stuff like that. It's like not work. When you're having one of those days where you just laugh the whole day, because it's just ... It's not like, I'd say, your desk job; it's fun.

Steffen, a Bremen apprentice car mechanic who quit *Gymnasium* after Grade 11, explains why working with cars was a more rewarding option for him at this point, although he says that to become a lawyer remains his life's goal:

WL: When you first continued at the *Gymnasium*, did you have any other career plans?

STEFFEN: Yes, I wanted to go to university.

WL: In what area?

STEFFEN: Law. I still hope to do that. You can still do that later through upgrading [*zweiter Bildungsweg*] ... To be a lawyer is still my ultimate goal ...

WL: Wouldn't it have made more sense then to do an apprenticeship in a more white-collar area?

STEFFEN: Yeah, maybe it would have been easier, but then I wouldn't have anything from which I could profit myself, you know ... and it's fun. That's just important, and I wouldn't know how to do anything with cars. If I was to apprentice in an administrative job, you sit in an office, and you don't have an office at home. I don't think anybody enjoys sitting at an office desk in their free time, except for maybe playing computer games.

Steffen does not seem concerned about the contradictions in his story. Specifically his ultimate goal of becoming a lawyer needs exactly that type of educational credential for which he seems to have such little patience.

Despite these efforts to construct biographies and to recast former dispositions and choices, for some youth apprentices there remains a lingering doubt about their decision and about the potential it may hold for their future. Julia, a young Bremen hairdressing apprentice who, like Steffen, quit *Gymnasium* after Grade 11, is a perfect example of a biography construction that begins to collapse on itself during the course of the focus group:

JULIA: I was just happy ... in the beginning, I would say that I'm happy that I now have a job that I know I want to do, that I enjoy. I said to myself, I don't care how much money I make. OK, by now you start thinking, the older I get the more plans I have, like moving out, a car, driver's licence. And you start thinking, yeah, I'll be able to afford only one of them. Either a car or an apartment, or holiday or clothes. You can always only afford one of them, you really have to figure out what you want. I guess that's kind of stupid. But I'm happy that the job is fun, and then I'd rather earn a little less money than making the big dough and sitting in an office all day, waiting for five o'clock.

A little later in the focus group, the very advantages she talks about above (a job that is fun rather than making money) have become disadvantages:

JULIA: I can't imagine standing behind a chair for 15 years, washing hair, blow-drying hair, cutting hair, always the same. It's the same all the time. I mean even now it's like "oh no, not another perm." You always think it's totally varied ... and it is, because you also do hair extensions and whatever, there are always new things to do. But what I wanted to say ... I don't know ... always the same ... And the money is terrible.

When I suggest that her school credentials could have opened up other opportunities, Julia and others in the group at once construct and deconstruct their choice to become hairdressers:

WL: You do have the *Realschule* diploma and even went to the *Gymnasium* for some time, which opens up a whole range of opportunities, for example in administrative or other white-collar apprenticeships. Why, in the end, did you decide to go into hairdressing?

JULIA: That was too boring for me, working in an office. I really didn't want to do that, although at one point I was pretty sure that I would end up in an office. I also wanted to become a teacher, totally conservative jobs, some-how. But then I just said to myself, no, I muck around on myself all the time, doing my nails, makeup, that totally interests me. Every weekend, disco and all, "hey, can you quickly fix my hair." I've always somehow liked doing that. Then I said to myself, working in an office, that's too boring for me, I need to meet people and not stare at a computer screen all day long.

ANNE: You know, now I wouldn't mind staring at a computer screen [laughs].

JULIA: Sometimes I think that, too. I wish I hadn't done this, all the stress.

ANNE: I think I will definitely still do something like that. Something that totally interests me, like we're learning communication and psychology here [at vocational school].

JULIA: Yeah, somehow I do feel ... not stupid, but kind of stuck. You're not challenged, and I miss that, challenging my head. You're physically exhausted, total creativity and all, great ... but educational, no, it's just not enough.

CONNIE: Somehow I've just had it with school, all the sitting around and blah, blah, blah. But I also don't want to stay stupid. Not being challenged enough, this feeling. ·

Adding to Julia's own sense of insecurity about her choice is the general disapproval from people around her. Her parents ("Really, they were rather against it, because they know how I did at school ... they said 'you can do better'"), her younger brother ("and my brother, he kept laying into me [with outraged voice] 'you can't become a hairdresser; youuuu! Have you gone nuts, or what?'"), and her friends all think that she could have done much better.

Julia's dilemma raises a number of important questions regarding agency. Given her parents' moderate levels of educational and occupational attainment, was her decision to drop out of *Gymnasium* to become a hairdresser one in which social status reasserts itself over agency? Bourdieu himself used the concept of *hysteresis of habitus* (Bourdieu 1990) to define a situation in which an option is available to an individual, but due to his or her habitus, this option is rejected. However, we do know that Julia did well enough at school, and that her parents, her brother, most of her friends, and her teachers reacted with varying degrees of horror to her decision to leave school to become a hairdresser. In other words, most of what I earlier discussed as habitus-reinforcing contexts (e.g., home, larger social environment, and schools) actually led to what we might call habitus modification. Yet, Julia's accounts of always having been interested in "mucking around" with her hair, nails, and makeup suggest some form of agency that is habitual. Although I subscribe to the notion of habitus as a durable yet open system of dispositions, Julia's story also shows how, for most individuals, "experiences will confirm habitus, because most people are statistically bound to encounter circumstances that originally fashioned their habitus" (Bourdieu and Wacquant 1992: 133). Julia tells how her dad himself had dropped out of school and how this somehow justifies leaving school and going into hairdressing:

JULIA: Yeah, my dad dropped out ... he himself had just had it with school. He himself lived his life like that. In a way, I want to start my life like he did ...

While the possibility of doing "something bigger," or of attending university in the future, remains important to some youth apprentices, most also reject the idea that higher post-secondary education is required for future career potential. Joelle, one of a group of Edmonton RAP hairdressers, explains:

WL: Do you think that not going to university is a disadvantage in the long run? Do you think you really have to go eventually, to make the best out of your life?
[some tentative Yeahs in the background]
JOELLE: I don't really think so, because I think it's like up to you, what you put into things. If you put all your effort into something, it doesn't matter. Because ... I don't know, like if you're not really into like the books and if you're not really into that place of going into university, you shouldn't really do it, because you're only doing it because it's like a stereotype. That it's something you should do after high school. You should just do whatever is motivating yourself, because you're just going to find yourself more successful at that.

Sven, a German youth in his second year of a hairdressing apprenticeship, would agree with Joelle about personal motivation and drive being more important than formal educational credentials. He gives his boss as an example:

SVEN: My boss doesn't even have *Hauptschule*, he quit *Hauptschule*, and as a hairdresser, he's now the trendsetter in Germany. He's on TV and stuff like that. I don't know, but if I look at him, I see ... I mean, I don't like him personally, but as a boss he's my role model. Because I know what he can do. And without even graduating from *Hauptschule*, he became a famous man. And that's why I think somehow that you don't need school anymore these days.

Rejecting schooling and denying value to higher post-secondary education is also a reflection of some RAP students' desire to "get on with their life":

WL: Did school become any more meaningful through RAP for you?
BRENT: Eh, not really. I think life in general became more meaningful. I just got the overview of what life is gonna be, you know, I really wanna get out of [school] and just start my life, start a career, get going.

Instead of being at school, work creates meaning in many RAP students' lives. They prefer to be at work because "it's fun" and because they begin to develop a social life with their usually older co-workers. This represents another important step in their journey to adulthood:

WL: [Between school and work], where do you like to spend your time more? Where do you have more fun?
DEBBIE: To tell you the truth, at work. I love being at work. 'Cause a lot of people say: "why do you like being at work." 'Cause they tell me that ... when you ask "how is work," people are like "yeah, it is boring, it isn't great." With me, when they ask me, I love it; it's great. And they usually don't hear that. And I actually like going to work, I don't mind it at all [with emphasis].

However, some cracks do appear in these narratives, particularly for the German apprentices who have in recent years seen traditional career patterns for skilled workers from the dual system erode as employers increasingly hire university graduates into mid-level supervisory positions. While this problem is not recognized by all, some like Kai, who apprentices as an electrician in Bremen, are aware of the greater range of opportunities open to those with higher levels of education:

WL: If you do look at your friends who are still at school, do you envy them?
KAI: A bit. But then again, we already make money and are [is interrupted]
KARL: [unintelligible] they're always on holidays.
KAI: Yeah, of course that sucks. But then again, I can say I'm young, I'll have my trades ticket by the time I'm 20, hopefully, and they don't. They won't have achieved anything real in their lives, somehow. I can say, I got something in my hands. I can go off and do something.

MARKUS: Those who are still at school doing their *Abitur* sometimes make more money in their part-time jobs than I do as an apprentice [laughs].

KARL: Yeah, I agree. My friend, he only works 8 hours a week and makes 250 Euro a month.

KAI: Yes, but look at it this way, when they're done with school and they start an apprenticeship, then they'll realize "oh, now we make less money than when we went to school." And then we're at a point that we can say, yes, we are making real money now.

KARL: OK, but when they're done, they'll make a lot more than we ever will.

KAI: Yeah, but then you'll have to go to school if you want to make more money. But you didn't. I mean, here you are, sitting here with us. Was your own decision, wasn't it?

The various forms of biography construction discussed above suggest that most youth apprentices are conscious of the potential disadvantage their educational and occupational attainment poses for their life course. Although the advantages of higher education are generally denied, there is still an undercurrent of doubt. The German youth apprentices with lower levels of secondary education, whose future access to higher education is much more limited because of Germany's heavily streamed education system, particularly express concerns about the long-term disadvantages they face vis-à-vis those with a *Gymnasium* or university education.

Embrace of Workplace Culture

The previous section showed that, not surprisingly, academic-track high-school students in both countries were much more confident and assured of the advantages of their post-secondary plans. While academic-track high-school students from lower socio-economic backgrounds had to deal with issues of greater risk and uncertainty, the advantage of going to university was still never in doubt. The biography construction we have seen among youth apprentices is largely absent among academic-track youth in both countries. It is also not important to them at this point in their life course to begin asserting independent adult identities. For youth apprentices, however, this is a crucial strategy in their biography construction.

Although I earlier rejected the notion that participation in youth apprenticeship is an act of resistance against the dominant, middle-class culture of educational mobility, my findings do match with those of Willis (and other resistance research) in two ways. First, as discussed earlier, youth apprentices clearly prefer applied over the-oretical learning. Mainstream education is accepted for its creden-tial function, but academic subjects are of little intrinsic interest. Second, and this is the focus of this section, youth apprentices clearly accept, almost embrace, the workplace culture as an anti-dote to their experiences at school, or the prospect of white-collar employment:

TED: The one thing about college is, when you're in there, you're in class-room learning. But with the RAP program, you're in hands-on learning. That's the way I gotta go. I gotta go hands-on ...

NICK: I don't really want to do an office job, because I'd rather be out actually doing work.

WL: Real physical work?

NICK: Yeah.

DEAN: Yeah, the physical in the work appealed to me too, instead of sitting at a desk for six hours.

DOUG: Yeah, that would be so boring.

Where school is often seen as meaningless and inconsequential, work is imbued with meaning. RAP students, in their own words, have now entered the "real world", unlike the "unreal world" of high school:

TED: You gotta be committed to do it [RAP]. If you're not committed, you won't last. You gotta be committed to do it.

DEAN: And you can't just work two days a week and not the other three. You have to do it consistently all day. Just ... yeah.

TED: It's not like school. You can't slack off every [is interrupted]

DEAN: yeah, it's not like you can come in and not write a single thing down in school. Like if you go into work and don't touch a single tool, there's not ... you're not ... no questions asked, there's no leniency. Like that, like we have it here. We have it easy here. There it's the real world ...

Interestingly, the discipline and regimen so readily accepted at work was resisted in school:

FRANK: School, you had more holidays than school; and getting up in the morning, you wouldn't take that too seriously either. And now at work, it's tough as nails, you couldn't just say, OK, I'm five minutes late. Everything is getting more strict, and school was much too lenient for that.

Almost all of the apprentices I interviewed considered working, drawing a regular salary, and taking on adult responsibilities as conferring a status in the "real world." This status transcends the possible disadvantages of social origin:

NICK: They [students at university] don't have the skills in the real world. That they haven't paid for everything themselves [Ted talks over Nick]
TED: They don't know the responsibility ...
NICK: it's gonna be new as soon as they start [working].

A socio-economic disadvantage is thus turned into a "real world" advantage: becoming independent, learning responsibility, and having a plan for your future. Bonnie and Liz, both apprenticing as hairdressers, echo Nick and Ted's comments when they suggest that they are already on a solid career path at a very young age, while their more privileged classmates will continue in a sort of limbo for another five to ten years before they will reach the same point in their life course:

WL: Do you think your lifestyle has changed quite a bit, compared to your friends that are just at school?
BONNIE: Oh yeah. We knew what we wanted to be. They didn't. They're going to university and are taking all these courses. They have no clue what they want to do. And in Grade 10, I knew what I wanted to be. There were how many people that knew what they wanted to be in Grade 10? So ... I felt kind of, not superior, but I felt like I was doing something better with my life, because I already knew, I was already working at it at such a young age. That's about it.
WL: What do you think makes you different from your friends?
LIZ: We have a life career, we can hold on to this, we can always make money ... We're only eighteen or nineteen years old, and we got a career for us, for ourselves already, that we can use for the rest of our lives. And these other people, they're twenty-five, thirty before they actually know what they want to do.

What emerges from these youth apprentices' interpretation of their role as full-time labour force participants is a sense that they have reached a level of adulthood and maturity that separates them from their peers who are still at school. This sense of maturity and superiority is yet another interpretive strategy youth apprentices employ to validate their career choices in the face of a powerful public discourse advocating high levels of educational attainment.

Accelerated Maturity

It has been argued that young people's coming of age is being delayed in advanced industrial societies (e.g., Coté and Allahar 1994). Young people remain dependent on their parents longer and become economically marginalized through their exclusion from the productive sphere, while, ironically, being increasingly targeted as consumers. Coté (2000) writes about arrested adulthood, suggesting that today's young adults are becoming more like adolescents in their tastes, attire, and general outlook on life and responsibility. The youth apprentices in this study, however, considered themselves to be much more mature than their academic schoolmates. Almost all saw this accelerated transition into adulthood as one of the key advantages of participation in RAP in Edmonton or the dual system in Bremen. Rather than shying away from adult responsibility, as Coté's arrested adulthood concept suggests, the youth apprentices in my study were eager to take on the increased responsibility of this new stage in their life course, or at least to talk about their eagerness to do so:

UWE: This thing about responsibility, that's true. You realize that you are growing up, because before, your parents would always tell you "study, because when you start working, you'll be wishing you could be at school." Now we can say, no, or yes, you were right. Now we know for ourselves.

Youth apprentices recognize and appreciate that they are no longer economically dependent, as Ted, an Edmonton welding apprentice, suggests:

TED: The way I look at it, most people are gonna rely on mom and dad for the first four or five years in their life [after high school] ... But I don't want to be like that. I don't want to have to rely on anybody. I want to go and make it on my own.

Brent apprentices as a cook and earlier in the interview commented that, although he had never been interested in going to university (his goal was always to become a chef), his parents could not afford to send him to university. Here is what he has to say about friends who look to their parents for financial support during their post-secondary education:

BRENT: Like most of my friends [puts on whiny voice], "Oh, my parents pay for university." I find that pointless. I mean, what does that teach you in life? You should be out working in your high school and save up for university, because then you learn how to save and you learn responsibility. So, when you go to [university], you're not an idiot. Some people, it just makes me sad to see that. 'Cause I like responsibility, it looks for you.

For youth apprentices, this new-found sense of maturity is a departure from their former life as high-school students and casual workers. It also serves as a reminder that they are now different from academic high-school students who "only" go to school. Here is Brent again, describing how his experience with RAP has readied him for "the rush into the real world," unlike most of his friends at school who still act like "really big goofs" or at least operate at a lower "maturity level":

WL: Do you think your outlook on life is different from being with older people at work? Do you see things differently from your friends in high school that haven't had this experience?

BRENT: Oh for sure ... Like most of my friends [unintelligible], 'cause a lot of them don't understand how the world is going to treat them when they're done. You know, they don't know what to expect, what it's going to be like. I'm bracing myself now for the rush into the real world.

WL: But do you find that sort of being more mature or feeling more mature has changed how you interact with friends at high school?

BRENT: Of course, 'cause a lot of times, they say something stupid, but now that you have the maturity level, you really don't find that funny. And you know, sometimes you can't really ... I don't know ... get really ... relate to them as much as you'd like to, because your thinking level is a little bit higher than theirs.

Similar sentiments are expressed by a group of apprentice car mechanics in Bremen, who argue that they have accepted adult responsibilities and matured by internalizing the discipline of the workplace. In contrast, their (sometimes former) friends at school are still childishly preoccupied with "playing":

WL: If you think back at what it was like at school, do you prefer working with older people now?

DETLEF: Much better. There is a calmness there.

STEFFEN: You're just being treated better. Especially if you show that you can work, then you'll be looked at as an adult and you'll be treated much better; compared to being at school with people my age, who still think about playing.

WL: Did you notice that you had to grow up a lot faster once you started regular work?

THOMAS: Absolutely. You can't goof around at work and fuck up. You have to get your work done.

For the male youth apprentices, an underlying machismo is often part of this new-found responsibility and maturity. Consider the following comments by Curtis, who apprentices as an automotive technician in Edmonton:

CURTIS: [Some] kids when they go to school, they don't know what their parents experience when they go to work. For me, second semester, I'm already working as a *man*, doing a *man's* job. I already know what it's like. Not like some kids who don't have a clue of what they have to do. (my emphasis)

A further expression of apprentices' new-found maturity is a change in their leisure behaviour and leisure companions, as Dean, a welding apprentice in RAP suggests:

WL: Have you changed in terms of what you do in your free time and who you do it with?

DEAN: Yeah. I found I hang around mostly with people that are done school and that are working ... more people that I can relate with.

WL: So you spend more time with people from work?

DEAN: Well not necessarily from work, but people who graduated two years ago or something like, ones that are just getting into the workforce. I find the people at school, they don't ... they just don't understand you the same way. They are not thinking on the same level as somebody who's obviously out in the workforce and doing the same thing you are. You're gonna get on better.

Luis, who apprentices as a chef, is even more explicit in his explanation of why he has changed his leisure behaviour and now spends more time with people from work, rather than school:

WL: Does that mean you feel more comfortable with your friends from work?

LUIS: From work. Because then they talk about things like chemistry and I don't even understand anything involved. Maybe some formulas and stuff. But like stuff that really doesn't matter.

WL: Your friends from school?

LUIS: Yes. So, it's like, why do I need to know this.

WL: When you hang out with your friends from work, what kind of stuff do you do?

LUIS: We usually go to the movies, or hang around talking. And we end up talking about music, sports, things that happen on the news. You know, stuff like that ...

WL: Do you think that you lost some friends because you're an apprentice?

LUIS: Yeah, I lost some because I don't talk to them anymore.

WL: Do you think that's a problem for you?

LUIS: It's not a problem for me at all. 'Cause they seem to change and so do I. And our views and what we see.

However, this new-found maturity and adult-like behaviour can only go so far. It is also important to retain a sense of mischievous youthfulness:

WL: Do you think you've become more mature?

DEAN: I think so.

TED: You have to be at work and stuff.

WL: How about your personal life?

DEAN: Yeah, I think my personal life's become more mature [Ted talks over Dean]

TED: Not really. I'm still living my life young.

DEAN: Oh yeah, I'm still young in living my life ... young and stupid. But I think I've matured quite a bit.

Fortunately, combining maturity and youthfulness is not too much of a problem, as colleagues at work still like to do "stupid stuff":

WL: You said earlier that you feel a little more focused and motivated now that you're decided to go into RAP. Do you think that it will make you more grown up ...?

BRAD: I think so.

WL: Have you found that already?

BRAD: Not really. I still like to joke around and do stupid stuff ... [Colleagues at work are] older and the kind of stuff they do is more fun that what we do [at school] ... Because, all the stuff they do is pretty stupid. And I'm thinking, oh, that's probably stuff me and my friends would do. So, I can kind of relate to them.

Others see in the relationship with their colleagues a reminder of their still inferior status as a high-school student, rather than a fully-accepted adult. Scott, who apprentices as an electrician and is the youngest person at his worksite considers himself a bit of an outsider in his workplace:

SCOTT: Yeah, I am the youngest person there.

WL: How is that?

SCOTT: Oh, it can be hard sometimes.

WL: In what way?

SCOTT: In like ... the guys go to the bar after work, or like the way people talk to you at the worksite, like you're younger and they don't expect you do know as much. You're like "downsized."

While Scott felt he was not taken seriously and was constantly being reminded of his relatively inferior status at work, or in his words "downsized," other apprentices are still not sure what to make of their new status as workers and adults. Note how Matt, an Edmonton apprentice chef, first mentions that his managers are not very nice and that this has caused him some difficulty when he started his apprenticeship. Yet, only seconds later, he says that his managers treat him more like an adult (compared to teachers at school) and that the freedom and trust they give him is probably a good thing:

WL: Was there anything, when you started work, that you found difficult to get used to?

MATT: Hmm, some of the managers, yeah. Some of them aren't very nice.

WL: So, you are being treated quite differently than you are at school by your teachers?

MATT: Ah, yeah.

WL: Can you talk about that a little more?

MATT: Mm, my managers treat me more like an adult than like my teachers do.

WL: Is that a good thing or a bad thing?

MATT: Uh ... that's good I guess.

WL: How is that different?

MATT: Mm, I don't know. They give me more freedom and stuff at work, yeah.

WL: Do they expect more from you?

MATT: Yeah, but they also have more trust in me.

WL: Is that stressful?

MATT: Sometimes, yeah.

WL: How do you deal with that?

MATT: I don't know, just do what they tell me to do.

This sense of confusion should probably be expected in a situation where high-school students continue to spend some of their time at school and the remainder in an adult workplace. As I have noted, programs such as RAP lack a mechanism to assist students to reflect on, discuss, and deal with these changes. Yet even with such mechanisms in place, as is the case in Germany, the hierarchy of workplaces and mistrust of older workers can prove to be difficult challenges for new apprentices, as the following conversation between a group of Bremen apprentice electricians demonstrates:

WL: At work, were you treated like adults right from the start?

[people talk over each other, some agreement]

SEBASTIAN: It depends, I think, on the journeymen that work there.

KAI: With some, no. You might take [a tool] in your hand, others would be totally OK with that, but he will take it right away from you and will tell you "no, not you!" But with others, you can even work with high voltage, or whatever.

MARKUS: Older journeymen always treat you more like a kid, I'd say.

KAI: Yeah, they'll make you follow them around [laughs].

MARKUS: That's right. But the younger ones, they treat you more like an equal. They clean up their own shit, and I'll clean up my shit, and that's it.

SEBASTIAN: Yeah, they'll let you work properly.

WL: Generally, how is the relationship with your co-workers?

[everybody says it is good, no complaints]

KAI: Well, there's always somebody in there you don't like, but ...

KARL: Well, I don't like my boss.

SEBASTIAN: Who likes his boss anyways? [laughs]

KARL: There are always people who are looking for stuff, you know, so they can get you.

SEBASTIAN: Yeah really, mean little fucks.

So far, my discussion of youth apprentices' sense of maturity has been restricted to their new roles as producers, as active members of the adult workforce, and their general perception of achieving adult status through their relationships with older colleagues at work. However, some youth apprentices have also begun to think about their future life-course plans and about the everyday responsibilities of adult life. Brent, the Edmonton RAP student apprenticing as a chef, comments on some of the worries he deals with, but which are still foreign to his high-school friends:

BRENT: [Some of my friends] don't have the real view on ... how much it's going to cost them to live on their own, how much a vehicle is, insurance, marriage, you know. They're not even thinking about any of that. To me that's wrong. You should plan this a little ... not fully, you don't want to plan your wedding this day, this year. Just, you know, have a guideline for yourselves, so you know what's going on.

Keith apprentices as an electrician and is one of the youngest participants in my study. Still, his early involvement with RAP has him thinking about his future with decidedly adult concerns about pensions and financial security:

KEITH: If you're an early journeyman, you got all your life ahead of you, you'll have a steady paycheque, if you can keep this job, because I've kept it for a long time now, they haven't fired me. And they said that's the kind of job you can keep for a long time, and I'm working with guys that have worked with the company for over 40 years. So, I can start up an RRSP, I have dental, I have ... I'll be protected.

Despite the RAP participants' confidence in their increased level of maturity, there is a counter-debate in the psychological literature about whether early work experience is an important and necessary step in the transition to adult status (Greenberger and Steinberg 1986; Mortimer, Shanahan, and Ryu 1994; Vondracek 1994). Advocates of youth employment argue that gaining maturity involves the ability to perform typical adult roles, such as being employed. Critics suggest that "a superficial ability to play adult roles can be achieved without commensurate development of self understanding or clarification of social experience," a state which may be better described as *pseudomaturity* (Greenberger and Steinberg 1986: 5). Citing the work of Erikson (1968), Greenberger and Steinberg (1986: 7) suggest that early, extensive commitment to a job "may actually interfere with the work of growing up." They argue that in a more individualized society, in which an active and reflexive engagement with one's environment becomes increasingly important, and in which traditional structural barriers are said to break down, young people need a longer period of time for identity clarification, and that early involvement in the workplace circumscribes this process drastically. The result of early extensive involvement in work is what the authors call *adultoid behaviour.* "'Adultoid' behaviour simply mimics adult activity without being accompanied by the underlying perceptions, beliefs, or understandings that a person who is psychologically adult would bring to a similar situation" (ibid.: 174).

Personal conversations I had with teachers/counsellors in different high schools responsible for overseeing RAP certainly indicated that, at least initially, students' confidence about their newly discovered sense of maturity was closer to pseudomaturity or adultoid behaviour. The teachers/counsellors felt that the students' sense of maturity was mostly expressed in the immediate purchase of status consumer goods (all of the RAP participants in the study seemed to own cell phones, for instance) upon receiving their first few paycheques. Dean sums up this need to consume best in the following quote:

DEAN: Yeah, if you wanted to ... like my main goal right now is to get as much stuff as I can before I move out. Like to accumulate as much stuff as I can, and when I move out, I don't have milk crates for coffee tables and stuff. That's my main ambition. So I went out and got like a DVD player, stereo, and all in my bedroom. I can do that ... I find it makes you happier, too, as a person, because if you want something, and it's your paycheque, you can get it. You don't have to ask mom and dad. Like if I want a Play Station 2, good for you, I want the red one, ok, you pay for it and you're done.

Nevertheless, RAP participants' preoccupation with adult concerns show that accelerated maturity is a real phenomenon for most of the youth apprentices in this study. They viewed this accelerated transition into adulthood as providing a key advantage over those who enter the labour market with higher post-secondary credentials, but older. Still, I consider this an *ex post facto* strategy of biography construction, as it appears that youth apprentices have to spend at least some time in the workplace in order to realize and articulate this advantage. This raises an absolutely fundamental and complex challenge to youth apprentices' perception of maturity and responsibility, namely that this very maturity has been gained as the result of an earlier decision that occurred when they were lacking the maturity to make a fully informed choice.

Nevertheless, apprentices are overwhelmingly positive regarding their employment potential and their future plans. Participation in youth apprenticeships was neither interpreted as creating life-course disadvantages nor understood as a result of socially or structurally reproductive processes. Like their academic-track counterparts, youth apprentices believed that trying hard and having the determination and willingness to achieve something would guarantee that achievement. Wyn and Dwyer (1999: 14) suggest that this overly optimistic (and often ambitious) outlook needs to be linked to a discussion of individualization, which in turn "implies an understanding of youth as an active process, rather than a stage of development." Given the underlying notion of individualization, namely that traditional, structured pathways are being rapidly eroded, young people need to rely on individual agency to establish (or envision) patterns "which give *positive meaning* to their lives" (ibid.: 14, emphasis in original).

This form of individualization recalls notions of late modernity (Beck 1992; Giddens 1990), which also suggests that reproductive processes need to be accounted for individually (Furlong and Cartmel 1997). In other words, if youth deny that disadvantages in the labour market are the result of persistent class or gender inequalities, any problems are then to be found in the young people themselves. It therefore becomes much more important to recast participation in programs such as RAP as the result of informed, active choice that promises a multitude of outcomes that are actually preferable to those achievable through, for instance, a university education. This raises a crucial question: do these strategies of construction imply increased agency? And given the pervasive theme of pride in manual labour as a reason for joining a trade, to what extent are these strategies still habitual or, in other words, structurally determined?

STRUCTURE IN AGENCY, AGENCY IN STRUCTURE

Archer (1988) has strongly argued for treating structure and agency as autonomous constructs. She considers any mutually constitutive relationship between structure and agency as a fallacy of central conflation, meaning that denying structure and agency autonomy makes it impossible to actually analyse their interplay (Emirbayr and Mische 1998: 1003). I suggest that insisting on an analytical separateness of agency and structure would constitute a fallacy of autonomy. Although I do not doubt that young people's claims of agency are a reflection of their beliefs about themselves at the point that these narratives are created (e.g., during the interviews and focus groups), they nevertheless need to be seen in a larger, structural context that is outside their frame of reference (Lehmann 2005b). Consider, for instance, the findings of Meulemann (2001), who, in a longitudinal study, analysed how German *Gymnasium* graduates' perceptions of success in life changed throughout their life course. While still at school, and at the time of graduation, most agreed that class attributes (in this case, family of origin) played no important part in becoming successful. Instead, talent and hard work were seen as the key indicators of achieving personal and occupational success. In hindsight, by their mid-forties, graduates viewed the influences of family or origin (and luck, no less) as far more important than initially expected. Meulemann (ibid.: 56–7) explains these remarkable findings by suggesting that: "Family of origin surely influences success in the life of a *Gymnasium* student more than the success in the life of a thirty or forty-three year old. But it is not until one reaches thirty or forty-three that one can see more clearly exactly how strongly family of origin influences the life course" (my translation).

No human action can be conceived of as free of any structural elements. I have shown, not surprisingly, that agency is always situated in a framework of institutions, objective structures, cultural practices, and ideologies. Furthermore, agency is not only circumscribed by the social reality in which individuals live, but also by the way in which they construct and interpret this reality. Bourdieu uses the metaphor of "feeling like a fish in water" when habitus encounters a social world of which it is the product (Bourdieu and Wacquant 1992: 127). Nash (2003: 49) provides a very lucid explanation for this Bourdieusian notion of socialized dispositions: "It seems, therefore, as if Bourdieu's sociological theory requires an agent endowed with dispositions able to translate structural principles of the culture into lived practice, with sufficient autonomy to allow observed social transformations to take place, but sufficiently conditioned as to effect the actual reproduction of social institutions."

Regardless of whether their plans reproduce or transform social background, individuals engage with their structural, institutional, and cultural environment and history to form dispositions that reflect their understanding of their position in this social structure. The young people in this study relied on their past experiences at home to develop dispositions toward certain career paths. Many of the male youth apprentices talked about "tinkering" at home with their fathers, grandfathers, or uncles and how these activities created and sustained interest in manual work. A substantial number of academic-track high-school students agreed that there was never any question about their plans to go to university, how this was always a given. Although participants expressed a sense of intentional agency, the range of school-work transition alternatives realistically under consideration was limited by their past experiences. In other words, while their formation of dispositions was not mechanical or determined, it was clearly circumscribed by habitus.

Witzel and Zinn (1998) provide a relevant empirical example. In their German longitudinal life-course study, these authors work with the assumption that individuals actively engage with their situation in educational or occupational contexts, despite the various claims of more structurally determined reproduction and life-course research. They use the term self-socialization processes (*Selbstsozialisationsprozesse*) to describe the ways in that individuals deal with and consolidate their own aspirations and the expectations of others (like parents or teachers), and how such processes result in choices and agency that may reproduce or modify social positions (ibid.: 28). They use the example of young apprentices moving into potential careers in the manual trades who attempt to compensate for their lack of formal educational credentials by arguing that they have always been more interested in applied, and practical, rather than theoretical work. Rather than assuming a deterministic social structure working behind individuals' backs, Witzel and Zinn acknowledge the transformative potential of agency. Unfortunately, their analysis of both qualitative and quantitative longitudinal data yields little that would shed light on the conditions of this transformative agency. As a matter of fact, they come to the conclusion that: "despite the hypotheses of individualized and accordingly differentiated vocational biographies, our analysis leaves us with the sombre realization that social inequalities persist in the transition to employment and the first years of employment and are only partly modified" (ibid.: 37, my translation).

To appropriate Bourdieu's analogy, these fish stayed in the water.

Nevertheless, this offers a framework to explain individuals' sense of purposive agency, despite overall reproductive outcomes. Emirbayr and Mische (1998: 980) argue that even though individuals operate with a habitually limited range of options, their decisions remain intentional because "it allows one to get things done through habitual interactions and negotiations (allowing Bourdieu to speak of the paradox of "intentionless intentions"). As Bourdieu notes, there may be much ingenuity and resourcefulness to the selection of responses from practical repertoires, even when this contributes to the reproduction of a given structure of social relationships."

The various strategies of biography construction and rationalization are evidence of such essentially reproductive ingenuity and resourcefulness, as individuals explained, evaluated (in hindsight), and justified their decisions. I interpreted these findings as both forms of self-socialization and *ex post facto* strategies to re-insert agency into essentially socially reproductive transition processes. While a sense of independent decision making is involved, dispositions about occupational choice were also affected or corrected by the opinions of others and by the social and institutional contexts in which these decisions took place. At the same time, young people engaged in a reality check vis-à-vis their educational attainment in order not to aim too high or too low. More importantly, youth apprentices reconstructed their occupational choices as a reflection of vocational preferences, despite an overwhelming public discourse that equates occupational success with increasingly high levels of formal education. Youth apprentices talked about their decisions to enter the trades as giving them various advantages over their university-bound peers. These advantages not only included getting a head start in a career and receiving a good income earlier in their life but also extended to more general life-course issues, such as becoming a more responsible and mature adult.

These strategies were not simply post-hoc rationalizations; they provide evidence that individuals actively engage with the structures and patterns that frame their dispositions and actions. Although the socially reproductive thrust of their dispositions and choices was not generally realized, the participants in my study did clearly understand and incorporate into their narratives where and how these dispositions were formed. This understanding and reflexive engagement with their habitus should be seen as an essential element of a projective or transformative dimension of agency. According to Emirbayr and Mische (ibid.), the projective dimension of agency relates to the generation of possible future trajectories in which the habitual element of agency might be creatively reconfigured. The authors argue, however, that to understand the projective and creative dimension of agency, it is necessary to shift attention away from the actor's orientation to the past, or in other words, their habitus (ibid.: 984): "as they respond to the challenges and uncertainties of the social life, actors are capable of distancing themselves ... from the schemas, habits, and traditions that constrain social identities and institutions."

In contrast, I suggest that individuals' potential for creative reconstruction and future projection is not achieved by an orientation away from the past, but by a reflexive understanding of the past. The projective dimension of agency, in its essence, has to be rooted in habitus. Thus, it becomes possible to understand young people's narratives regarding their decision to become youth apprentices as reflecting independent choices infused with agency and working-class pride, even though these choices are situated in a context of social reproduction. The majority of youth apprentices interpreted their choice to enter the world of manual labour not only as a career move with future potential but also as the expression of a preference for, and identity with, the ideals of manual work. Youth apprentices see their entry into the trades as congruent with the formation of positive vocational identities and the possibility of a successful life course that is not in opposition to dominant middle-class ideals of education, mobility, and achievement.

Finally, we may want to challenge our very own understanding of reproduction processes, which are rooted in middle-class notions of social mobility and meritocracy. Why do we consider the decision of a plumber's son or daughter to become a plumber a social problem, but not that of a lawyer's daughter or son to become a lawyer? Would it be more desirable if the plumber's child spends ten years in possibly alienating institutions of higher education to become an unsuccessful lawyer, even though he or she might be happier doing physical work? And what about the few children of lawyers who might find themselves working on construction sites? Why did even Willis (1977) feel compelled to consider his lads condemned, while at the same time celebrating their rebellion?

This is not, I must stress, a functionalist argument suggesting that because we need plumbers and carpenters and hairdressers, because we will always need to build homes and our hair will always grow (as these young people often argue themselves), who better to fill these positions than the sons and daughters of those who have always fulfilled these functions. This is most certainly not the argument I wish to make. And, given the findings of this study, I am not oblivious to the fact that a great many young people might end up doing this work because they could not find anything else, which is hardly the condition for positive identity formation along the lines I am discussing here. There is no denying, however, that much of the social inequality we discuss under the umbrella of structural reproduction hinges on the different life-course outcomes of individuals from different socio-economic backgrounds and in different vocational trajectories. In other words, there is ample evidence that individuals with a higher socio-economic status will enjoy more stable careers, higher incomes, better health, and longer life. But is this necessarily a result of a reproductive vocational choice, or the result of the social and economic values placed on these choices? It is, after all, our value system that typically celebrates intellectual achievement over physical and manual competence. What creates social stratification in the first place is therefore not a reproductive choice, but a system that affords such different rewards to different accomplishments. In this regard, even the most well-intended and critical research tends to walk into a "hegemonic trap" that takes for granted certain capitalist relations of production and ideologies in which participation in manual labour has to be considered "problematic." Thus, we need to ask ourselves whether we can reduce social inequality only by promoting upward mobility, or whether it may first be necessary to look at the ways in which different forms of work receive such different recognition, both socially and economically. Maybe we should take a moment to ponder this hypothetical situation: It is minus 30 Celsius in January (this is Canada, after all), your heating and plumbing system has just broken down, you are sitting in your cold home, and both your plumber and your lawyer are enjoying themselves on a Caribbean cruise. Who will you miss more?

APPENDICES

Profile of Participants

LOCATION, GENDER, AGE, AND ETHNICITY

Of the 105 participants, 52 were interviewed in the four Edmonton schools and 53 in Bremen. Sixty-five of the participants were youth apprentices (29 of them in Edmonton and 36 in Bremen) and 40 were academic-track high-school students (23 in Edmonton and 17 in Bremen) (see table A.1). The vast majority of youth apprentices participating in the study were male, in both the Edmonton and the German samples. The Edmonton apprentice sub-sample included only five women, all of whom apprenticed as hairdressers. Although I tried to include young women apprenticing in traditionally male trades, there was none in the schools selected for my study. One young woman had started RAP as an automotive technician in the previous year, but by the time the school made contact with her, she had quit the apprenticeship.

Essentially the same picture emerged for the German youth apprentices. Out of 36 participants, 11 were female. Again, none of the female youth apprentices was in a traditionally male trade, although at least two were not in hairdressing but apprenticed as chefs. When I asked a female teacher at the school for metal-based trades in Bremen about efforts to increase female participation in male-dominated trades, she said that such efforts, although they do exist, have been very unsuccessful and even abandoned in recent years (Personal conversation, 30 May 2002). Similarly, there are few efforts in Alberta to increase female participation in traditional male trades. There are no equity programs or initiatives (at least at the high-school level) that try to increase participation of women in

Table A.1. Participation by location, type of program, and gender

| | Edmonton | | | Bremen | | | Total |
	Total	Male	Female	Total	Male	Female	
Apprentices	29	23	6	36	25	11	65
Academic	23	12	11	17	2	15	40
Total	52	35	17	53	27	26	105

Table A.2: Participation by average age (rounded)

	Edmonton	Bremen
Apprentices	17	19
Academic	17	18
Total	17	19

male-dominated apprenticeships. Generally, it is seen as sufficient to ensure that young women are aware of the opportunities in the trades (Taylor and Lehmann 2002).

As is to be expected, given enrolment statistics in higher education in both Canada and Germany and my attempt to construct a representative sample, female participation was much higher in the academic student samples. Eleven of the 23 academic-track Edmonton high-school students and 15 of the 17 grammar-school participants in Bremen were female. Most participants fell into the 16 to 19 age range, both in the apprenticeship and the academic groups (see table A.2).

German youth apprentices were slightly older (average age 19) than Canadian youth apprentices (average age 17) and both academic-track comparison groups. The higher average age for German youth apprentices is largely explained by shifts in educational attainment, which have seen more students opting for the middle or higher school qualifications and thus staying in school for longer. Furthermore, the German apprentice sub-group contained two older participants (aged 26 and 31) who were in retraining and this pushed up the average age for this sub-group. Nevertheless, I chose to include them in the final analysis, as they added further insights into the study of life-course events.

As for participation of visible minorities, 15 per cent (or four) of the Edmonton youth apprentices were members of visible minority groups, compared to 26 per cent (or six) in the Edmonton academic-track sample. The four visible minority youth apprentices were one African-Canadian, one Hispanic, and two East-Asian students. None of the youth apprentices identified themselves as First Nation Canadians. In contrast, two of the six academic-track high-school students in the Edmonton sample identified themselves as Aboriginals and four were East-Asian.

The Bremen youth apprentice sample and the academic-track students both included only two members of ethnic minority groups. The ethnic minority youth apprentices in Bremen were Turkish, while the two academic-track ethnic minority students were of Middle Eastern descent. This low number of participants in both apprenticeship programs and academic programs is a reasonably accurate representation of ethnic minorities in German postsecondary programs. For instance, in 2003, only 5 per cent of all apprentices were not of German descent (Bundesministerium für Bildung und Forschung 2005, 133). This under-representation of women and visible minorities is seen to stem from the fact that apprenticeship positions are distributed via the labour market (Alba, Handl, and Müller 1994, Damm-Rüger 1994). In other words, hiring biases in apprenticeship programs reflect racist and sexist practices in the labour market overall.

LIVING ARRANGEMENTS

While all Edmonton youth apprentices were still living with either both, or one of their parents, a third of the Bremen apprentices (33 per cent) had left their parental home and lived either on their own (17 per cent) or with others (17 per cent), including partners and roommates. This difference reflects the higher average age of German youth apprentices, but could also be because the German youth apprenticeship program is a post-secondary program (rather than secondary, as is the case with RAP). Thus, some of the Bremen youth apprentices had to move from rural areas into the city to find employment in their chosen career and to attend technical training at vocational schools. This was the case for two of the participants apprenticing as chefs. Although they grew up and went to secondary school in rural areas, their career ambitions encouraged them to seek employment with higher-end restaurants in the city. Similarly, one of the apprentices in the metal trades (shipbuilding) originally hailed from landlocked central Germany. In the academic-track samples, only one student in both Edmonton and Bremen lived with somebody other than their parents.

Table A.3. Trades/occupations of youth apprentices, by location

Edmonton	N	Bremen	N
Automotive, motorcycle & RV technicians, heavy equipment technicians	8	Automotive technician, heavy equipment technician	5
Electrician	3	Electrician	5
Carpenter	2	Carpenters/roofers	5
Welder, millwright, pipefitter	6	Metal (welding does not exist in Germany as a discrete trade)	5
Hairdressers	5	Hairdressers	10
Chefs	4	Chefs	6
Landscaping	1		
Total	29		36

APPRENTICESHIP OCCUPATIONS

Compared to Germany's dual system, with over 300 occupations in which apprenticeship training is possible, apprenticing in Alberta is restricted to approximately 50 occupations that can be largely classified as trades occupations (Alberta Apprenticeship and Industry Training Board 2005). Although many trades occupations are classified differently in Germany, I matched the occupations of Bremen youth apprentices as closely as possible to those in the Edmonton sample (see table A.3). This was easy for most of the construction (e.g., carpenters and electricians) and vehicle-type (e.g., automotive mechanics) occupations. However, welding is one of the most important trades in Alberta, but does not exist as such in Germany. Instead, I chose a group of apprentices working in a range of "metal" trades (e.g., shipbuilding) for whom welding is an integral component of their training and work.

EDUCATIONAL ATTAINMENT OF APPRENTICES

I was also interested in the educational background of the German youth apprentices. As discussed in chapter 2, apprenticeships in the trades were traditionally entered by students graduating from the *Hauptschule* stream. However, increased enrolment in the two higher-level secondary streams (*Realschule* and *Gymnasium*) has led to displacement competition, in which graduates from higher school streams are now entering apprenticeships that were previously the domain of *Hauptschule* graduates. It is therefore not surprising to find that more than half of the apprentices in my Bremen sample had graduated from the two higher-level secondary schools. Seventeen of the 36 Bremen apprentices (47 per cent) were graduates from the *Hauptschule*, 18 (or 50 per cent) had finished the middle-school stream (*Realschule*), and one had graduated from the *Gymnasium*. Although there was a mix of *Hauptschule* and *Realschule* graduates in all six occupational groups represented in the sample, there is also some evidence that there is a hierarchy of occupations within the trades, with the higher-status occupations being domi-nated by *Realschule* graduates. For instance, most of the car mechanics, electricians, and chefs had entered their apprentice-ships with a *Realschule* diploma, whereas most of the metal workers, roofers/carpenters, and hairdressers had attended *Hauptschule*.

Edmonton apprentices were asked to comment on their average marks in Grade 10 (i.e., prior to entering RAP). None of the Edmonton apprentices had average marks above 80 per cent and only two fell under the 50 per cent range. Twelve participants (44 per cent) said that their average marks in Grade 10 fell into the 65 to 79 per cent range, and 13 (48 per cent) fell into the 50 to 64 per cent range. While this shows that few high-achieving students are attracted into the program, it also suggests that RAP may actually be out of reach for students with educational attainment problems, despite the fact that "at-risk" students are one of the target groups for this program.

ACADEMIC-TRACK POST-SECONDARY PLANS

Research on career aspirations of high-school students in Canada has shown an increasing preference for careers in the professions (e.g., Lowe and Krahn 2000). The post-secondary education and career plans of both Edmonton and Bremen academic-track partic-ipants included occupations in law, medicine, teaching, business, and engineering. Six of the 23 Edmonton participants hoped to enter engineering programs, while four considered a career in teaching. However, some students in both Edmonton and Bremen reported somewhat more unusual career plans. One Edmonton high-school student hoped to embark on a career as a recording artist, although he was also considering a degree in education. Other career plans in Edmonton included police officer, para-medic, military pilot, conservation biologist, nursing, and social

Table A.4. Post-secondary education plans of academic-track students, by location

Type of Post-Secondary Education	Edmonton		Bremen		Total	
	No.	%	No.	%	No.	%
University	16	70	12	70	28	70
College	6	26	3	18	9	23
Apprenticeship	1	4	2	12	3	7
Total	23	100	17	100	40	100

worker. Two respondents admitted to an interest in sociology, while only one Edmonton respondent considered an apprenticeship (as automotive technician) as his first choice upon completion of high school. Two of the Edmonton participants were still undecided about a career or post-secondary program, but were committed to enter university.

Given the very low number of male participants in the Bremen academic sample, engineering was not mentioned as a career option. Instead, career plans in the Bremen sample gravitated more toward law (three participants), teaching (two participants), business administration (two participants), and medicine (two participants). Still located within the field of medicine, one Bremen participant hoped to begin training as a dietician a few months later, and another young woman planned to become a midwife. Two participants were hoping to enter the field of design, two others were interested in studying psychology, one young man hoped to become a journalist, and another young woman was planning to study biology. As these career plans indicate, the majority of participants in both the Edmonton and Bremen samples (70 per cent) were hoping to enter university upon completion of secondary education (see table A.4).

Data and Methodology

Between November 2001 and October 2002, I interviewed 105 high-school students and youth apprentices in Edmonton, Alberta, and in Bremen, Germany, using either one-on-one semi-structured interviews, or focus groups. Schools in Edmonton were selected based on enrolment levels in the Registered Apprenticeship Program (RAP). Participating youth apprentices in Germany were matched, as far as possible, to those in Edmonton based on age and occupation. All but two participants also completed a survey at the end of their interview or focus group. The following sections explain in more detail my selection of specific research sites, my sampling strategies, and my methods of data collection.

SELECTION OF RESEARCH SITES

The Edmonton sample was drawn from four different schools, chosen because of their above-average enrolment in RAP. Enrolment statistics for RAP were obtained from three sources: 1. Alberta Education, the ministry responsible for secondary education; 2. Alberta Apprenticeship and Industry Training Board, the body responsible for apprenticeship training in the province; and 3. *Careers: The Next Generation,* a non-profit, private foundation established to promote RAP in schools and the business community. In the 2000/2001 school year, 980 students participated in RAP across the province (Alberta Apprenticeship and Industry Training Board 2002). As these 980 students were spread throughout schools in the province, and school boards have become increasingly hesitant to allow researchers into their schools because they disrupt, to whatever degree, the school's everyday activities, I chose to concentrate data collection in one locality (Edmonton) and a few representative schools within Edmonton.

As any university-based researcher can appreciate, data collection is always preceded by a lengthy, albeit necessary, research ethics approval. Particularly research to be carried out with minors in an institutional setting requires approval at a number of different levels. After being approved by the university's research ethics office, research proposals are also reviewed by school boards before they are approved and the research request is passed on to individual schools and their principals. My choice of research sites was further complicated by a lengthy teachers' strike within the Edmonton Public School Board that began just as I was ready to take research into the field. Although I recognize this strike as a necessary negotiation tactic of the Alberta Teacher Federation vis-à-vis Alberta's conservative, deficit-obsessed government, the suspension of normal school operations for several months put a bit of a kink, to say the least, into the data collection process. The solution to the problem entailed a switch to Edmonton's Catholic School Board, which operates under a different collective agreement from that of the Edmonton Public School Board, but still has similar programs and student demographics. Thus, two of the four research sites are part of the Edmonton Catholic School Board, the other two schools are in the Edmonton Public School Board.

All four sites were chosen for their above-average student enrolment in RAP, but also because they offered a range of other high-school programs and options, appealing to a diverse student body. The four Edmonton schools were located in neighbourhoods in the north, west, and south of the city. This further assured that participants were drawn from a variety of Edmonton neighbourhoods and socio-economic backgrounds.

Bremen is a city in northern Germany that is similar in size to Edmonton and is also, like Edmonton, a provincial (*Land*) capital. While Edmonton's industrial base is in the oil and gas industry, Bremen is located just downstream of the North Sea coast and has had an important seaport and shipbuilding industry. However, in recent years Bremen has largely lost its status as a seaport, as bigger freighters are using the more chartable waters of Rotterdam and Hamburg, as well as Bremen's satellite harbour in Bremerhaven. As a result, Bremen's shipbuilding industry has declined in recent years, but the city still has a strong industrial base that includes an assembly plant for Mercedes Benz automobiles, a world-renowned brewery (Beck's), and production plants for large multinational food brands such as Kellogg's and Kraft. Although recently Bremen, as the rest of Germany, has had much higher levels of unemployment than Alberta, the city does have an industrial base that provides apprenticeship-training possibilities in similar or identical trades to the ones I chose to study in Edmonton.

Although it is common to assert that the selection of research sites is purely driven by theoretical and conceptual considerations, access and convenience tend to play an important role in reality. It seems only fair to admit that Bremen also presented itself as an ideal location for the comparison study as I was able to draw upon active academic relationships several members of the Department of Sociology at the University of Alberta have established over the years with researchers at the University of Bremen. At the time, faculty members of the University of Bremen had also been involved for many years in a collaborative research project entitled *Special Collaborative Centre 186: Status Passages and Risks in the Life Course*, in which they carried out substantial research on similar topics and had developed contacts with school and apprenticeship board authorities in Bremen that were most useful in organizing my data collection.

Unlike the selection of research sites in Edmonton, which aimed at choosing representative schools, selection of sites in Bremen (at least for youth apprentices) was dictated by the trades I chose to compare. Youth apprentices in Germany's dual system have already left the secondary school system and are employed as full-time workers. They attend vocational school for technical training and classes in general education either once or twice a week, or during a block release for a longer period of time. All apprentices in a specific occupational cluster (e.g., metal trades, construction trades, cooking and hospitality, transportation, beauty trades) attend the same vocational school in their geographic region. Added to the five vocational schools included in the study were two *Gymnasien* (grammar schools), chosen to provide a comparison with academic-track high-school students in Edmonton. Like the four Edmonton high schools, these two schools were located in different parts of Bremen and had a diverse student body, although diversity in a German *Gymnasium* is limited because of the streaming processes in

Table B.1. Sample matrix

	Edmonton	*Bremen*
Apprentices	First and second year youth apprentices (grades 11 and 12) who started their apprenticeship program in high school through RAP	First, second, and third year apprentices within Germany's dual system
Academic	Grades 11 and 12 high-school students enrolled in an academic program	Grade 11 and 12 Gymnasium (grammar school) students

Germany's tripartite education system (see chapter 2). Access to these schools was once again facilitated through the contacts of the University of Bremen colleagues.

SAMPLING

The study aimed at discovering both class-cultural and institutional elements of school-work transitions. Hence, the comparison of academic and vocational-track students in Edmonton and Bremen resulted in a fourfold sampling matrix (see table B.1) of a relatively large size, for qualitative research. This fourfold comparison led to a rather large sample, compared to many other qualitative studies. However, using focus groups for data collection provided a useful alternative for collecting qualitative (and quantitative) data from this relatively large sample.

Edmonton RAP

This group included first- and second-year youth apprentices (Grades 11 and 12) who had started their apprenticeship program in high school through RAP. Interviews and focus groups were arranged through the four schools' RAP co-ordinators. Students' work status at the time of interview determined whether they could be included in the study or not. While some RAP students work and attend school at the same time, others work for one semester and attend school the next semester. All RAP participants were drawn from among part-time students or from those who were currently in their school semester. All interviews and focus groups were carried out at the school site, usually in a conference room or an available classroom. Given these restrictions (i.e., relatively low levels of enrolment and school-workplace scheduling), student availability eventually determined which trades and occupations were covered in the study. However, the range of occupations that eventually resulted from this sampling process, and the fact that the distribution of occupations reflects that of adult apprentices in Alberta, leave me confident that the participating youth apprentices in the study are reasonably representative of the larger population of RAP participants.

Edmonton Academic

This group included Grades 11 and 12 high-school students either already enrolled in academic high-school programs leading to university entrance, or planning to enrol in post-secondary programs at the community college or university level. To increase comparability between this group and the RAP students, participants were drawn from the same schools as the RAP sample. My aim was to include male and female students from different socio-economic backgrounds. I was particularly interested in the participation of students from working-class or lower socio-economic backgrounds in order to draw comparisons with RAP students of a similar background and to understand why some developed dispositions toward manual labour and others toward more academic post-secondary education. I relayed these criteria to school principals and teachers, who insisted that they be in charge of the final selection of students for the interviews and focus groups. Despite the active involvement of teachers and principals in the sampling process, the academic-track sample came to include a mix of female and male students from varied socio-economic and ethnic backgrounds, with various higher-level post-secondary goals. As with the RAP group, all interviews and focus groups were carried out at the high school, on release from classes, during lunch or other free time.

Youth Apprentices in Bremen

This group included first, second, and third year apprentices within Germany's dual system. Unlike RAP in Alberta, Germany's apprenticeship system is no longer part of secondary schooling. German youth apprentices have graduated from one of the three school streams described earlier (chapter 2), spend the majority of their time in the workplace, and attend occupation-specific vocational schools (*Berufschule*) either once a week or on a block-release basis. As all apprentices in a specific occupational cluster attend the same vocational school for their technical training, I decided to arrange data collection through these schools. Vocational schools and students were selected to match, as closely as possible, the types of occupations held by interview participants in Edmonton. Data collection was carried out at the vocational schools, usually in a classroom or conference room. Given the tight timetable of apprentices during their once-a-week visit to vocational school, I had to rely on teachers' willingness to release students from their classes for a period of time. Given this restriction, I opted for focus groups only for my data collection in Germany, as this method allowed for a larger number of participants with minimal disruption to the schools. While this switch to focus groups was partly motivated by the specific conditions at the schools, they also emerged as my preferred method to generate richer data, as I describe in more detail below.

Academic High-School Students in Bremen

This group included Grades 11 and 12 *Gymnasium* (grammar school) students. German youth apprentices have already left the secondary school system by the time they start their apprenticeship, making comparison a little more difficult. However, schools and students were selected to approximate the types of schools included in Edmonton and to ensure that participants came from a cross-section of socio-economic backgrounds. As with vocational schools, contacts with teachers and principals were facilitated through researchers at the University of Bremen. Furthermore, to be methodologically consistent with the data collection for German apprentices, only focus groups were used. They were carried out at the schools, with students released from class for the requested period of time (usually 60 to 90 minutes).

This comparative, four-cell sampling strategy resulted in a total sample of 105 participants. Of these, 65 were youth apprentices, and 40 were academic-track high-school students. Fifty-two were interviewed in Edmonton and 53 in Bremen (see table B.2). Twenty-nine of the 52 Edmonton participants were youth apprentices in RAP, and 23 were academic students. In Germany, 36 of the 53 partici-

Table B.2: Study participants by location, type of program, and data collection method

	Edmonton	Bremen	Total
Apprentices	18 individual interviews	No individual interviews	
	3 Focus groups (11)	7 Focus groups	
	2 groups of 4	6 groups of 5;	
	1 group of 3	1 group of 6	
	N=29	N= 36	N= 65
Academic	5 individual interviews	No individual interviews	
	3 Focus groups (18)	3 Focus groups	
	1 group of 5	2 groups of 6	
	1 group of 6	1 group of 5	
	1 group of 7		
	N= 23	N= 17	N= 40
Total	N= 52	N= 53	N= 105

pants were youth apprentices in the dual system, and 17 were academic students in grammar schools (*Gymnasium*). Table B.2 also shows the distribution of participants contacted via individual interviews and those who participated in focus groups.

DATA COLLECTION STRATEGIES

Interviews and Focus Groups

The main purpose of this study was to explain how both structure and agency are implicated in the reproduction of social inequality. To explore the role of agency in these reproductive processes, it was important to engage with participants' at an in-depth, individual level. I approached this study with an image of high-school students and youth apprentices, not as mere dupes being streamed, tracked, and sent off on predetermined life-course paths, but as active individuals who make choices, who have some understanding of how these choices may be affected by their social origin, and who engage in a construction of the social reality in which they live. More specifically, I used a mix of individual semi-structured interviews and focus groups, both with a flexible interview guide. Although the interview guide was designed to give participants as much control over the interview process as possible, it served as a tool to ensure that all interviews covered the same range of questions, themes, and issues. Participants were asked to reflect on their dispositions and motivations for joining RAP (in the case of Edmonton youth apprentices) or for the reasons behind their post-secondary education plans (in the case of academic-track high-school students). These sets of questions allowed participants to construct narratives of agency and independence, if they so chose. The interview then proceeded to ask about the influence of parents, siblings, peers, teachers, and others on the formation of these dispositions. These influences were assessed both directly (e.g., participants' own accounts of discussions with parents) and indirectly. Questions about indirect influences asked about the overall relationships with parents, family life, and attitudes about schooling and working. Through this relatively wide set of questions, asked in an open format, it was possible to analyse consistencies and inconsistencies in individuals' accounts of agency and independence.

My first few individual interviews revealed at least two important response patterns that required some modification to the interview guide and more flexibility in the data collection strategy. For instance, I recognized early on that youth apprentices were keen to talk about the new responsibilities they were granted in the workplace and how this led to a sense of maturity beyond that of their peers at school. I recognized these narratives as important elements in the way youth apprentices made sense, at least in hindsight, of their decisions to enter youth apprenticeships. They also contained important elements demarcating themselves from their friends and peers in mainstream school programs. Although I was aware of the literature on maturity, pseudo-maturity, and the influences of working on youth development (e.g., Greenberger and Steinberg 1986), I had not initially expected this theme to be of great importance to the study of agency and structural constraints in school-work transitions. Yet, realizing its role in these processes, I included this theme in my semi-structured interview guide for all subsequent interviews and focus groups.

An even more methodologically important need for reflexivity in the research process was my realization that focus groups might prove to be a better data collection strategy than individual interviews. This shift in preference was partly determined by schools' reluctance to commit too much time to this project and to allow an outside person in the school for too long. School timetables are a very intricate arrangement of the time-space continuum, and my continued presence in the school, as well as my ongoing request to remove individual students from classrooms created logistical problems for some school administrators. Asking to spend 90 minutes with groups of four or five students proved to be a much easier "sell" than trying to conduct 45 minute individual interviews with the same four or five students.

However important the move from individual interviews to focus groups may have been for the maintenance of positive relationships with teachers and administrators, it also offered two crucial sampling and data collection benefits. First, in terms of sampling strategy, my four-cell sampling matrix required a relatively large number of participants to gain any valuable insights. Focus groups offer the potential of increasing the quantity of responses, while at the same time retaining many of the strengths of individual interviews. Second, from a data quality perspective, I found that young people, particularly those who may be considered less articulate (or willing to talk), appeared far more engaged and talkative in groups. Few of the participants in the focus groups showed the kinds of inhibitions I had observed with some participants in early individual interviews. Being able to respond to the ideas of others in the group brought unexpected stories and insights into the discussion. I might not have heard these stories had I followed my interview guide in individual interviews. For instance, the dynamics of focus groups, particularly in the male-dominated focus groups with trades apprentices, revealed some rich insights into the banter and attitudes of working-life masculinity that would not have been obvious in individual interviews.

Some social researchers look at focus groups with suspicion, possibly due to their association with market research, in which they are used extensively (Morgan 1988). However, this should not detract from the advantages they offer social scientists. Madriz (2000: 836–7) confirms my observations in this study when she argues that focus groups offer the advantage of observing interaction between participants, generating spontaneous responses that ease involvement and participation, and limiting the interference of the interviewer in the interview process. Madriz proposes the use of focus groups in feminist research, particularly with women in severely disadvantaged situations. My study has shown that using focus groups might also be effective in youth research, as many young people may not yet have acquired the confidence to openly speak about experiences with a stranger (who appears to them, it should be noted, in a position of authority). Instead, both their school and private lives are probably more characterized by activities carried out in groups. Speaking to a researcher in a group thus may be more in tune with their social experiences, and offers the further advantage of making the researcher appear as a less authoritative figure.

Focus groups can thus not only increase the quantity of responses but also increase the quality, through observable interaction, emergence of unexpected themes and topics, and the potential of creating a more natural interaction between participants and researcher than a one-on-one interview (Stewart and Shamdasani 1990). Of course, these strengths are also tempered by some disadvantages. Just as focus groups have the potential to make interactions more natural and to generate spontaneous responses, they can also mean a loss of control of the researcher over the interview process and a blurring of lines between truly individual responses (i.e., responses an individual would have given in a one-on-one interview) and responses meant to conform to the attitudes and dynamics of the group (Morgan 1988: 21). The last criticism is particularly crucial, as it affects the validity and reliability of data generated through focus groups. Carey (1994: 234–6) writes that "members in a group are interactive, dynamic suppliers of information. Participation is interactive in the sense that a member's contribution exists in a social context affected by previous statements and other factors, such as conformity and censoring."

These concerns are not to be taken lightly. However, as I carried out both individual interviews and focus groups in this study, I was able to assess individual responses in focus groups in comparison to responses received from other participants in individual interviews. While the focus groups provided invaluable insights into interactions, similar responses and the emergence of similar themes in both one-on-one interviews and focus groups suggested to me that problems of conformity and censorship in focus groups were minimal. Two examples may illustrate this point.

Since the best mix of focus groups and individual interviews was obtained in the sub-group of Edmonton RAP students, I took a closer look to see whether individual responses and response patterns using the two different data collection strategies were similar. Without any prompts on my part, issues of how careers might be affected by motherhood and women's responsibility for raising a family were discussed by female RAP students in both focus groups and individual interviews (the same was also true for Edmonton female academic-track students). Similarly, all respondents in both individual interviews and focus groups discussed at great length the influence participation in RAP has had on their sense of maturity and responsibility. I already indicated how this emerged as a strong pattern early on and how I modified my interview guide accordingly. However, in almost all instances, this issue emerged on its own, without me resorting to the interview guide. As there are similar examples for the Edmonton academic sub-group, I was confident that I could combine and compare data collected with the two different strategies, and that the benefits of switching from individual interviews to focus groups outweighed any possible disadvantages.

Survey

A survey was administered after the interview or focus group and was completed by all but two of the participants. This survey provided a means of collecting socio-economic data on which an initial structural analysis could be based. For ethical reasons, some of these data were difficult to obtain in focus groups. Answering questions regarding family income or parents' occupational and educational attainment in a focus group is likely to cause discomfort with some participants. Instead, using a survey to obtain this socio-economic background data was less intrusive and seemed a more reliable way of collecting this type of potentially sensitive information (although in most cases, students spoke quite willingly and unprompted about their family backgrounds).

Slightly modified (and translated) questionnaires were used for participants in each of the four sub-samples. All participants were asked the same questions regarding age, gender, ethnicity, and family socio-economic status. I also included a range of items intended to assess notions of cultural capital, both in their current lives (e.g., participation in high and low culture, like going to the theatre or the movies) and in their homes (the emphasis their parents placed on manual/physical versus intellectual skills). While these items provided background information that was not obtained during the interviews or focus groups, the questionnaires also included some Likert-scale items intended for triangulation purposes. For instance, participants were asked to rate structural factors (e.g., class, gender, ethnicity, locality) that might constrain individual agency in school-work transitions. As these issues were also addressed in the interviews, the questionnaire items could be used to assess validity and also for theory construction. Silverman (2001) suggests that even the inclusion of a few simple counts in qualitative studies can support qualitative findings as they may convince more skeptical readers who otherwise only have the researchers' word vouching for validity and reliability. As a potential measure of validity, they confirm (or contradict) participants' narratives.

DATA ANALYSIS

Given the tremendous amount of data accumulated through interviews and focus groups with 105 participants, as well as extensive field notes on focus group interactions, non-verbal communications, and emerging themes and concepts, I turned to NUDIST (Version 6) for my data analysis. NUDIST was a particularly useful tool as it allows for complexity in the coding process, but has easy data access and recall.

I administered and coded the surveys, conducted all the interviews, and transcribed all interviews and focus groups myself. The German focus groups were transcribed in German, and only the quotes and excerpts used in this book were translated into English. In the translation, I made every effort possible to take account of and preserve slang and colloquialisms. On occasions, this required some poetic license, particularly as participants' language and expression turned to the more flowery and ornate. All participants were given unique pseudonyms to protect their identity, but to make it possible to identify them as individual speakers throughout the data analysis. Thus I was able to follow some individuals whose stories emerged as particularly salient for the different empirical and theoretical themes and concepts.

My multiple roles as the sole data collector, transcriber, translator, and analyst gave me the advantage of being fully immersed in the narratives of these young people. For months, the stories, experiences, and concerns of the 105 young men and women in Edmonton and Bremen became my life. I believe that this full immersion increased the reliability of the data analysis. For instance, during the transcribing process, I was able to supplement the transcripts with field notes and my recollections of the interactions and non-recorded events and gestures that took place during the interviews and focus groups. This process was aided by the fact that I would transcribe interviews and focus groups as immediately as possible. Following narratives of individual respondents throughout the analysis was supported by the fact that I actually knew them, albeit not in the same, intense sense of knowing as is the case with ethnographic research. Yet there is still the risk that my specific status as a male, university-based researcher affected the relationships with respondents in ways that might leave important issues and themes undiscovered. I would counter this concern with two arguments: 1. my own background as a working-class kid whose father worked in the trades and who ended up at university has made me sensitive to the concerns of both the academic-track students and youth apprentices in the sample; 2. the fact that the young women in the study felt comfortable enough to raise issues of marriage and motherhood without my specific prompting suggests that they were not inhibited by my gender. In any case, I hope that I have been able to do justice to the experiences, concerns, and hopes of the young people at the centre of this book.

Notes

INTRODUCTION

1 The concepts of class and socio-economic status (SES) are used inter-
changeably throughout this study. Socio-economic status represents a
more clearly defined empirical category (including measures of education and occupational attainment and income), and I use it when referring to the importance of these measures. However, I also use the various
concepts of class to more explicitly address issues concerning the reproduction of social status. Furthermore, the notion of social class throughout the book has a cultural rather than purely empirical meaning.

CHAPTER ONE

1 Throughout the book, the five-point Likert scales have been transformed
into dichotomies of "important" and "not important." In some of the
tables and figures the responses indicate levels of agreement with a statement rather than a rating of importance, in which case the recoded,
dichotomous variables are "agree" and "disagree." The main purpose of
this transformation is simplicity, in terms of both the argument made and
the presentation of data. The cut-off point for all tables and figures based
on Likert scales is the mid-category three: responses one to three were
recoded into "not important" or "disagree" and responses four and five
into "important" or "agree." The justification for this cut-off point is simple. I am not interested in relatively fine differences in responses, but in
broadly understanding who agrees with a certain statement or rates a certain issue as important. Therefore, I consider a response of three, which

indicates "neither important nor unimportant" or "neither agree nor disagree," as one that is closer to "not important" or "disagree."

CHAPTER TWO

1 I am referring to Alberta's apprenticeship system as an "adult" apprenticeship system, because most apprentices in Alberta enter their apprenticeship after numerous years in the workforce, usually in casual labour without any post-secondary credentials. On average, Alberta apprentices do not start their apprenticeships until they are in their mid-20s (Alberta Apprenticeship and Industry Training Board 1996). In contrast, apprentices in Germany's dual system start their apprenticeships immediately after completing their schooling, at an average age of around 17 (Heidenreich 1998: 327).

2 Similarly, young men are not entering hairdressing.

3 The primary reason for making education a responsibility of the *Länder* was to avoid a centralization of the educational system as was experienced during the Nazi era from 1933 to 1945 (Führ 1989).

4 In some of the educational jurisdictions, Grades 5 and 6 constitute a so-called *orientation level*, generally offered at one of the rare comprehensive schools, with the purpose of making transferability between the streams easier (Führ 1989). This is to give individual students an idea about their abilities and interests and to help determine which school type would be most appropriate. Orientation levels and quasi-comprehensive school types have typically only been introduced in the federal states (*Länder*) governed by the less conservative social democrats, which has made any debate about their success or failure also an ideological and political one. These controversies have flared up recently with Germany's rather poor results in the recent PISA (*Programme for International Student Assessment*) study, which also revealed differences within Germany (i.e., between the different *Länder*).

5 Percentages do not add up to 100 per cent, as some apprentices enter the dual system without formal school-leaving certificates or after having attended school-based courses and preparatory schemes and programs.

6 The agencies formerly known as *Arbeitsamt* have recently been renamed *Agentur für Arbeit*.

CHAPTER FOUR

1 This argument can, of course, be extended beyond class issues, to include gender, race, and ethnicity. In Canada, for instance, low levels of educa-

tional attainment of Aboriginal students are often traced to the existence of a white, middle-class school curriculum and culture (Wotherspoon 2004).

2 The index comprised seven "high culture" activities: reading literature, writing, learning a musical instrument, going to classical music concerts, going to the theatre, listening to classical music, and going to the museum. Scores from 0 to 3 were considered "low cultural capital," and from 4 to 7 "high cultural capital."

3 These findings are confirmed in a logistic regression in which gender is shown to have the most effect on cultural capital, although the sample is too small to draw overly confident, generalizable conclusions from such a finding (see also Note 5 for findings regarding habitus in the logistic regressions).

4 The various discourses on the educational gains made by girls are tempered by an understanding that education continues to reproduce traditional gender roles and inequalities. This is evidenced in the educational areas boys and girls choose and in classroom interactions and behaviours (see Warrington and Younger 2000).

5 Using logistic regression models to predict both cultural capital and RAP participation, the measures for middle-class habitus are shown to have strong effects on both, although the sample is too small to draw overly confident, generalizable conclusions from such a finding (see also note 3 on gendered findings in logistic regressions). In particular, the relationship between middle-class habitus and high cultural capital confirm the findings discussed in chapter 4.

6 Fordism is based on mass production and mass consumption. Post-Fordism is characterized by flexibility (Burrows and Loader 1994). At the global level, this flexibility can be seen in the deregulation of international markets (most notably financial markets). In industry, flexibility means a move away from mass production to batch production of diversified products, small-scale (service) industries, and flexible production with different employment relationships. We see the polarization between core and periphery jobs, skilled and unskilled work, a growth of non-standard employment, etc. (Pierson 1998).

7 See also Sennett and Cobb (1972), who wrote about how the American ethos of social mobility affects parents.

8 A number of key studies that have critically engaged with Willis's landmark ethnography of working-class lads in an English school (McFadden 1995). These works have criticized his male-oriented ethnography (McRobbie 1991), romanticized notion of male working-class culture

(Walker 1988), misinterpretation of loutish ritual and clowning (McLaren 1993), and consideration of merely organized trouble (Graham and Jardine 1990) as acts of working-class resistance.

CHAPTER FIVE

1 For a more in-depth discussion of the concepts of employability skills in different countries see, for example, Crouch et al. (1999) for the UK; Evers et al. (1998) for the U.S.; and Krahn et al. (2002) or Taylor (1998) for Canada.
2 See Lehmann (2000) for a more in-depth discussion regarding the future of Germany's dual system.

Bibliography

Alba, Richard, Johann Handl, and Walter Müller. 1994. Ethnische Ungleichheiten im deutschen Bildungssystem. *Kölner Zeitschrift für Soziologie and Sozialpsychologie* 46 (2):209–37.

Alberta Apprenticeship and Industry Training Board. 1996. *A Vision for the Future: A Discussion Paper.* Edmonton: Alberta Apprenticeship and Industry Training Board.

– 2002. *2001/2002 Annual Report: Responding to a Strong Economy.* Edmonton: Alberta Apprenticeship and Industry Training Board.

– 2005. *2004/2005 Annual Report: Going Strong.* Edmonton: Alberta Apprenticeship and Industry Training Board.

Alberta Chamber of Resources and Construction Owners of Alberta. 1990. *Alberta Resource Developments in the 1990s: A Response to Potential Skill Shortages.* Edmonton: Alberta Chamber of Resources.

Alberta Education. 1984. *Review of Secondary Programs.* Edmonton: Alberta Education.

– 1991. *A Vision for the Nineties: A Plan for Action.* Edmonton: Alberta Education.

– 1994. *Meeting the Challenge: Three-Year Business Plan.* Edmonton: Alberta Education.

– 1996. *Framework for Enhancing Business Involvement in Education.* Edmonton: Alberta Education.

Alberta Finance. 2000. *Careers: The Next Generation: 2000 Satisfaction Survey.* Edmonton: Alberta Finance.

Andres, Lesley. 1993. "Life Trajectories, Action, and Negotiating the Transition from High School." In *Transitions: Schooling and Employment in Canada.* P. Anisef and P. Axelrod, eds. Toronto: Thompson Educational Publishing, Inc.

Andres, Lesley, Paul Anisef, Harvey Krahn, Dianne Looker, and Victor
    Thiessen. 1999. "The Persistence of Social Structure: Cohort, Class and
    Gender Effects on the Occupational Aspirations and Expectations of
    Canadian Youth." *Journal of Youth Studies* 2 (3):261–82.
Andres, Lesley, and Harvey Krahn. 1999. " Youth Pathways in Articulated
    Postsecondary Systems: Enrolment and Completion Patterns of Urban
    Young Women and Men." *Canadian Journal of Higher Education* 29
    (1):47–82.
Anisef, Paul, Paul Axelrod, Etta Baichman-Anisef, Carl James, and Anton
    Turrittin. 2000. *Opportunity and Uncertainty: Life Course Experiences of the
    Class of '73*. Toronto: University of Toronto Press.
Archer, Margaret. 1988. *Culture and Agency: The Place of Culture in Social
    Theory*. Cambridge: Cambridge University Press.
Aries, E., and M. Seider. 2005. "The Interactive Relationship Between
    Class Identity and the College Experience: The Case of Lower Income
    Students." *Qualitative Sociology* 28 (4): 419–43.
Arum, Richard, and Yossi Shavit. 1995. "Secondary Vocational Education
    and the Transition from School to Work." *Sociology of Education* 68
    (3):187–204.
Baumert, J., R. Benkmann, J. Fuchs, D. Hopf, H. Köhler, B. Krais, L.
    Krappmann, A. Leschinsky, J. Naumann, P. M. Roeder, and L
    Trommer. 1994. *Das Bildungswesen in der Bundesrepublik Deutschland:
    Strukturen und Entwicklungen im Überblick*. Reinbek bei Hamburg:
    Rowohlt Taschenbuch Verlag.
Beck, Ulrich. 1992. *Risk Society: Towards a New Modernity*. London: Sage
    Publications.
Becker, Gary S. 1993. *Human Capital: A Theoretical and Empirical Analysis,
    with Special Reference to Education*. 3rd ed. Chicago: University of
    Chicago Press.
Benson, Charles S. 1997. "New Vocationalism in the United States: Potential
    Problems and Outlook." *Economics of Education Review* 16 (3):201–12.
Berger, Klaus, Harald Brandes, and Günter Walden. 2000. *Chancen der
    dualen Berufsausbildung: Berufliche Entwicklungsperspektiven aus betrieblicher
    Sicht und Berufserwartungen von Jugendlichen*. Bielefeld: Bertelsmann.
Bertin, Oliver. 2000. "Builders Facing Worker Shortage." *Globe and Mail*,
    4 December 2000, B1/B5.
Betcherman, Gordon, and Norm Leckie. 1997. *Youth Unemployment and
    Education Trends in the 1980s and 1990s*. Ottawa: Canadian Policy
    Research Network Inc.

Betcherman, Gordon, Kathryn McMullen, and Katie Davidman. 1998. *Training for the New Economy*. Ottawa: Renouf Publishing Co. Ltd.

Blau, Peter Michael, and Otis Dudley Duncan. 1967. *The American Occupational Structure*. New York: John Wiley & Sons, Inc.

Boudon, Raymond. 1974. *Education, Opportunity and Social Inequality*. New York: Wiley.

Bourdieu, Pierre. 1977. *Outline of a Theory of Practice*. New York: Cambridge University Press.

– 1984. *Distinction : a Social Critique of the Judgment of Taste*. Cambridge, Mass.: Harvard University Press.

– 1986. "The Forms of Capital." In *Handbook of Theory and Research for the Sociology of Education*. J. G. Richardson, ed. New York: Greenwood Press.

– 1990. *The Logic of Practice*. Cambridge: Polity.

Bourdieu, Pierre, and Jean Claude Passeron. 1977. *Reproduction in Education, Society and Culture*. London: Sage.

Bourdieu, Pierre, and Loïc J. Wacquant. 1992. *An Invitation to Reflexive Sociology*. Chicago: University of Chicago Press.

Bowles, Samuel, and Herbert Gintis. 1976. *Schooling in Capitalist America*. New York: Basic Books.

Brown, Phillip. 1987. *Schooling Ordinary Kids: Inequality, Unemployment and the New Vocationalism*. London and New York: Tavistock Publications.

– 1995. "Cultural Capital and Social Exclusion: Some Observations on Recent Trends in Education, Employment and the Labour Market." *Work Employment and Society* 9 (1):29–51.

Büchtemann, C.F., J. Schupp, and D. Soloff. 1994. "From School to Work: Patterns in Germany and the United States." In *Labour Market Dynamics in Present Day Germany*. J. Schwarze, F. Buttler and G. G. Wagner, eds. Frankfurt: Campus Verlag.

Bundesministerium für Bildung und Forschung. 2000. *Ausbildung und Beruf*. Bonn: Bundesministerium für Bildung und Forschung.

– 2002. *Berufsbildungsbericht 2002*. Bonn: Bundesministerium für Bildung und Forschung.

– 2004. *Grund- und Strukturdaten 2003/2004*. Bonn: Bundesministerium für Bildung und Forschung.

– 2005. *Grund- und Strukturdaten 2005*. Bonn: Bundesministerium für Bildung und Forschung.

Bundesministerium für Bildung und Wissenschaft. 1994. *Berufsausbildung im dualen System in der Bundesrepublik Deutschland: Eine Investition für die Zukunft*. Bonn: Bundesministerium für Bildung und Wissenschaft.

Burrows, Roger, and Brian Loader, eds. 1994. *Towards a Post-Fordist Welfare State?* London: Routledge.

Bynner, John, and Ken Roberts, eds. 1991. *Youth and Work: Transition to Employment in England and Germany.* London: Anglo-German Foundation.

Canadian Association of University Teachers. 2004. *CAUT Almanac of Post-Secondary Education in Canada 2004.* Ottawa: CAUT.

Careers: The Next Generation. 1998. *Annual Report 97–98.* Edmonton: Careers: The Next Generation.

Carey, Martha Ann. 1994. "The Group Effect in Focus Groups: Planning, Implementing and Interpreting Focus Group Research." In *Critical Issues in Qualitative Research Methods.* J.M. Morse, ed. Thousand Oaks: Sage Publications.

Collins, Randall. 1979. *The Credential Society: An Historical Sociology of Education and Stratification.* San Diego: Academic Press.

Coté, James E. 2000. *Arrested Adulthood: The Changing Nature of Maturity and Identity.* New York: New York University Press.

Coté, James E., and Anton L. Allahar. 1994. *Generation on Hold: Coming of Age in the Late Twentieth Century.* Toronto: Stoddard.

Crouch, Colin, David Feingold, and Mari Sako. 1999. *Are Skills the Answer? The Political Economy of Skill Creation in Advanced Industrial Countries.* Oxford: Oxford University Press.

Curtis, Bruce, David Livingstone, and Harry Smaller. 1992. *Stacking the Deck: The Streaming of Working Class Kids in Ontario Schools.* Toronto: Our Schools/Our Selves.

Damm-Rüger, Sigrid. 1994. "Duale Berufsausbildung und Berufserfolg: Junge weibliche und männliche Fachkräfte im Vergleich." In *Die Zukunft der dualen Berufsausbildung: Eine Fachtagung der Bundesanstalt für Arbeit.* S. Liesering, K. Schobing, and M. Tessaring, eds. Nürnberg: Institut für Arbeitsmarkt- und Berufsforschung der Bundesanstalt für Arbeit.

Davies, Scott. 1994. "Cultural Theories of Class Inequality in Canadian Education." In *Sociology of Education in Canada: Critical Perspectives on Theory, Research and Practice.* L. Erwin and D. MacLennan, eds. Toronto: Copp Clark Longman.

– 1995. "Reproduction and Resistance in Canadian High Schools: An Empirical Examination of the Willis Thesis." *British Journal of Sociology of Education* 46 (4):662–87.

– 2004. "Stubborn Disparities: Explaining Class Inequalities in Schooling." In *Social Inequality in Canada: Patterns, Problems, and Policies.* J. Curtis, E. Grabb, and N. Guppy, eds. Toronto: Pearson Prentice Hall.

de Broucker, P., and L. Lavallée. 1998. "Getting Ahead in Life: Does Your Parents' Income Count?" *Canadian Social Trends* Summer:6–10.

du Bois-Reymond, Manuela 1998. "I Don't Want to Commit Myself Yet: Young People's Life Concepts." *Journal of Youth Studies* 1 (1):63–79.

Duncan, Otis, and Robert W. Hodge. 1963. "Education and Occupational Mobility: A Regression Analysis." *American Journal of Sociology* 68 (6):629–44.

Economic Council of Canada. 1992. *A Lot to Learn: Education and Training in Canada: A Statement.* Ottawa: Economic Council of Canada.

Emirbayr, Mustafa, and Ann Mische. 1998. "What is Agency?" *American Journal of the Sociology of Education* 103 (4):964–1022.

Erikson, Erik H. 1968. *Identity: Youth and Crisis.* New York: Norton.

Esping-Andersen, Gøsta. 1990. *The Three Worlds of Welfare Capitalism.* Cambridge: Polity Press.

Evans, Karen. 2002. "Taking Control of Their Lives? Agency in Young Adult Transitions in England and the New Germany." *Journal of Youth Studies* 5 (3):245–69.

Evans, Karen, and Walter R. Heinz. 1995. "Flexibility, Learning and Risk: Work, Training and Early Careers." *Education and Training* 37 (5):3–11.

Evans, Karen, Maurice Taylor, and Walter Heinz. 1993. "Studying Forms of Transition: Methodological Innovation in a Cross-National Study of Youth Transition and Labour Market Entry in England and Germany." *Comparative Education* 29 (2):145–58.

Evers, Frederick T., James Cameron Rush, and Iris Berdrow. 1998. *The Bases of Competence: Skills for Lifelong Learning and Employability.* San Francisco: Jossey-Bass.

Evetts, J. (2000). "Analysing Change in Women's Careers: Culture, Structure and Action Dimensions." *Gender, Work and Organization* 7 (1):57–67.

Fenwick, Tara. 2004. "What Happens to the Girls? Gender, Work and Learning in Canada's 'New Economy'." *Gender and Education* 16 (2):169–85.

Ferrer, Ana, and W. Craig Riddell. 2001. *The Role of Credentials in the Canadian Labour Market. WRNET Working Paper 01.05.* Vancouver: Western Research Network on Education and Training.

Finlayson, David. 2003. "Trades Scrambling as Labour Shortages Loom." *Edmonton Journal,* 12 February 2003, A1, 11.

Fortin, M. 1987. *Accessibility to and Participation in the Postsecondary Education System in Canada.* Saskatoon: National Forum on Postsecondary Education.

Friebel, Harry, Heinrich Epskamp, Brigitte Knobloch, Stefanie Montag, and Stephan Toth. 2000. *Bildungsbeteiligung: Chancen und Riskiken. Eine Längsschnittstudie über Bildungs- und Weiterbildungskarrieren in der " Moderne."* Opladen: Leske & Budrich.

Friedman, S.R., and C.S. Weissbrod. 2005. "Work and Family Commitment and Decision-Making Status among Emerging Adults." *Sex Roles* 53 (5/6):317–25.

Führ, C. 1989. *Schools and Institutions of Higher Education in the Federal Republic of Germany.* Bonn: Inter Nationes.

Furlong, Andy, and Fred Cartmel. 1997. *Young People and Social Change: Individualization and Risk in Late Modernity.* Buckingham: Open University Press.

Gallagher, Paul, Robert Sweet, and Rick Rollins. 1997. *Intermediate Skill Development in British Columbia: New Policy and Research Directions.* Vancouver: BC Ministry of Education, Skills and Training.

Gambetta, Diego. 1987. *Were They Pushed or Did They Jump? Individual Decision Mechanisms in Education.* Cambridge: Cambridge University Press.

Gaskell, Jane. 1985. "Course Enrollment in the High School: The Perspective of Working Class Females." *Sociology of Education* 58 (1):48–59.

– 1992. *Gender Matters from School to Work.* Milton Keynes: Open University Press.

Geißler, Karlheinz A. 1991. "Das dual System der industriellen Berufsausbildung hat keine Zukunft." *Leviathan* 19 (1):68–77.

– 1994. "Vom Lebensberuf zur Erwerbskarriere: Erosionen im Bereich der beruflichen Bildung." *Zeitschrift für Berufs- und Wirtschaftspädagogik* 90 (6):647–54.

Geller, Gloria. 1996. "Educational, Occupational and Family Aspirations of Women: A Longitudinal Study." In *Youth in Transition: Perspectives on Research and Policy.* B. Galaway and J. Hudson, eds. Toronto: Thompson Educational Publishing.

Gellert, Claudius. 1996. "Recent Trends in German Higher Education." *European Journal of Education* 31 (3):311–19.

Giddens, Anthony. 1984. *The Constitution of Society: Outline of the Theory of Structuration.* Cambridge: Polity Press.

– 1990. *The Consequences of Modernity.* Stanford: Stanford University Press.

Goldthorpe, John H. 1996. "Class Analysis and the Reorientation of Class Theory: The Case of Persisting Differentials in Educational Attainment." *British Journal of Sociology* 47 (3):481–505.

Graham, P.R., and D.W. Jardine. 1990. "Deviance, Resistance, and Play: A Study in the Communicative Organization of Trouble in Class." *Curriculum Inquiry* 20 (3):283–304.

Granfield, R. 1991. "Making It by Faking It: Working-class Students in an Elite Academic Environment." *Journal of Contemporary Ethnography* 20 (3):331–51.

Greenberger, E., and L. Steinberg. 1986. *When Teenagers Work: The Psychological and Social Costs of Adolescent Employment.* New York: Basic Books.

Greinert, Wolf-Dietrich. 1994a. *The "German System" of Vocational Education: History, Organization, Prospects.* M. Carroll, trans. Baden Baden: Nomos Verlagsgesellschaft.

– 1994b. "Berufsausbildung und sozio-ökonomischer Wandel: Ursachen der Krise des dualen Systems der Berufsausbildung." *Zeitschrift für Pädagogik* 40 (3):357–72.

Grenfell, Michael, and David James. 1998. *Bourdieu and Education: Acts of Practical Theory.* London: Falmer Press.

Grubb, Norton W. 1996. "The New Vocationalism: What It is, What It Could Be." *Phi Delta Kappan* 77 (8):535–66.

Guppy, Neil. 1984. "Access to Higher Education in Canada." *Canadian Journal of Higher Education* 14 (3):79–93.

Haag, Eugen. 1982. *The Contribution of Vocational Education to the Economic Development in Partner Countries: Report: International Seminar from September 20th to October 2nd, 1982.* Bonn: German Foundation for International Development Industrial Occupations Promotion Centre.

Hamilton, Stephen F. 1990. *Apprenticeship for Adulthood: Preparing Youth for the Future.* New York and London: Free Press; Collier Macmillan.

Hamilton, Stephen F., and Klaus Hurrelmann. 1993. "Auf der Suche nach dem besten Modell für den Übergang von der Schule in den Beruf: ein amerikanisch-deutscher Vergleich." *Zeitschrift für Soziologie der Erziehung und Sozialisation* 13 (3):194–207.

– 1994. "The School-to-Career Transition in Germany and the United States." *Teachers College Record* 96 (2):329–44.

Hargreaves, David H. 1967. *Social Relations in a Secondary School.* London: Routledge.

HarGroup Management Consultants Inc. 2001. *A Study to Evaluate the Promotion, Administration and Effectiveness of the Registered Apprenticeship Program.* Edmonton: Alberta Learning and Alberta Apprenticeship and Industry Training Board.

Hatcher, Richard. 1998. "Class Differentiation in Education: Rational Choices?" *British Journal of Sociology of Education* 19 (1):5–24.

Heidenreich, Martin. 1998. "Die duale Berufsausbildung zwischen industrieller Prägung und wissensgesellschaftlichen Herausforderungen." *Zeitschrift für Soziologie* 27 (5):321–40.

Heinz, Walter. 2003. "The Restructuring of Work and the Modernization of Vocational Training in Germany." In *Integrating School and Workplace Learning in Canada.* Hans G. Schuetze and Robert Sweet, eds. Montreal and Kingston: McGill-Queen's University Press.

Heinz, Walter, Helga Krüger, Ursula Rettke, Erich Wachtveitl, and Andreas Witzel. 1987. *Hauptsache eine Lehrstelle: Jugendliche vor den Hürden des Arbeitsmarkts.* Weinheim: Deutscher Studien Verlag.

Henz, Ursula, and Ineke Maas. 1995. "Chancengleichheit durch die Bildungsexpansion." *Kölner Zeitschrift für Soziologie and Sozialpsychologie* 47 (4):605–33.

Hodkinson, Philip. 1998. "Career Decision Making and the Transition from School to Work." In *Bourdieu and Education: Acts of Practical Theory.* M. Grenfell and D. James, eds. London: Falmer Press.

Hodkinson, Phil, and Andrew C. Sparkes. 1997. "Careership: A Sociological Theory of Career Decision Making." *British Journal of Sociology of Education* 18 (1):29–44.

Human Resources Development Canada. 1998. *The Transition from Initial Education to Working Life: A Canadian Report for an OECD Thematic Review.* Ottawa: Public Works and Government Services Canada.

Jencks, C., J. Crouse, and P. Mueser. 1983. "The Wisconsin Model of Status Attainment: A National Replication with Improved Measures of Ability and Aspiration." *Sociology of Education* 56 (1):3–18.

Jenkins, Richard. 1992. *Pierre Bourdieu.* London: Routledge.

Jonsson, Jan O., Colin Mills, and Walter Müller. 1996. "A Half Century of Increasing Educational Openness? Social Class, Gender, and Educational Attainment in Sweden, Germany, and Britain." In *Can Education Be Equalized? The Swedish Case in Comparative Perspective.* R. Erikson and J.O. Jonsson, eds. Boulder: Westview Press.

Kantor, Harvey. 1994. "Managing the Transition from School to Work: The False Promise of Youth Apprenticeship." *Teachers College Record* 95 (4):442–61.

Kelle, Udo, and Jens Zinn. 1998. "School-to-Work Transition and Occupational Careers: Results from a Longitudinal Study in Germany." In *Understanding the School-to-Work Transition: An International Perspective.* T. Lange, ed. Commack, NY: Nova Science Publishers.

Kerckhoff, Alan C. 1995. "Institutional Arrangements and Stratification Processes in Industrial Societies." *Annual Review of Sociology* 15:323–47.

Kincheloe, Joe L. 1999. *How Do We Tell the Workers? The Socioeconomic Foundations of Work and Vocational Education.* Boulder: Westview.

Koch, Richard, and Jochen Reuling. 1994. "The Responsiveness and Regulation of Training Capacity and Quality." In *Vocational Training in Germany: Modernisation and Responsiveness.* Paris: OECD.

Krahn, Harvey. 1996. *School-Work Transitions: Changing Patterns and Research Needs.* Ottawa: Human Resources Development Canada.

– 2004. "Choose Your Parents Carefully: Social Class, Post-Secondary Education, and Occupational Outcomes." In *Social Inequality in Canada: Patterns, Problems, and Policies.* J. Curtis, E. Grabb, and N. Guppy, eds. Toronto: Pearson Prentice Hall.

Krahn, Harvey, Graham Lowe, and Karen Hughes. 2007. *Work, Industry, and Canadian Society.* 5th ed. Toronto: Thomson Nelson.

Krahn, Harvey, Graham S. Lowe, and Wolfgang Lehmann. 2002. "Acquisition of Employability Skills by High School Students." *Canadian Public Policy* 28 (2):275–96.

Krahn, Harvey, and C. Mosher. 1992. *The Transition from School to Work in Three Canadian Cities, 1985–89: Research Design and Methodological Issues.* Edmonton: Population Research Laboratory (University of Alberta).

Krüger, Helga. 2001. "Social Change in Two Generations: Employment Patterns and Their Costs for Family Life." In *Restructuring Work and the Life Course.* V.W. Marshall, W.R. Heinz, H. Krüger, and A. Verma, eds. Toronto: University of Toronto Press.

Lehmann, Wolfgang. 2000. "Is Germany's Dual System Still a Model for Canadian Youth Apprenticeship Initiatives?" *Canadian Public Policy* 26 (2):225–40.

– 2004. "'For Some Reason, I Get a Little Scared': Structure, Agency, and Risk in School-Work Transitions." *Journal of Youth Studies* 7 (4):379–96.

– 2005a. "'I'm Still Scrubbing the Floor': Experiencing High School Based Youth Apprenticeships." *Work, Employment, and Society* 19 (1):107–29.

– 2005b. "Choosing to Labour: Structure and Agency in School-Work Transitions." *Canadian Journal of Sociology.* 30 (3):325-50.

Lehmann, Wolfgang, and Alison Taylor. 2003. "Giving Employers What They Want? New Vocationalism in Alberta." *Journal of Education and Work* 16 (1):45–67.

Lempert, Wolfgang. 1995. "Das Märchen vom unaufhaltsamen Niedergang des dualen Systems." *Zeitschrift für Berufs- und Wirtschaftspädagogik* 91 (3):225–31.

Livingstone, David W. 2004. *The Education-Jobs Gap: Underemployment or Economic Democracy.* Toronto: Garamond Press.

Looker, E.D., and P.A. Magee. 2000. "Gender and Work: The Occupational Expectations of Young Women and Men in the 1990s." *Gender Issues* 18 (2):74–88.

Looker, Dianne. 1993. "Interconnceted Transitions and Their Costs: Gender and Urban/Rural Differences in the Transitions to Work." In *Transitions: Schooling and Employment in Canada.* P. Anisef and P. Axelord, eds. Toronto: Thompson Educational Publishing.

Looker, E. Dianne, and Peter Dwyer. 1998. "Education and Negotiated Reality: Complexities Facing Rural Youth in the 1990s." *Journal of Youth Studies* 1 (1):5–22.

Looker, E. Dianne, and P.C. Pineo. 1983. "Social Psychological Variables and Their Relevance to the Status Attainment of Teenagers." *American Journal of Sociology* 88 (6):1195–219.

Lowe, Graham, Harvey Krahn, and Jeff Bowlby. 1997. *1996 Alberta High School Survey Report of Research Findings.* Edmonton: Population Research Laboratory.

Lowe, Graham S., and Harvey Krahn. 1999. "Reconceptualizing Youth Unemployment." In *Young Workers: Varieties of Experience.* J. Barling and E. K. Kelloway, eds. Washington, DC: American Psychological Association.

– 2000. "Work Aspirations and Attitudes in an Era of Labour Market Restructuring: A Comparison of Two Canadian Youth Cohorts." *Work, Employment and Society* 14 (1):1–22.

Madriz, Esther. 2000. "Focus Groups in Feminist Research." In *Handbook of Qualitative Research.* N.K. Denzin and Y.S. Lincoln, eds. Thousand Oaks: Sage Publications.

Mansel, Jürgen. 1993. "Zur Reproduktion sozialer Ungleichheit: soziale Lage, Arbeitsbedingungen und Erziehungsverhalten der Eltern im Zusammenhang mit dem Schulerfolg des Kindes." *Zeitschrift für Soziologie der Erziehung und Sozialisation* 13 (1):36–60.

Marquardt, Richard. 1998. *Enter at Your Own Risk: Canadian Youth and the Labour Market.* Toronto: Between the Lines.

Max Planck Institute for Human Development and Education. 1983. *Between Elite and Mass Education: Education in the Federal Republic of Germany.* Albany: State University of New York Press.

McDowell, Linda. 2003. *Redundant Masculinities: Employment Changes and White Working Class Youth.* Oxford: Blackwell.

McFadden, Mark G. 1995. "Resistance to Schooling and Education: Questions of Structure and Agency." *British Journal of Sociology of Education* 16 (3):293–308.

McLaren, P. 1993. *Schooling as a Ritual Performance: Towards a Political Economy of Educational Symbols and Gestures*. London: Routledge.

McLaughlin, Maryann. 1992. *Employability Skills Profile: What Are Employers Looking For?* Ottawa: Conference Board of Canada.

McRobbie, A. 1991. *Feminism and Youth Culture: From Jackie to Just Seventeen*. London: Macmillan.

Meulemann, Heiner. 2001. "Ankunft im Erwachsenenleben: Identitätsfindung und Identitätswahrung in der Erfolgsdeutung einer Kohorte ehemaliger Gymnasiasten von der Jugend bis zur Lebensmitte." *Zeitschrift für Soziologie der Erziehung und Sozialisation* 21 (1):45–59.

Michelson, Roslyn A. 1990. "The Attitude-Achievement Paradox among Black Adolescents." *Sociology of Education* 63 (1):44–61.

Ministère de l'Éducation. 2001. *Education in Québec: An Overview*. Québec: Gouvernement du Québec.

Morgan, David L. 1988. *Focus Groups as Qualitative Research*. Newbury Park: Sage Publications.

Mortimer, Jeylan T., Michael Shanahan, and Seongryeol Ryu. 1994. "The Effects of Adolescent Employment on School-Related Orientation and Behaviour." In *Adolescence in Context: The Interplay of Family, School, Peers, and Work in Adjustment*. R. K. Silbereisen and E. Todt, eds. New York: Springer Verlag.

Müller, Walter, and Dietmar Haun. 1994. "Bildungsungleichheit im sozialen Wandel." *Kölner Zeitschrift für Soziologie und Sozialpsychologie* 46 (1):1–42.

Münch, Joachim. 1995. *Vocational Education and Training in the Federal Republic of Germany*. Berlin: European Centre for the Development of Vocational Training.

Murphy, Raymond. 1988. *Social Closure: The Theory of Monopolization and Exclusion*. Oxford: Clarendon Press.

– 1994. "A Weberian Approach to Credentials: Credentials as a Code of Exclusionary Closure." In *Sociology of Education in Canada*. L. Erwin and D. MacLennan, eds. Toronto: Copp Clark Longman.

Nash, Roy. 2003. "Social Explanation and Socialization: On Bourdieu and the Structure, Disposition, Practice Scheme. *The Sociological Review* 51 (1):43–62.

Bibliography

Oakes, J. (2005). *Keeping Track: How Schools Structure Inequality.* 2nd ed. New Haven and London: Yale University Press.

O'Connor, J. 1996. "From Women in the Welfare State to Gendering Welfare State Regimes." *Current Sociology* 44 (2):1–124.

Oppel, W. 1994. "Aus der Sicht des Deutschen Gewerkschaftsbundes (DGB): Zukunftschancen durch Reformationen." *Informationen für die Beratungs- und Vermittlungsdienste der Bundesanstalt für Arbeit* 6:497–503.

Organisation for Economic Co-operation and Development. 2000. *Education at a Glance: OECD Indicators.* Paris: OECD.

Orloff, A. 1996. "Gender in the Welfare State." *Annual Review of Sociology* 22:51–78.

Pierson, Christopher. 1998. *Beyond the Welfare State: The New Political Economy of Welfare.* 2nd ed. University Park, Pennsylvania: Pennsylvania State University Press.

Pritchard, R. 1992. "The German Dual System: Educational Utopia?" *Comparative Education* 28 (2):131–41.

Ray, Carol Axtell, and Roslyn Arlin Mickelson. 1993. "Restructuring Students for Restructured Work: The Economy, School Reform and Non-College-Bound Youth." *Sociology of Education* 66 (1):1–20.

Reskin, B., and I. Padavic. (1994). *Women and Men at Work.* Thousand Oaks: Pine Forge Press.

Rieble-Aubourg, Sabine. 1996. "Institutional Arrangements of Germany's Vocational Education System: What Are the Policy Implications for the U.S.?" *International Journal of Comparative Sociology* 37 (1–2):174–91.

Roberts, Ken, S.C. Clark, and Claire Wallace. 1994. "Flexibility and Individualisation: A Comparison of Transitions into Employment in England and Germany." *Sociology* 28 (1):31–54.

Rosenbaum, James. 2001. *Beyond College for All: Career Paths for the Forgotten Half.* New York: Russel Sage Foundation.

Rudd, Peter, and Karen Evans. 1998. "Structure and Agency in Youth Transitions: Student Experiences of Vocational Further Education." *Journal of Youth Studies* 1 (1):39–62.

Schlicht, Michael. 1994. "Das duale Ausbildungssytem: Geschichtliche Entwicklung und aktueller Stand." *Informationen für die Beratungs- und Vermittlungsdienste der Bundesanstalt für Arbeit* 6:471–4.

Schmidt, H. 1988. "The Federal Institute of Vocational Education and Training (Bundesinstitut für Berufsbildung): Structure, Tasks and Research Results." In *Vocational and General Education in Western Societies.* H. Röhrs, ed. London: Symposium.

Schober, Karen. 1984. "The Educational System, Vocational Training and Youth Unemployment in West Germany." *Compare* 14 (2):129–44.

Sennett, Richard, and Jonathan Cobb. 1972. *The Hidden Injuries of Class.* New York: Knopf.

Sharpe, Andrew. 2003. "Apprenticeship in Canada: A Training System under Siege?" In *Integrating School and Workplace Learning in Canada.* H.G. Schuetze and R. Sweet, eds. Montreal and Kingston: McGill-Queen's University Press.

Shavit, Yossi, and Hans-Peter Blossfeld. 1996. "Equalizing Educational Opportunity: Do Gender and Class Compete?" In *Can Education Be Equalized? The Swedish Case in Comparative Perspective.* R. Erikson and J.O. Jonsson, eds. Boulder: Westview Press.

– eds. 1993. *Persistent Inequality: Changing Educational Attainment in Thirteen Countries.* Boulder, CO: Westview Press.

Shilling, Chris. 1987. "Work-Experience as a Contradictory Practice." *British Journal of Sociology of Education* 8 (4):407–23.

Silverman, David. 2001. *Interpreting Qualitative Data: Methods for Analysing Talk, Text and Interaction.* 2nd ed. London: Sage Publications.

Skof, K. (2006). "Trends in Registered Apprenticeship Training in Canada." *Education Matters: Insights on Education, Learning, and Training.* http://www.statcan.ca/english/freepub/81-004-XIE/2006002/regappr.htm

Solga, Heike, and Dirk Konietzka. 2000. "Das Berufsprinzip des deutschen Arbeitsmarktes: Ein Geschlechtsneutraler Allokationsmechanismus?." *Schweizerische Zeitschrift für Soziologie* 26 (1):111–47.

Solga, Heike, and Sandra Wagner. 2001. "Paradoxie der Bildungs-expansion: die doppelte Benachteiligung von Hauptschülern." *Zeitschrift für Erziehungswissenschaft* 4 (1):107–27.

Statistics Canada. 1999. *The Daily.* 4 August 1999. Ottawa: Statistics Canada.

– 2000a. *1999 Labour Force Survey.* Ottawa: Statistics Canada.

– 2000b. *Women in Canada: A Gender-Based Statistical Report; Cat. No. 89–503–XPE.* Ottawa: Statistics Canada.

– 2001. *2001 Census of Canada.* Ottawa: Statistics Canada.

– 2003a. *The Daily.* 24 February 2003. Ottawa: Statistics Canada.

– 2003b. *The Daily.* 20 November 2003.Ottawa: Statistics Canada.

– 2004. Labour Force Historical Review, 2003. Ottawa: Statistics Canada.

– 2006. Labour Force Survey: February 2006. *The Daily.* 10 March 2006, 2–8.

Statistics Canada, and Council of Ministers of Education Canada. 2003. *Education Indicators in Canada: Report of the Pan-Canadian Education Indicators Program 2003*. Ottawa: Statistics Canada.

Stewart, David W., and Prem N. Shamdasani. 1990. *Focus Groups: Theory and Practice*. Newbury Park: Sage Publications.

Swartz, David. 1997. *Culture and Power: The Sociology of Pierre Bourdieu*. Chicago and London: The University of Chicago Press.

Taillon, Jacques, and Mike Paju. 1999. *The Class of '95: Report of the 1997 National Graduate Survey of 1995 Graduates*. Ottawa: Statistics Canada.

Tanner, Julian. 1990. "Reluctant Rebels: A Case Study of Edmonton High School Dropouts." *Canadian Review of Sociology and Anthropology* 27 (1):74–94.

Tanner, Julian, Harvey Krahn, and Timothy F. Hartnagel. 1995. *Fractured Transitions from School to Work: Revisiting the Dropout Problem*. Toronto: Oxford University Press.

Taylor, Alison. 1998. "Employability Skills: From Corporate " Wish List" to Government Policy." *Journal of Curriculum Studies* 30 (2):143–64.

– 2001. *The Politics of Educational Reform in Alberta*. Toronto: University of Toronto Press.

Taylor, Alison, and Wolfgang Lehmann. 2002. "Reinventing Vocational Education Policy: Pitfalls and Possibilities." *Alberta Journal of Educational Research* 48 (2):139–61.

Thiessen, Victor, and E. Dianne Looker. 1999. *Investing in Youth: The Nova Scotia School-to-Work Transition Project*. Hull, QC: Human Resources Development Canada.

Vondracek, Fred W. 1994. "Vocational Identity Development in Adolescents." In *Adolescence in Context: The Interplay of Family, School, Peers, and Work in Adjustment*. R. K. Silbereisen and E. Todt, eds. New York: Springer Verlag.

Walker, J.C. 1988. *Lotus and Legends: Male Youth Culture in an Inner City School*. Sydney: Allen & Unwin.

Warrington, Molly, and Michael Younger. 2000. "The Other Side of the Gender Gap." *Gender and Education* 12 (4):493–508.

Weiner, Gaby, Madeleine Arnot, and Miriam David. 1997. "Is the Future Female? Female Success, Male Disadvantage, and Changing Patterns in Education." In *Education: Culture, Economy, Society*. A.H. Halsey, H. Lauder, P. Brown, and A. Stuart Wells, eds. Oxford and New York: Oxford University Press.

Willis, Paul. 1977. *Learning to Labour: How Working Class Kids Get Working Class Jobs*. Farnborough: Saxon House.

Witzel, Andreas, and Jens Zinn. 1998. "Berufsausbildung und soziale
Ungleichheit: Sozialstruktur und Biographie beim Übergang von der
Schule in die Erwerbstätigkeit." *Diskurs* 8 (1):28–39.

Wotherspoon, Terry. 2004. *The Sociology of Education in Canada: Critical
Perspectives.* 2nd ed. Toronto: Oxford University Press.

Wyn, Johanna, and Peter Dwyer. 1999. "New Directions in Research on
Youth in Transition." *Journal of Youth Studies* 2 (1):5–21.

Index